D0012427

Fishing
Colorado

Help Us Keep This Guide Up to Date

Every effort has been made by the author and editors to make this guide as accurate and useful as possible. However, many things can change after a guide is published—regulations change, techniques evolve, facilities come under new management, etc.

We would love to hear from you concerning your experiences with this guide and how you feel it could be improved and kept up to date. While we may not be able to respond to all comments and suggestions, we'll take them to heart, and we'll also make certain to share them with the author. Please send your comments and suggestions to the following address:

The Globe Pequot Press
Reader Response/Editorial Department
P.O. Box 480
Guilford, CT 06437

Or you may e-mail us at:

editorial@GlobePequot.com

Thanks for your input, and happy travels!

Fishing
Colorado

RON BAIRD

FALCON®

GUILFORD, CONNECTICUT
HELENA, MONTANA
AN IMPRINT OF THE GLOBE PEQUOT PRESS

A FALCON GUIDE ®

Copyright © 2003 by The Globe Pequot Press

All rights reserved. No part of this book may be reproduced or transmitted in any form by any means, electronic or mechanical, including photocopying and record-ing, or by any information storage and retrieval system, except as may be expressly permitted by the 1976 Copyright Act or by the publisher. Requests for permission should be made in writing to The Globe Pequot Press, P.O. Box 480, Guilford, Connecticut 06437.

Falcon and FalconGuide are registered trademarks of The Globe Pequot Press.

All photos by Ron Baird unless otherwise noted.
Text design by Casey Shain
Maps created by Trailhead Graphics © The Globe Pequot Press

Library of Congress Cataloging-in-Publication-Data is available.

ISBN 0-7627-1098-5

Manufactured in the United States of America
First Edition/First Printing

The Globe Pequot Press assumes no liability for accidents happening to, or injuries sustained by, readers who engage in the activities described in this book.

Contents

Southeast Colorado

Denver Metro Area

Map Legend

Featured Fishing Site

Interstate Highway

U.S. Highway

State Highway

County, Local, or
Forest Road

Trail

Railroad

Boat Ramp

Campground

Parking

Trailhead

Ranger Station

Ski Area

Point of Interest

Picnic Area

Pass

Bridge

Mountain, Peak,
or Butte

River, Creek,
or Drainage

Reservoir or Lake

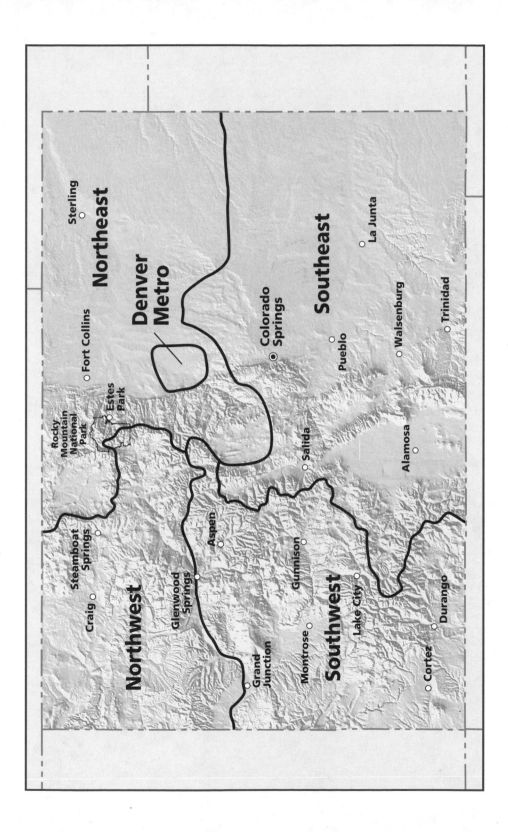

Acknowledgments

I could not have written this book without the help of John Alves, Dan Brauch, Ken Kehmeier, Mike Japhet, Greg Gerlich, Jim Melby, Charlie Bennett, Jay Stafford, Kevin Rogers, Steve Puttman, Dave Langlois, Sherman Hebein, and Doug Krieger, who, as aquatic biologists for the Colorado Division of Wildlife, have the difficult job of balancing the demand for recreation with the protection of resources, yet undertake the challenge with passion and dedication.

Thanks also to DOW Aquatic Manager Eddie Kochman for sharing with me the complexity of the challenge; to Hatchery Chief Eric Hughes, for sharing the complexity of growing fish for Colorado waters in a rapidly changing world; to Todd Malmsbury, for letting me in the door in the first place; and to Dave Buchanan, of the *Grand Junction Daily Sentinel,* and Charlie Meyers, of the *Denver Post,* for inspiration.

Introduction

Colorado is primarily known as trout-fishing country. Although it boasts many fine warm-water fisheries, two-thirds of all resident anglers list trout as the type of fish they prefer to pursue. Out-of-state anglers come to Colorado almost exclusively to fish for trout.

Trout-fishing in Colorado these days is complicated by the presence of whirling disease: lack of fish to stock due to hatchery renovations and new policies to prevent the spread of the disease. Nevertheless, opportunities abound for anglers to catch their limit of trout at easily accessible Front Range lakes, to land wild trout in the scenic Rockies, and even to haul in some trophy-size fish from world-famous tailwater rivers or high-country lakes.

After trout, walleye get the most attention from anglers in Colorado. An up-and-coming sport fish is the wiper—a cross between the white and striped bass—known for its fighting nature. Opportunities likewise abound to take the limit of warm-water species like bass, saugeye, wiper, crappie, bluegill, perch, catfish, and walleye. But this too has become more complicated due to reservoir low-water levels in recent years. The good news is that many of these fisheries rebound quickly once the water levels come back up.

I wrote this book to provide anglers with a reasonable chance of success in their chosen endeavors, whether it be a day of family fishing fun, or the more serious pursuit of trophy-size fish, or simply partaking of the Rocky Mountain experience of fishing the high country.

The first key to success is finding waters where there are fish. I've drawn upon the knowledge of the Colorado Division of Wildlife's local aquatic biologists, whose job it is to know where the fishing is good. They conduct stream population and creel surveys and talk to their friends and neighbors. I have also drawn upon my years of experience in fishing many of these waters and upon the expertise of numerous experienced anglers.

Generally, my criteria for selecting the waters covered in this book were that they have been consistent producers for at least five years and would likely be consistent for five years after the book is published. These criteria are not ironclad, and I have noted exceptions that could affect the fishing. If anything, my approach has been conservative. When the hatchery renovations are completed, many mountain lakes and some streams and rivers will be stocked with greater numbers of whirling-disease-negative fish. But for now, the information in this book reflects the most current, accurate information on fishing in Colorado.

The second key to angling success is understanding the habitat preference, choice of prey, and daily and seasonal movements of the type of fish you want to catch. I have addressed these factors in the species profiles and in the descriptions of the various fisheries.

The last key to success, as every angler knows, is luck! With so many variables involved in catching fish, it's possible to do nearly everything correctly and still get skunked. It's also possible to do nearly everything incorrectly and still catch fish. But using the first two keys will enhance your success.

Whirling Disease

Whirling disease is caused by a parasite that attacks the soft cartilage of young trout. (It has primarily affected rainbow trout.) The clinical signs of whirling disease include skeletal deformities and a whirling motion while swimming. Many, if not most, of the fish that develop these symptoms die from starvation or predation, as the whirling motion reduces their ability to feed and elude predators. Once the trout reach 3 to 4 inches in length, the soft cartilage becomes bone, and the fish, while they can still carry the organism, are no longer susceptible.

While some trout species other than rainbow are known to be susceptible, no other species have so far shown dramatic, localized population declines. Brown trout, for the most part, are resistant to the disease; in fact, their numbers have increased in areas where rainbow trout numbers have declined.

Colorado Division of Wildlife researchers have documented population-level declines, primarily of rainbow and brook trout, on river and stream reaches totaling 400 miles out of the estimated 8,000 miles open to the public. These whirling-disease-impacted waters include portions of the Cache La Poudre, upper Colorado, Dolores, Fraser, Fryingpan, upper and lower Gunnison, Middle Fork of the South Platte, Rio Grande, Roaring Fork, South Fork of the Rio Grande, South Platte, and Williams Fork Rivers, as well as Beaver Creek (South Fork of the Rio Grande drainage), Cottonwood Creek (Arkansas River drainage), and Spring Creek (Taylor River drainage). By contrast, 7,600 miles of public trout rivers and streams are either free of the whirling-disease parasite or there is no evidence of population-level effects on trout. These waters are referred to as "negative."

Many cold-water reservoirs and lakes have tested positive for whirling-disease organisms, but so far the fish, including rainbows, have shown no population-level declines. The reason for this is unclear, but it may have to do with the whirling-disease organisms' tendency to settle to the bottom in still waters, thereby minimizing their contact with susceptible young fish. Therefore, there is no reference to whirling disease in sections discussing these waters.

Whirling-disease organisms are not found in warm-water environments, and the organisms have no effect on humans.

How You Can Help

While it isn't clear to what degree anglers can spread whirling disease on their equipment, officials ask—just to be safe—that anglers clean all mud from their boots, waders, boats, and trailer tires after fishing in trout habitat. However, cleaning an infected fish and disposing of entrails in the water is definitely a way to spread the disease. Burn or bury the entrails or pack them out. Whirling-disease-positive fish are completely safe to eat.

Hatchery Renovations and Stocking

In order to rid Colorado fish hatcheries of the whirling-disease organism, a $13 million renovation was begun in 1998. At present 11 facilities have been certified as free of whirling disease. An estimated 2.2 million catchable-size (10-inch) trout will be stocked in 2003, including 700,000 whirling-disease-free fish into mountain streams, rivers and lakes. The remainder, which show no signs of the disease but are considered lightly infected because they come from hatcheries that haven't been certified whirling-disease-free, will be stocked in low elevation lakes, primarily along the Front Range or adjacent to urban areas.

Drought

Colorado experienced serious drought conditions in 2001 and 2002. However, there were no major fish kills due to low water or high water temperatures during that time in any of the selections featured in this book. The main effect of low water conditions in mountain streams and rivers was to reduce or even eliminate the high runoff associated with a normal snowpack and to move up the hatches of insects by three to four weeks. Fish census surveys indicated that trout in some rivers actually seemed to grow larger during the drought years, possibly because the feeding season was prolonged.

In May 2003 snowpack in both the Northwest and Northeast regions was at or above normal levels, and most reservoirs were either full or expected to be full by the end of the summer. Snowpack in the Southeast region was about 50 percent of normal and, while decent flows were anticipated for streams and rivers, the mountain and eastern plains reservoirs were expected to remain low. Snowpack in the Southwest region was about 60 percent of normal, and the situation was similar to the Southeast—decent stream and river flows but unfilled reservoirs.

Low water in reservoirs doesn't necessarily mean the fishing will be poor. It may be a problem getting boats into the water, however, because some water levels are below the boat ramps.

To find out about conditions on lakes you want to fish, call the contact number listed at the end of the description, or check one of the Web sites listed in the appendix. All these sources have up-to-date information.

Wildlife

Wildlife is certainly a part of fishing in Colorado. In the lower-elevation canyons and among the high-mountain lakes and streams on the Eastern Slope (east of the Continental Divide), anglers can see bighorn sheep and mountain goats frolicking on the canyon rims and highest mountainsides. In the mountains of the upper Poudre Canyon and North Park, the hiker occasionally stumbles on a moose in a swampy thicket.

Deer are more a presence in populated areas and will mainly be a concern of anglers while driving to a fishing spot.

In the Front Range foothills and the lower elevations of the Western Slope, a backcountry angler might hear the warning rattle of a rattlesnake. In recent memory no one has died from a rattlesnake bite. Mountain lions and bears are here, too. But in thirty years of backcountry hiking and fishing, I've only seen three bears and three mountain lions, all near my cabin in the mountains west of Boulder. Neither poses a significant threat to anglers, but those spending the night in the mountains should clean their dishes, pack away refuse, and hang food from a tree. Food and refuse are both strong attractants to bears.

In the past thirty years, I only recall one person killed by a lion and two by bears in Colorado. Compare this to car crashes, lightning strikes, falls, hypothermia, drowning, and even bee stings, and you realize that statistically the danger from mountain lions and bears is negligible. Still, the Colorado Division of Wildlife has brochures that describe how to handle encounters with bears and other potentially dangerous wildlife. Pay attention to your surroundings, and even those rare encounters can usually be avoided.

Weather

On the other hand, weather, particularly lightning, contributes to many deaths in Colorado each year. In the mid- to late summer, thunderstorms in the high country can be on you in minutes, even in clear, sunny weather. Try to get on and off the mountain by early afternoon. If caught, get rid of fishing rods and any metal, and try to find a low spot to let it blow over. These storms often last less than a half hour, and once they have passed, it's safe to move. Be prepared when hiking the backcountry with food, water, extra clothing, and rain protection, as well as a first-aid kit. Don't count on a cell phone to get you out of trouble—they don't work in many remote areas of the state. Use common sense instead.

Wind is another factor to consider, especially when out on the water. On a small lake in the Front Range foothills, we once beached during a high wind, only to see our canoe blown up a 12-foot bank. If the wind comes up, head for shore.

Finding Your Way

I made every effort to provide accurate directions, mileages, and maps to the fishing places described in this book, driving the various routes myself. When cross-referencing my data with published maps, however, I learned that nearly every one varies to some extent. In these cases I generally depended on my figures first and government maps second and estimated some distances by averaging the different figures. I believe that all the mileages are fairly accurate, but try to obtain detailed local maps of areas you intend to visit.

Catch and Release

Catch-and-release fishing helps maintain healthy fish populations. In many of the areas I profiled in this book, it is also required. The Colorado Division of Wildlife guidelines to handling and releasing fish are:

- Do not play a fish to exhaustion.
- Keep the fish in the water as much as possible when handling.

- Remove a hook as gently as possible. Do not squeeze the fish or put your fingers in its gills. If deeply hooked, cut the line.
- Release a fish only after its equilibrium is restored. If necessary, hold the fish facing the current and move it back and forth to get oxygen into its gills.
- Wet your hands before holding a fish.
- Use barbless hooks or mash the barbs down.

Hiking

A fact of Colorado fishing, particularly in the mountain areas, is that some hiking is required. Many anglers believe that, all other things being equal, the more difficult it is to get to a fishing spot, the better the fishing will be. Most of the places described in this book should not be too difficult to reach for a person in good physical condition and acclimated to the altitude. The high-mountain lakes involving more than 3 miles of hiking should only be attempted by those in good condition and acclimated to the altitude.

Fishing Regulations

New fishing regulations were adopted in 2001 and are in effect until 2006. Obtain a copy of the regulations from any Colorado Division of Wildlife office or any store that sells licenses or fishing gear. Exceptions to the general regulations—and there are many—are noted in the descriptions of specific fisheries in this book.

Colorado Gamefish

Walleye *(Stizostedion vitreum)*

General description: Walleye bodies are long and rounded with a forked tail. The bottom lobe of the tail is silvery or white. Its sides are silvery to mottled brown. The walleye's back has two separated dorsal fins, with the front dorsal containing fourteen or fifteen sharp spines. Its eyes are a milky color. A typical walleye will average 4 to 5 pounds, but they can grow to three times that size, with the state record at 18.8 pounds, 34 inches.

Distribution: The walleye was introduced into the state in 1949 and now inhabits at least thirty-six large reservoirs along the Front Range and in eastern Colorado. The state record walleye was caught at Standley Lake in 1997. Top walleye fisheries are Pueblo and Cherry Creek Reservoirs.

Points to ponder: Walleye are considered one of the best-tasting sport fish. They are also among the most elusive, inspiring a cultlike following among anglers. They typically will stay in deep water over beds of rock or gravel. Small fish are their primary prey.

Saugeye *(Stizostedion vitreum x S. canadense)*

General description: The saugeye is the fertile hybrid of the walleye and sauger, both of which it closely resembles. It has a long, round body and silvery to mottled-brown sides. The saugeye can be differentiated from the walleye by the faded saddle markings extending down its sides, blurred spots on its dorsal fin, and no white spot on its tail. The state record saugeye is 8.8 pounds, 27 inches.

Distribution: Because saugeye are able to crossbreed with walleye, they are not stocked in any walleye brood lakes but otherwise can be found in thirty large, deep lakes along the southern Front Range and in eastern Colorado. Saugeye were brought to Colorado in the early 1990s to offset losses of walleye when the large reservoirs in southeast Colorado were drawn down for irrigation. Walleye, which tend to run downstream, were being drawn into irrigation ditches. Saugeye tend to run upstream and avoid being swept into reservoir outflows. The state record saugeye was caught at John Martin Reservoir in 1999.

Points to ponder: Saugeye are very tasty fish and reportedly a little easier to catch than walleye but fight just as hard. Saugeye, like walleye, prefer deep water and sandy or gravel bottoms. Their prime feeding times are evening into nightfall and early morning. Slow retrieval of lures and spoons imitating bait fish is the primary method to catch saugeye.

Northern Pike *(Esox lucius)*

General description: Northern pike have long, thin bodies, as if sculpted for speed. Their snout is flat like a duck's bill, and their jaws are lined with razor-sharp teeth. Their color can range from light to dark green, depending on their habitat. Their sides feature cream to yellow, irregularly shaped spots. A typical northern pike will average 10 pounds. The state record is 30.4 pounds, 43.5 inches.

Distribution: While pike have not been stocked extensively in Colorado waters since the early 1980s, fish have escaped or have been "planted" illegally by "bait bucket biologists" in Colorado waters other than where they were intended to be, sometimes repeatedly. In western Colorado officials have documented northern pike in at least five reservoirs where they were never stocked, causing extensive damage to trout fisheries. The Colorado Division of Wildlife's Fishing Map guide lists twenty-five waters that offer northern pike. The state record northern pike was caught in Williams Fork Reservoir in 1996. A 39-inch northern pike was caught on a fly rod and released in the Yampa River in 1997.

Points to ponder: Northern pike are problematic because as they are such voracious predators, they can decimate other fish species populations. As problematic as they are, northern pike are still popular sport fish because they're such good fighters. They can pull like runaway freight trains when they realize they've been duped by a lure, fly, or bait. Pike will typically lurk in vegetation in shallow water during daylight hours and attack any prey that happens by, including ducks, muskrats, songbirds, rodents, frogs, and other fish. In order to help control pike populations, bag limits for pike have been eliminated throughout the state. Anglers are encouraged to keep and kill all the pike they catch.

Tiger Muskie *(Esox masquinongy x E. lucius)*

General description: The most notorious warm-water hybrid in Colorado, the tiger muskie is a cross of the muskellunge and northern pike. Their sides are marked with distinctive tigerlike stripes, and their mouths are full of razor-sharp teeth. These fish are ferocious predators and have been called freshwater barracuda. They can grow to lengths exceeding 30 inches in five to six years. The state record tiger muskie—40.1 pounds, 53 inches—was caught at Quincy Reservoir in 1994. A 58-inch tiger muskie was caught and released at Quincy in 1997. While they resemble pike in shape and size, tiger muskies in the upper sizes increase their girth more than mature pike.

Distribution: Tiger muskies are sterile and are stocked in limited numbers in carefully selected impoundments due to the potential havoc such a large predator can wreak upon a fishery. Stocking began in eastern Colorado and on the Front Range in 1984. Tiger muskies were first stocked on the Western Slope in Harvey Gap Reservoir in 1995. They have been stocked in sixty impoundments over the past fifteen years but have successfully provided a fishery in about twenty waters.

Points to ponder: Their predacious nature makes the stocking of tiger muskies a good management tool to control suckers, carp, or other species that tend to become overabundant. Tiger muskies are not easy to catch, preferring large lures with bait, but are highly prized by a small but devoted number of warm-water anglers. Some of the best tiger muskie fisheries are Quincy, Lon Hagler, and Horseshoe Reservoirs.

Wiper *(Morone saxatilis x M. chrysops)*

General description: The wiper—a cross between a female striped bass and a male white bass—closely resembles the white bass in appearance, with a body shape similar to a slightly flattened football. Its silvery sides are marked with distinct horizontal black stripes, and it has two slightly separated dorsal fins, the front one sharp and spiny. But the wiper gets its size and growth rate from the striped bass, with fish in excess of 20 pounds sometimes caught in the big eastern Colorado reservoirs. The average-size wiper in most lakes runs 3 to 10 pounds. The state record is a 23.9-pound, 34-inch fish.

Distribution: Wiper populations are listed in twenty-one reservoirs, mostly along the Front Range and in eastern Colorado. Wipers are sterile, and populations are maintained by stocking.

Points to ponder: The wiper could well become a poster fish for the concept of hybrid vigor, combining the best traits of both parents. Its fighting ability is quickly becoming legendary. Voracious predators, wipers feed on gizzard shad and other bait fish, as well as on smaller game fish. During cooler times of the day or year, wipers will attack schools of bait fish in the shallows with a fury resembling a shark feeding frenzy. In warm weather schools of wiper will lie in deep water waiting for a school of small fish to pass over. Wipers also appear to be incredibly adaptable and have in several cases found new forage sources, such as crayfish, when the forage-fish population crashes. The most effective flies and lures resemble 3- to 6-inch fish. Some of the top wiper fisheries are Nee Noshe (which produced the state record in 1996), Pueblo and John Martin Reservoirs in southeast Colorado; North Sterling Reservoir in northeast Colorado; and Cherry Creek and Union Reservoirs in the Denver metro area.

Largemouth Bass *(Micropterus salmoides)*

General description: Largemouth bass vary from silvery green to dark olive and have a white belly. Their mouths extend past the hind margins of their eyes, which are brown. The dorsal fins are separated. The state record largemouth is 11.4 pounds, 22.5 inches.

Distribution: Largemouth bass, the undisputed old-timer of warm-water fisheries, were introduced into Colorado in 1878. The species is listed in forty-five Colorado waters in the Colorado Fishing Map guide but can be found in many more warm-water impoundments, from farm ponds, to suburban lakes, to gravel quarries. The state record was caught in Archuleta County in 1997.

Points to ponder: Largemouth bass favor warmer waters with extensive weed beds, lily pads, and other surface and subsurface cover from which they ambush prey like small fish, mice, birds, and frogs. These areas are best fished in the morning and evening. During the day, particularly sunny days, they tend to be found in deeper water off points of land, underwater river channels, and submerged weed beds.

Smallmouth Bass *(Micropterus dolomieui)*

General description: The smallmouth bass's color ranges from brown to olive, depending upon the type of water they inhabit. Their sides are marked with dark, blotchy vertical bars running the length of the fish's body. The mouth does not extend beyond the hind margins of the eyes. The state record is 5.75 pounds, 22 inches.

Distribution: Smallmouth bass were introduced into Colorado in 1951 and can now be found in at least twenty-one impoundments. Their range is restricted by a pref-erence for cooler, clearer water with rocky or gravel bottoms but often overlaps their largemouth cousins'.

Points to ponder: Smallmouth bass will normally be found in 12 to 25 feet of water above rocky shoals and gravel beds and along shoreline drop-offs and riprap at dams. In Colorado smallmouth have shown a preference for crayfish and small forage fish. Pueblo, McPhee, and Chatfield Reservoirs are among the top smallmouth fisheries in the state. The lower Yampa River is the only smallmouth river fishery in the state.

White Crappie *(Pomoxis annularis)*

General description: White crappies have olive-colored backs, silvery sides with vertical dark stripes, and white bellies. They average from 4 to 12 inches long. The state record is 4.25 pounds, 17 inches.

Distribution: Introduced into Colorado in 1882, white crappies have adapted successfully and are now found throughout the state in warm-water impoundments, preferring areas around submerged brush.

Points to ponder: Crappie anglers pursue the fish for its delicate flavor. The state record white crappie was caught in Northglenn Lake in 1975. Among the top crappie fisheries are John Martin and Nee Noshe Reservoirs in southeast Colorado and Jumbo Reservoir in northeast Colorado.

Channel Catfish *(Ictalurus punctatus)*

General description: The channel catfish has a silvery gray body with a white belly, a deeply forked tail, and a small head with whiskers around the mouth. Large adults and spawning males may be much darker. Channel catfish as large as 30 pounds have been caught. The state record is 33.5 pounds, 38 inches.

Distribution: Channel catfish, the only true native warm-water sport fish, is listed in the Colorado Fishing Map guide as being present in fifty-two of the sixty-one warm- and cold-water fisheries profiled. Unlike many of the introduced warm-water sport fishes, channel cats do well in river systems as well as impoundments.

Points to ponder: Top channel catfish fisheries include John Martin and Pueblo Reservoirs in the southeast, Horseshoe Reservoir west of Walsenburg, and Harvey Gap Reservoir on the Western Slope. Big channel cats can also be caught in the lower Yampa and Colorado Rivers. Channel catfish prefer clear lakes and streams with bottoms composed of rocks or sand but can be found in a wide range of waters. They typically feed at night and are not fussy about what they eat as long as it is bait, but they are more likely to feed in water temperatures from 50 to 70 degrees.

Rainbow Trout *(Onchorhynchus mykiss)*

General description: Rainbow trout have green backs and silvery sides covered with irregularly shaped dark spots, a horizontal reddish-pink stripe on each side of the body, and pink gill covers. Lake-dwelling rainbows might not have the red stripe on their sides. The average fish most anglers will catch is 8 to 12 inches, with some as large as 20 inches in wild-trout water and up to 8 to 10 pounds in some tailwaters directly below dams. The state record is 18.5 pounds, 32 inches.

Distribution: Rainbow trout have been heavily stocked for more than a century throughout the state, including most cold- and cool-water habitats, as well as some warm-water reservoirs and high-altitude lakes where they are incapable of reproduction. Today, their range has been diminished to a certain degree by whirling disease in some popular, mainstem rivers (see section on whirling disease), but they still persist in many rivers and fast-running streams. The Colorado Division of Wildlife has replaced rainbows in high-altitude waters with native cutthroat trout and cutthroat trout hybrids. The state record was caught in the South Platte River in 1972.

Points to ponder: Where they persist, rainbows are still the favorite quarry of anglers because they are relatively easy to catch and put up an acrobatic fight. Rainbows will hold in relatively fast water, even during daylight hours if there is some cover, and feed opportunistically and selectively throughout the day primarily on insects but as they grow in size, also on small fish.

Brown Trout *(Salmo trutta)*

General description: Brown trout have olive to brown backs, lighter colored sides with black and red spots, and yellowish bellies. The head is relatively large for a trout, and as they grow older, males develop a hooked jaw, which becomes pronounced during spawning. Anglers can catch browns from 6 inches all the way up to 26 inches in some tailwaters and mountain reservoirs. The state record is 30 pounds, 36 inches.

Distribution: Brown trout can be found in nearly all cold-water habitats, from small mountain streams to slow, silt-bottomed meandering rivers, as well as mountain lakes and reservoirs. The state record was caught at Roaring Judy Hatchery in 1988.

Points to ponder: Young brown trout are similar to rainbows in their food preferences and habitats, but by the time they reach 16 inches or so, they have become secretive and tend to feed at night. Bigger browns tend to find protected, slow-water areas off moderate currents to hold in and will remain in those areas most of their lives, except during nightly feeding forays and spawning. They will come out during heavy hatches but prefer to eat small fish, leeches, and bigger insects like stoneflies and grasshoppers. When hooked, brown trout will often attempt to tangle the line in any nearby obstructions, such as tree limbs or roots, so the angler should be aware of these and attempt to pull the fish into open water if possible.

Cutthroat Trout *(Onchorinchus clarki)*

General description: These fish are among the most beautiful in the aquatic kingdom, with a crimson slash along the gill covers and with equally striking shadings of orange and golden yellow over a golden or brassy background color. Their black spots vary in size and are concentrated near the tail. Habitat limitations restrict cutthroat growth, so the average fish in streams will be 8 to 10 inches long. Some lake cutthroat may grow to 18 inches, though they are rare. The state record is 16 pounds. There are three widely recognized subspecies of cutthroat trout in Colorado: the greenback, the Colorado River, and the Rio Grande.

Distribution: Remaining populations of native cutthroat trout are largely relegated to headwater streams and alpine lakes. Colorado River cutthroat are found west of the Continental Divide. Greenback cutthroat are primarily in Rocky Mountain National Park east of the Continental Divide as well as in the headwaters of the Cache La Poudre and Arkansas Rivers. The state record was caught in Twin Lakes in 1964. Rio Grande cutthroat are found primarily in the Rio Grande basin.

Points to ponder: Genetically pure populations of Colorado's native trout are few and generally under special management to protect them from overharvest. Most of the cutthroat trout that anglers will catch are slightly hybridized (with other cutthroat) and are now being stocked in timberline lakes in place of rainbow trout. These fish are stocked for recreational fishing, although catch-and-release fishing is allowed for most protected populations. If in doubt, return cutthroat trout quickly to the water.

Fine-Spotted Snake River Cutthroat Trout *(Onchorhynchus clarki behnkei)*

General description: These fish are silvery colored, with lighter red gill covers than most cutthroat and a profusion of small black spots on their sides. For the most part, they are similar in size to river-run rainbows, averaging from 8 to 20 inches. In productive lake habitats they can grow to 15 pounds but will usually be 3 to 5 pounds.

Distribution: As Snake River cutthroat are more resistant to whirling disease, look for them in future years in waters heavily impacted by the disease, as well as in larger mountain reservoirs.

Points to ponder: Look for Snake River cutthroat in rainbow trout habitat and use similar fishing methods.

Kokanee *(Onchorynchus nerka)*

General description: Kokanees, landlocked sockeye salmon, are silvery-sided fish with green backs. During their spawning runs the males develop a pronounced snarling curve in their jaws, and both sexes turn red in color with dark-green heads. They live in reservoirs for three to four years, attaining a weight of 3 to 5 pounds, before making a spawning run and dying.

Distribution: Kokanees are found in Vallecito, McPhee, and Blue Mesa Reservoirs, among others. In the fall they can be found on their spawning runs in streams feeding the reservoirs. Fishing is allowed, with restrictions, in the Gunnison River during the spawning run.

Points to ponder: Deep-trolling with flashy lures is the best way to catch kokanee salmon.

Lake Trout *(Salvelinus namaycush)*

General description: Lake trout, also known as mackinaw, are by far the largest trout in Colorado, averaging 10 to 15 pounds, with many caught in excess of 30 pounds. The state record is 38 pounds, 39.5 inches. They are gray to brown, and their sides are profusely decorated with beige spots.

Distribution: Lake trout are found in relatively few Colorado waters—generally large, deep reservoirs in the mountains. The best lake trout fishing is at Blue Mesa Reservoir, where the state record fish was caught in 1998.

Points to ponder: Lake trout are generally found in deep water in large water bodies, and successful anglers will need a boat with a fish finder to locate them. Trolling lures that imitate small fish, such as chrome Flatfish or silver Rapalas, is the method of choice. Many anglers use meat on the lures or drop a sucker meat-baited hook on the bottom.

Brook Trout *(Salvelinus fontinalis)*

General description: Brook trout are one of the most colorful fish in Colorado, with wavy lines on their greenish backs and upper sides, giving way to yellow and red spots circled by a ring of blue. In Colorado streams they rarely exceed 10 inches, while some lake-dwelling brook trout reach 5 pounds. The state record is 7.8 pounds.

Distribution: Brook trout can be found in nearly all headwater streams and beaver ponds in the high mountains, with some small populations in lower-elevation streams. The state record brookie was caught in Cataract Lake in 1947.

Points to ponder: The brook trout's favored habitat, the coldest headwater streams, puts them in direct competition with cutthroat trout. In fact, brook trout are one of the main factors in cutthroat trout declines in the past fifty years. Even in the absence of cutthroat, brook trout proliferate to the point where many are undernourished, even starving. Colorado officials encourage anglers to catch and keep their limit of brook trout, which is easy to do because many believe they are the best-tasting trout.

Using This Guide

This book is organized into five sections: Southwest, Northwest, Northeast, Southeast, and Denver Metro Area.

In some cases, information is not repeated on closely situated lakes to save the reader time. The numbers of the various fisheries, as well as places of interest such as campgrounds and river access points, correspond to numbers on the maps. The descriptions of the fisheries in this book are organized as follows:

Key species: This section contains a list of the most prominent game fishes found at the site.

Description: Terrain and water conditions at each site are described in this section. Due to the length and changing nature of many Colorado rivers, some are detailed in multiple sections. Where appropriate, information on nearby campgrounds is also included.

Tips: This section contains specific information related to successful fishing techniques, safety, and other related material.

The fishing: Various techniques and considerations relevant to angler success for the key species, as well as prime locations, times to fish, and public access, are contained in this section. Public access is also noted on the maps when possible.

Stream census data: When available, stream sampling data showing the composition, abundance, and size of the key species are listed here.

Whirling disease: The presence of whirling disease and any ramifications to the site are noted here, if applicable.

Directions: Directions to fishing sites and nearby campgrounds from the nearest towns or cities are detailed in this section to complement the maps.

Additional information: This section includes special regulations, historical and environmental facts, safety considerations, fees, facilities such as boat ramps, and other services important to the angler.

Contact: The names and phone numbers of government agencies responsible for specific areas are given here.

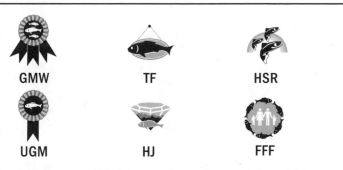

GMW State-designated Gold Medal waters for numbers and sizes of fish

UGM Undesignated, but meets or exceeds Gold Medal standards

TF Trophy-size fish

HJ Hidden jewel; good fishing and scenery off the beaten path

HSR Heavily stocked with rainbow trout on a regular basis

FFF Family fishing fun; easy access with lots of easily caught fish

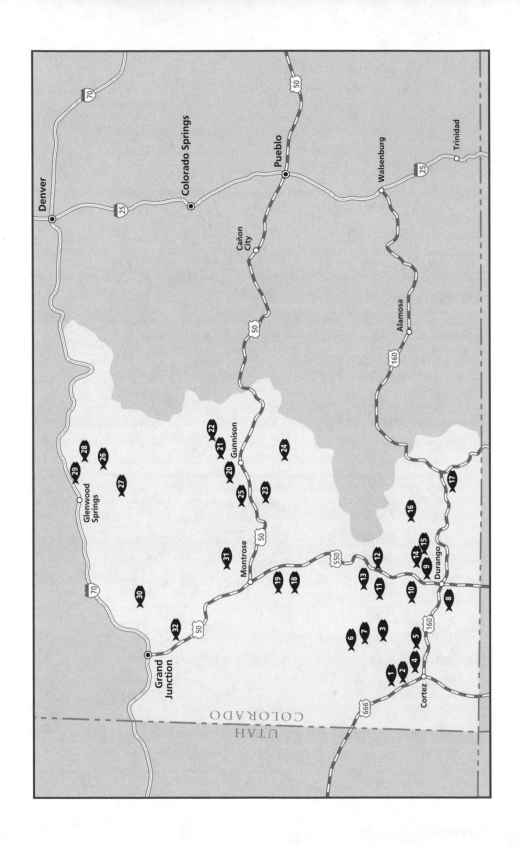

Southwest Colorado

1 Dolores River below McPhee Reservoir

Key species: Brown trout, rainbow trout, Snake River cutthroat trout.

Description: The lower Dolores River below McPhee Reservoir is a tailwater trout fishery stretching 12 miles northeast through the high desert in the southwest corner of Colorado, maybe a few miles farther depending on flow and clarity. It eventually joins the San Miguel River a few miles from the Utah border.

Tips: The fish are extremely wary despite relatively low fishing pressure. This river was severely hurt by drought in 2002, and it may take some time to bounce back.

The fishing: Browns are predominate in this stretch, and while their numbers are down, nearly a fourth of those caught are larger than 14 inches. The introduction of fingerling rainbows and Snake River cutthroat in 1999 has brought some catches of these fish up to 14 to 16 inches. The fish here are strongly oriented to key insect hatches. The best fishing is between late April and early June. In summer hopper patterns and natural dry-fly imitations of caddis flies, pale morning duns, and midges work best because heavy moss from warming water fouls nymphs, streamers, and spinners. During the warm summer months, fish morning or evening. In the fall water temperatures cool, and blue-winged olives start to come off midday.

Stream census data: Seventy percent of the fish in the 12-mile stretch are brown trout. Anglers are taking an average of one fish per hour.

Whirling disease: Positive. Natural reproduction of rainbow trout has nearly ceased, but supplemental stocking of rainbow trout fingerlings should reestablish the population to a certain degree.

Directions: From Cortez, take U.S. Highway 666 north for 21 miles to Forest Road 505, turn east and stay on the road to Bradfield Bridge, then follow Forest Road 504 along the river to the dam.

Additional information: Heavy recreational rafting clogs the river as long as seasonal water flows are high enough to navigate it, which could be mid-May to mid-July. Flies-and-lures-only and catch-and-release regulations are in effect for all fish from McPhee Reservoir to Bradfield Bridge.

Contact: Colorado Division of Wildlife, Montrose; (970) 249–3431.

2 McPhee Reservoir

Key species: Kokanee, rainbow trout, smallmouth bass.

Description: This reservoir, at 4,400 acres the largest mixed warm-water/cool-water fishery in western Colorado, is located in the piñon and juniper hills west of Dolores.

Tips: McPhee Reservoir's springtime smallmouth bass fishing is among the best in the state.

The fishing: Use Gitzit tube jigs, curly-tail grubs, spinners, and crankbaits to catch up to 14-inch smallmouths, with some larger than 15 inches, in the coves. Troll for kokanees and trout up to 14 inches in the Dolores River inlet area with lures, spinners, and bait in the spring and deep-troll in the old river channel all summerlong. The best bank-fishing is along the southwest shore and in the cove at the House Creek Recreation Area.

Directions: From Cortez, take U.S. Highway 160 west for 2 miles, then go north for 8 miles on Colorado Highway 145 to Colorado Highway 184 and proceed west to fishing access areas and boat ramps.

Additional information: Bank access is steep around most of the lake, necessitating the use of a boat. Smallmouth and largemouth bass must be 15 inches or larger to be kept. Kokanees must be returned to the water from the Dolores River inlet upstream to the confluence with the West Fork of the Dolores River.

Contact: Colorado Division of Wildlife, Montrose; (970) 249–3431.

2A Camping: McPhee Reservoir Recreation Area

This campground, sitting on a high bluff overlooking the reservoir, has modern facilities and a marina. From Cortez, take U.S. 160 west for 2 miles, then go north for 8 miles on CO 145 to CO 184 and proceed west 6 miles to the recreation area entrance.

2B Camping: House Creek Recreation Area

This campground, on the east side of the reservoir, has drinking water, some electrical hookups, rest rooms, an RV dump station, and a boat ramp. From Dolores, go northeast on Forest Road 526 for 7 miles, then turn west on Forest Road 528 and drive 6 miles.

3 Upper Dolores River

Key species: Cutthroat trout.

Description: This is a classic freestone river draining Lizardhead Pass. From its headwaters to the town of Rico, the river is productive. Mining pollution below Rico and lack of stocking limit fishing to small brookies until just outside Dolores.

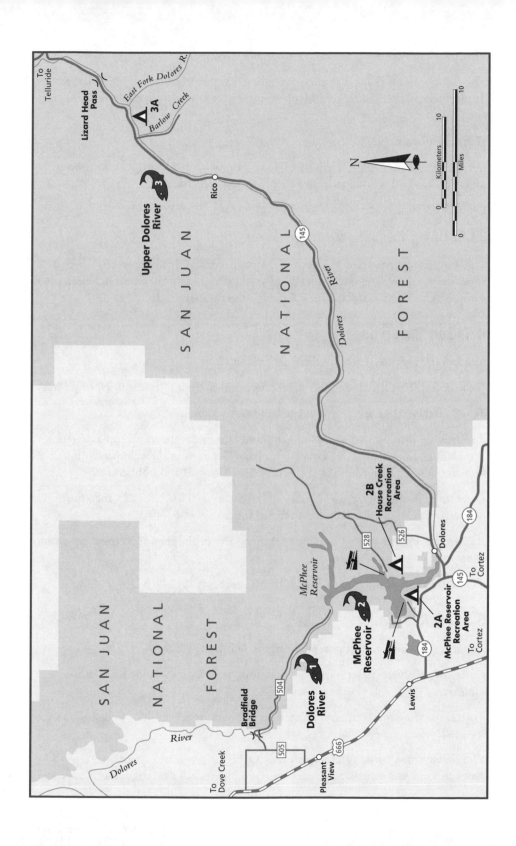

Tips: Dry-fly attractor patterns are especially effective.

The fishing: From the end of runoff to fall, use small Stimulators, Humpies, Royal Trudes, terrestrials, red or gold Mepps spinners, or worms to haul in up to 10-inch cutthroat.

Whirling disease: Negative.

Directions: From Dolores, take Colorado Highway 145 northeast for about 30 miles to Rico and work upstream as the river parallels the road.

Contact: Colorado Division of Wildlife, Montrose; (970) 249–3431.

3A Camping: Cayton Area

This busy campground on the upper Dolores River has drinking water, tables, rest rooms, and a dump station. From Dolores, take CO 145 northeast for 42 miles, then turn east on Forest Road 578 for 0.5 mile to the campground.

4 Totten Reservoir

Key species: Northern pike, bluegill, largemouth bass.

Description: This lake lies in the scrub piñon and juniper hills northeast of Cortez.

Tips: Northern pike are overpopulated and easily caught.

The fishing: Fishing shallow water early and late in the day with top-water plugs produces good-size pike and largemouth bass. Go deep in the summer with baited lures resembling fish. Bluegills are susceptible to worms and bobbers.

Directions: From Cortez, go east on U.S. Highway 160 for 3.5 miles, then north on Montezuma County Road 29 for 1 mile to the lake.

Additional information: Camping and fires are prohibited. Wakeless boats are allowed.

Contact: Colorado Division of Wildlife, Montrose; (970) 249–3431.

5 Puett Reservoir

Key species: Walleye, northern pike, largemouth bass, yellow perch.

Description: Puett Reservoir is a high-altitude lake surrounded by piñon and juniper.

Tips: Depending on weather, access may require a four-wheel-drive vehicle or a hike for the last half mile.

The fishing: Bank-fishing early and late in the day with buzz bait and top-water plugs around weed beds and snags will produce good-size largemouth bass and

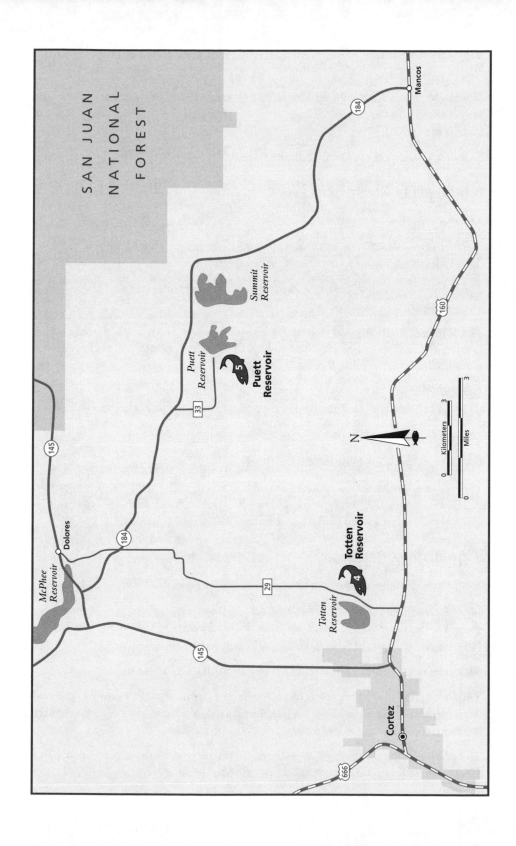

pike. Crayfish patterns fished along submerged rock formations will bring in small-mouth bass.

Directions: From Mancos, take Colorado Highway 184 northwest for 10 miles to Montezuma County Road 33, then go 1 mile south to the trailhead, then east 0.5 mile to the lake.

Contact: Colorado Division of Wildlife, Montrose; (970) 249–3431.

6 Miramonte Reservoir

Key species: Rainbow trout.

Description: This 420-acre reservoir is in a meadow surrounded by scrub timber on the north side of Lone Cone Peak in the San Juan Mountains.

Tips: Heavy fingerling stocking makes this a premium rainbow trout fishery that is known mostly to locals.

The fishing: Fishing is good from the banks for rainbow trout up to 16 inches. Use crayfish fly or lure imitations, or, of course, the crayfish themselves, as they are the trout's main forage food in this lake.

Directions: From Norwood, go 1.5 miles east on Colorado Highway 145 to Forest Road 610 (Norwood-Dolores Road), then go 17 miles south to the reservoir.

Contact: Colorado Division of Wildlife, Montrose; (970) 249–3431.

6A Camping: Miramonte Reservoir Area

This remote, lakeside campground has drinking water, shelters, an RV dump station, and a boat ramp. From Norwood, go 1.5 miles east on CO 145 to FR 610 (Norwood-Dolores Road), then go 17 miles south to the reservoir.

7 Groundhog Reservoir

Key species: Rainbow trout, brook trout, brown trout, cutthroat trout hybrids.

Description: This high-altitude, 667-acre meadow reservoir, surrounded by panoramic peaks and forested mesas, is at the headwaters of the North Fork of the Dolores River.

Tips: The isolated location keeps fish populations high and healthy.

The fishing: Open regulations allow rainbows and cutthroat to be taken by standard flies, lures, and bait from shore or wakeless boats. Work the inlet and outlet early morning and evening. Go deep during the heat of the day.

Directions: From Dolores, go 25 miles north on the well-maintained Forest Road 526 to Forest Road 533, then 5 miles northeast to the reservoir.

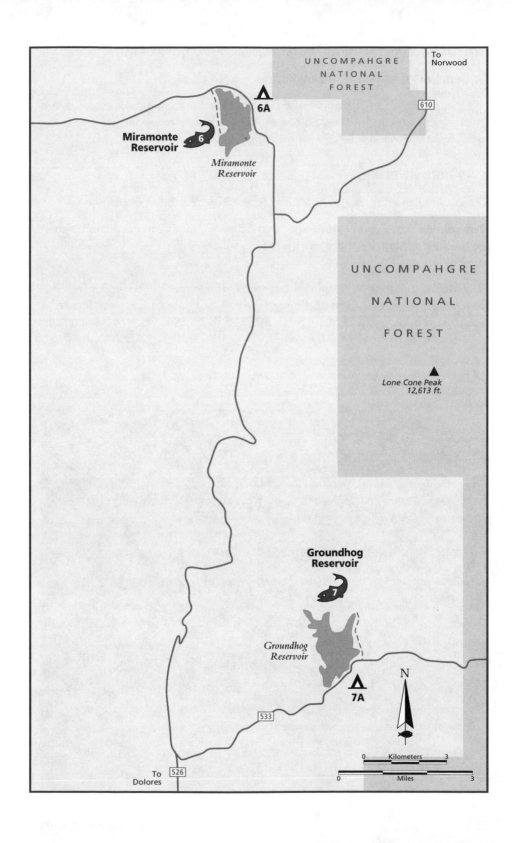

To Norwood

UNCOMPAHGRE
NATIONAL
FOREST

610

**Miramonte
Reservoir**

6

6A

*Miramonte
Reservoir*

UNCOMPAHGRE

NATIONAL

FOREST

▲ Lone Cone Peak
12,613 ft.

**Groundhog
Reservoir**

7

*Groundhog
Reservoir*

7A

N

533

To
Dolores   526

0   Kilometers   3

0   Miles   3

Contact: Colorado Division of Wildlife, Montrose; (970) 249–3431.

7A Camping: Groundhog Reservoir Area

This campground has drinking water, rest rooms, a boat ramp, and a store. From Dolores, go 25 miles north on FR 526 to FR 533, then 5 miles northeast to reservoir. The campground is just across the dam.

8 Animas River

Key species: Brown trout, rainbow trout, Snake River cutthroat trout.

Description: The Animas River begins in the Red Mountain mining district high in the San Juan Mountains and flows freely for about 60 miles to the Colorado–New Mexico border.

Tips: Mining pollution has stunted fish reproduction in much of the upper river but has abated enough that a stretch through the city of Durango has been declared a Gold Medal fishery. A prolific trico mayfly hatch in 2002 has resulted in significant trout growth in the river in Durango.

The Animas River in Durango

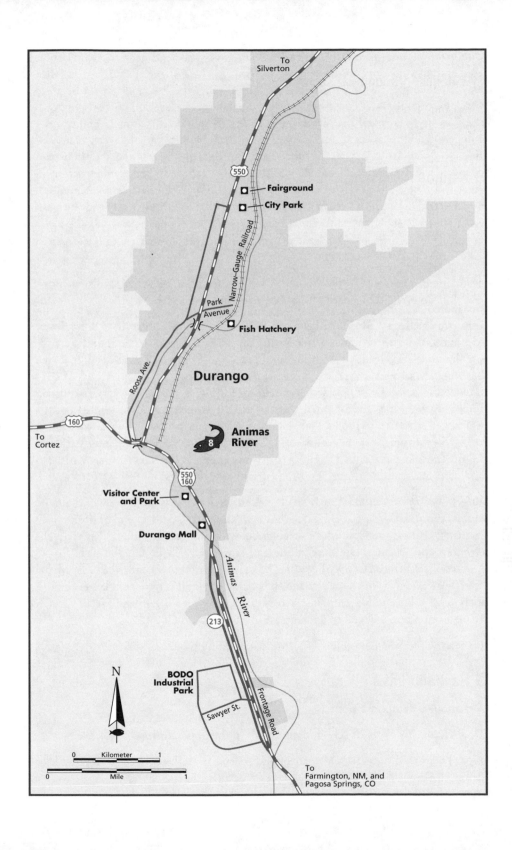

To
Silverton

550

■ **Fairground**
■ **City Park**

Narrow-Gauge Railroad

Park
Avenue

■ **Fish Hatchery**

Roosa Ave.

Durango

160

To
Cortez

8 **Animas
River**

550
160

**Visitor Center
and Park** ■

■

Durango Mall

Animas River

213

N

BODO
Industrial
Park

Sawyer St.

Frontage Road

0   Kilometer   1

0   Mile   1

To
Farmington, NM, and
Pagosa Springs, CO

The fishing: The Animas River through Durango is wide and deep and experiences tremendous runoff from May to July, so fishing is best in the spring, late summer, and fall. The fish are very hatch-oriented. Blue-winged olives and midges begin to hatch before the water comes up. As the water starts to clear and come down, caddis flies begin to hatch. Brown trout will also respond to streamers and Woolly Buggers. Spin fishers can use Rooster Tails in yellow, brown, and black combinations to good effect. Heavier lures are required for higher water and should be cast across slack water behind boulders and quickly retrieved. The 2-mile section of river south of the U.S. Highway 160 bridge to the Purple Cliffs area is designated a Gold Medal fishery, with about a 60/40 brown trout to rainbow trout ratio. Fish can reach 18 to 20 inches. A surprise in recent years is the appearance of Snake River cutthroat, which probably migrated upriver from the Southern Ute Reservation, where they have been stocked.

Whirling disease: In 1999 the Animas River was found to be whirling-disease positive, but no population-level effects have been noticed so far.

Directions: Using the bridge where U.S. Highway 160 splits off from U.S. Highway 550 and crosses the Animas River, upstream fishing access can be found by proceeding to the west side of the bridge and turning north onto Roosa Avenue, which becomes Park Avenue. At the end of Park Avenue, access to the next stretch of river is available at the Durango Hatchery and by following the narrow-gauge railroad tracks to the north end of town. Access to that stretch can also be made at the Durango City Park or the La Plata County Fairgrounds.

Downstream from the bridge, take U.S. 160/550 to the visitor center park and follow the bike path, which parallels the river. Or exit at La Plata County Road 213 and continue south to the BODO Industrial Park; turn east on Sawyer Street.

Additional information: Nearly all the Animas River within Durango is public access. From the U.S. 160 bridge 2 miles downstream to the lower end of the BODO Industrial Park is the Gold Medal stretch. Below Durango, the Animas River quickly enters the Southern Ute Reservation and requires a tribal fishing license. Above Durango to Hermosa Creek, the river is on private property. Fishing the Gold Medal stretch is limited to flies and lures and the possession limit is two trout larger than 16 inches. Very little public camping is available in the immediate vicinity; however, a KOA campground is located 8 miles east of Durango on U.S. 160.

Contact: Colorado Division of Wildlife, Montrose; (970) 249–3431.

9 Haviland Lake

Key species: Rainbow trout.

Description: This is a 70-acre impoundment in the upper Animas River Valley.

Tips: The season runs from May through September, with easy access to good lake fishing.

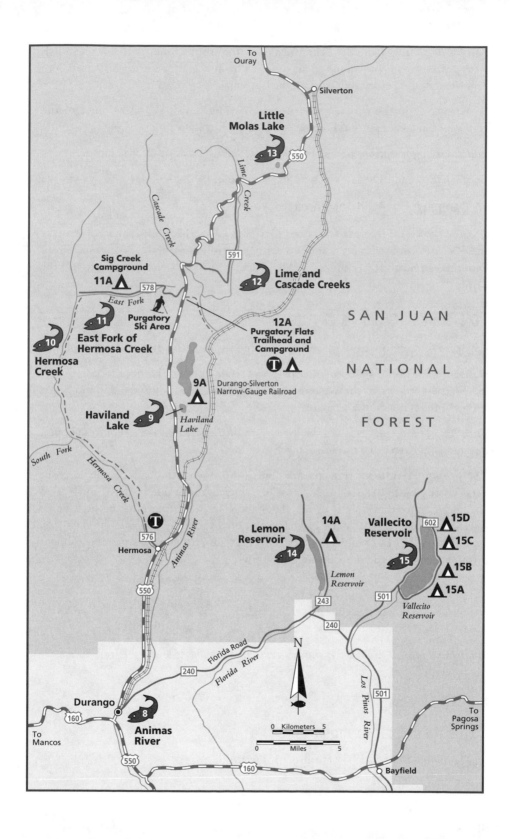

The fishing: Midges and damselflies make up the trout's food on this lake, so fish these patterns or throw some small spinners from a belly boat toward shore and retrieve, letting the lure stay close to the bottom.

Directions: From Durango, go north on U.S. Highway 550 for 18 miles to the Haviland Lake Campground on the east side of the highway.

Additional information: Boats must be propelled by hand or electric motor.

Contact: Colorado Division of Wildlife, Montrose; (970) 249–3431.

9A Camping: Haviland Lake Area

Located between Hermosa Cliffs and Haviland Lake, this campground offers tent and RV sites with drinking water, vault toilets, fire grates, and a boat dock. From Durango, go north for 17 miles on U.S. 550, then turn east on Forest Road 671 for 1 mile.

10 Hermosa Creek

Key species: Rainbow trout, brook trout, rainbow/cutthroat hybrid (cutbow).

Description: This 20-mile-long stream flows south through Hermosa Park, one of the prettiest valleys in the western part of the state, and joins the Animas River about 10 miles north of Durango.

Tips: An 18-mile trail parallels the lower part of the stream, but it requires about a one-hour hike from the trailhead to get close to the water.

The fishing: Hermosa Creek has developed into one of the better rainbow trout fisheries in southwest Colorado, possibly due to the limited access and varied stream structure throughout its length. Anglers are reporting catching high numbers of fish, some in the 12- to 14-inch range, on a variety of general flies and lures, as well as on bait. Even with a trail, the hike presents challenges, as the river plunges through canyons and winds through meadows.

Whirling disease: Negative.

Directions: From Durango, take U.S. Highway 550 for about 8 miles north to Forest Road 576, then turn west and drive 3 miles to the trailhead.

Additional information: Backcountry camping is available along the trail. There are no developed sites.

Contact: Colorado Division of Wildlife, Montrose; (970) 249–3431.

11 East Fork of Hermosa Creek

Key species: Colorado River cutthroat trout, brook trout.

Description: This little creek comes off the backside of the Purgatory Ski Area and meanders 2.5 miles through a grassy meadow before tumbling into a forested stretch at Sig Creek Campground for another 2 miles until it joins Hermosa Creek.

Tips: Absolute stealth, fine tippit, and delicate delivery are required to catch the cutthroat.

The fishing: The upper stretch, above a waterfall adjacent to the national forest campground, holds a recovery population of pure Colorado River cutthroat up to 10 inches long. Any small dry-fly natural or attractor pattern will provoke a strike as long as the fish don't see you. Stay well back and drop the fly into pools or against undercut banks. If the fish aren't suspicious, the strike will be immediate. After two or three tries, move to the next spot. These small cutthroat will spook at anything resembling a predator fish, making lures and spinners virtually worthless. Below the waterfall East Hermosa Creek is chock-full of brookies, which should be fished with worms or dry flies.

Whirling disease: Negative.

Directions: From Durango, drive 25 miles north on U.S. Highway 550 to the Purgatory Ski Area, then turn west on Forest Road 578. About 3 miles in, the creek parallels the road.

The East Fork of Hermosa Creek holds Colorado River cutthroat trout.

Additional information: All cutthroat trout must be returned immediately to the water. Anglers are encouraged to catch and keep their limit of brookies to help control the population.

Contact: Colorado Division of Wildlife, Montrose; (970) 249–3431.

11A Camping: East Fork of Hermosa Creek Area

This south-facing campsite offers rustic sites with drinking water, rest rooms, and fire grates. From Durango, drive 25 miles north on U.S. 550 to the Purgatory Ski Area, then turn west on FR 578 and drive 5 miles to the Sig Creek Campground.

12 Lime and Cascade Creeks

Key species: Rainbow trout, brown trout, brook trout, cutthroat trout.

Description: Lime Creek's headwaters are in the basin below 10,900-foot Molas Pass south of Silverton, where three alpine tributaries join in a rugged canyon below a 10-mile historic mining road. Six miles downstream, Lime Creek joins Cascade Creek, and they flow 2 miles through a rugged, remote canyon into the Animas River.

Tips: The easiest access is by taking the Denver and Rio Grande narrow-gauge railroad out of Durango and getting off at the Cascade Creek trailhead.

The fishing: This is wild country and wild water, and the fish are suckers for attractor dry flies. Some of the bigger fish lurk in pools that are inaccessible until low water and are quite willing to take small lures and weighted nymphs. Worms and salmon eggs should allow anglers to take their limit of smaller fish in short order. A big fish in these streams is going to be about 12 inches long, but the challenge is fishing in such a beautiful, remote area.

Whirling disease: Negative.

Directions: From Durango, drive 25 miles north on U.S. Highway 550 to the Purgatory Flats Campground and trailhead, which are on the east side of the highway across from the Purgatory Ski Area, and hike 3 miles down to Cascade Creek.

Contact: Colorado Division of Wildlife, Montrose; (970) 249–3431.

12A Camping: Purgatory Flats Area

This shady campsite is near the highway and offers small tent and vehicle camping with rest rooms, water, and fire grates. From Durango, drive 25 miles north on U.S. 550. The campsite is just off the highway across from the ski area.

13 Little Molas Lake

Key species: Rainbow trout, brook trout.

Description: This is a 7-acre natural lake at 11,000 feet, west of the rugged Needles Peaks in the San Juan National Forest.

Tips: Little Molas is an excellent float-tubing lake.

The fishing: Regular stocking of fingerling rainbow trout keeps this little lake a productive, if out-of-the-way, sport fishery. Trout grow up to 12 inches in this lake and can be taken on spinners, bait, streamers, or flies. Damselfly nymphs and caddis emergers are proven fly patterns. Fish at various depths to figure out where the fish are feeding.

Directions: From Silverton, drive south on U.S. Highway 550 for 6 miles to the turnoff for Little Molas Lake on the west side of the road.

Contact: Colorado Division of Wildlife, Montrose; (970) 249–3431.

14 Lemon Reservoir

Key species: Brown trout, rainbow trout, kokanee.

Description: Lemon Reservoir is a 600-acre impoundment in a narrow mountain valley just outside the southwestern corner of the Weminuche Wilderness in the San Juan Mountains.

Tips: Medium-size rainbow trout and some big browns congregate at the Florida River inlet in the spring and again in the late summer.

The fishing: Midges are the primary hatch during the spring and fall, and midge and mosquito dry-fly patterns are effective. Woolly Buggers and small gold or silver spinners fished from the shore will bring up the browns and an occasional kokanee. Salmon eggs are effective fished near the bottom in shallow areas or at the inlet in spring and fall. Trolling flashers with a Rooster Tail will produce trout, and trolling flashers with a Cherry Bobber will take kokanees. Above the reservoir a road runs along the Florida River, and the 2-mile stretch up to the Transfer Park Campground offers easy access to the river. Above the campground the river runs through a scenic but difficult to access canyon. Small rainbows, brookies, and browns are in the river but are easily spooked. Small mayfly nymph patterns delicately presented, as well as yellow caddis dry flies, will take some fish, mostly in the 8- to 10-inch range.

Directions: From Durango, drive 9 miles northeast on La Plata County Road 240 (Florida Road) to County Road 243, then go north 3 miles to the reservoir.

Additional information: Camping fees are charged. There is one boat ramp on the north side of the reservoir. The Florida River below the reservoir is entirely private.

Contact: Colorado Division of Wildlife, Montrose; (970) 249–3431.

14A Camping: Miller Creek Area

This lakeside campground offers tent and RV camping with drinking water, vault toilets, fire grates, tables, and a boat ramp. From Durango, drive 9 miles northeast on La Plata CR 240 (Florida Road) to CR 243, then go north 3 miles to the reservoir. The campsite is about 1.5 miles past the dam.

15 Vallecito Reservoir

Key species: Brown trout, northern pike, rainbow trout, kokanee.

Description: At 7,600 feet in altitude and 2,700 acres, Vallecito Reservoir is big water that produces big fish.

Tips: Shore action is going to be limited. If you don't have a boat, use a float tube but keep an eye out for sudden windstorms.

The fishing: Brown trout up to 20 inches, pike in excess of 20 pounds, kokanees up to 4 pounds, and rainbows from 12 to 16 inches are caught regularly in this impoundment. Look for northern pike in the spring, and cast large lures into shallow shoreline coves. Brown trout can be taken by trolling silver Rapala spoons along the north end of the reservoir, near the islands, or along the dam. Kokanees should be fished from a boat by trolling pop gear trailed by a Kokanee Killer. Rainbows can be taken all summerlong by trolling flashers tipped with a worm or from shore with PowerBait or salmon eggs rigged to float just off the bottom.

Directions: From Durango, go east on U.S. Highway 160 for 19 miles to Bayfield, then north for 12 miles on La Plata County Road 501 to the reservoir.

Additional information: Camping and boating fees are required. There are three boat ramps available. The reservoir is a high-use recreation area—expect crowds.

Contact: Colorado Division of Wildlife, Montrose; (970) 249–3431.

15A Camping: Graham Creek Area

The first of four campgrounds on the east side of Vallecito Reservoir, Graham Creek is best suited for tents and small RVs and features drinking water, tables, and rest rooms. From Durango, go east on U.S. 160 for 19 miles to Bayfield, then north for 12 miles on La Plata CR 501 to the reservoir. Take Forest Road 603 across the dam and go 3 miles.

15B Camping: North Canyon Area

A little more secluded than its nearly neighbors, North Canyon has vault toilets, fire grates, picnic tables, and drinking water. From Durango, go east on U.S. 160 19 miles to Bayfield, then north for 12 miles on La Plata CR 501 to the reservoir. Take FR 603 across the dam and go 3.5 miles.

15C Camping: Pine Point Area

This campground is suited for large RVs, with plenty of shade and the same facilities as other Vallecito campsites. From Durango, go east on U.S. 160 for 19 miles to

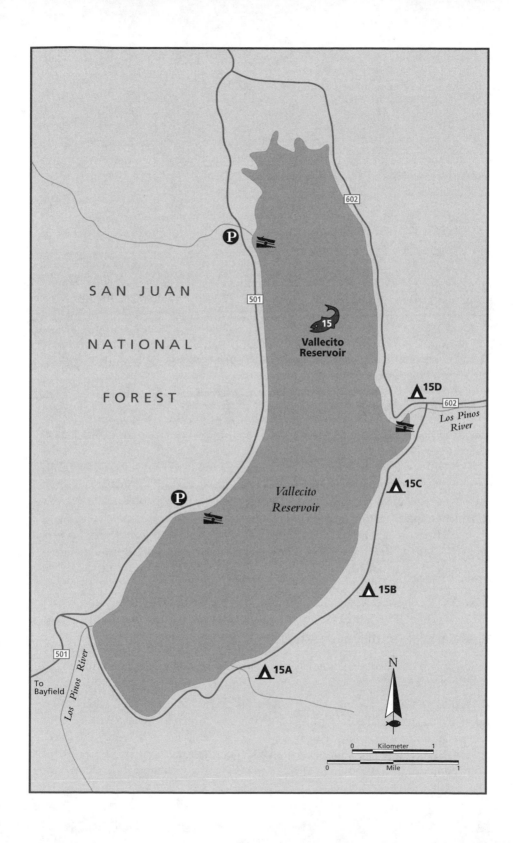

Bayfield, then north for 12 miles on La Plata CR 501 to the reservoir. Take FR 603 across the dam and go 4 miles.

15D Camping: Middle Mountain Area

Situated on a sloping hill above the reservoir, this site offers a good view of the lake and access to the water, along with the basic facilities. From Durango, go east on U.S. 160 for 19 miles to Bayfield, then north for 12 miles on La Plata CR 501 to the reservoir. Take FR 603 across the dam and go 4.5 miles to Forest Road 602, then west 0.5 mile.

16 Piedra River

Key species: Brown trout, rainbow trout.

Description: The Piedra River drains the south side of the Weminuche Wilderness in the San Juan Range and has cut a spectacular 20-mile canyon through the mountains as it winds its way to the rolling hills and mesas of the Southern Ute Reservation.

Tips: Be prepared for a strenuous hike, as the main river can only be accessed by vehicle at two points in its entire reach.

The fishing: Due to the extreme terrain, the lower 10-mile section of river is virtually inaccessible during high water. The upper section, however, has a trail well above the river and offers river access all summer long. Even so, mid- to late June is about the earliest the river can be fished due to runoff. The fish range up to 16 inches. Hatches begin with stoneflies, salmonflies, and caddis flies at the end of runoff, with mayflies beginning a couple of weeks later, followed by terrestrials—all in a season just two and a half months long. Along with the varied structure of the river, this makes for an anything-goes approach. Take standard attractors like Royal Wulffs, Humpies, and Stimulators and old standbys like bead-head Prince, Hare's Ear, and Pheasant Tail nymphs. Or consult local fly shops to get up-to-date information on the current hatches. Likewise, lures can run the gamut but should be heavier for high water. Be prepared to lose some—trees from the wooded slope above the river occasionally end up in the water. The Middle Fork of the Piedra River, which joins with the East Fork and Williams Creek to become the main river, is accessible by car and has hatches similar to those on the main river. The Middle Fork is primarily brown trout water, with fish up to 14 inches regularly caught.

Whirling disease: Negative.

Directions: To access the upper Piedra River, Williams Creek, or the East and West Forks of the Piedra, take Forest Road 631 (Piedra Road), which is 2.5 miles west of Pagosa Springs on U.S. Highway 160, northwest for 20 miles. To reach the lower Piedra River from Pagosa Springs, take U.S. 160 west for 20 miles to Forest Road 622 (First Fork Road) and drive 11 miles to the river. Forest Service Trail 596 con-

Ron Baird fishing a nice hole in Second Box Canyon on the Piedra River.

nects the upper and lower river on the north bank. The Sheep Creek access to First Box Canyon is about 6.5 miles up FR 622 on the west side of the road. Second Box Canyon, which is accessible during low water, is about 2 miles up Trail 596 from the First Fork Campground.

Additional information: The entire mainstem Piedra River is flies and lures only, and the possession limit is two trout. A 3-mile stretch below Sheep Creek is private property.

Contact: Colorado Division of Wildlife, Montrose; (970) 249–3431.

16A Camping: Lower Piedra River Area

This riverside campground has vault toilets, tables, and fire grates but no drinking water. From Pagosa Springs, take U.S. 160 west for 20.5 miles to Forest Road 621, just west of the Piedra River, turn north and go 1.5 miles.

16B Camping: First Fork Area

This riverside campground has informal sites and a vault toilet. From Pagosa Springs, take U.S. 160 west for 20 miles to FR 622 (First Fork Road) and drive 11 miles.

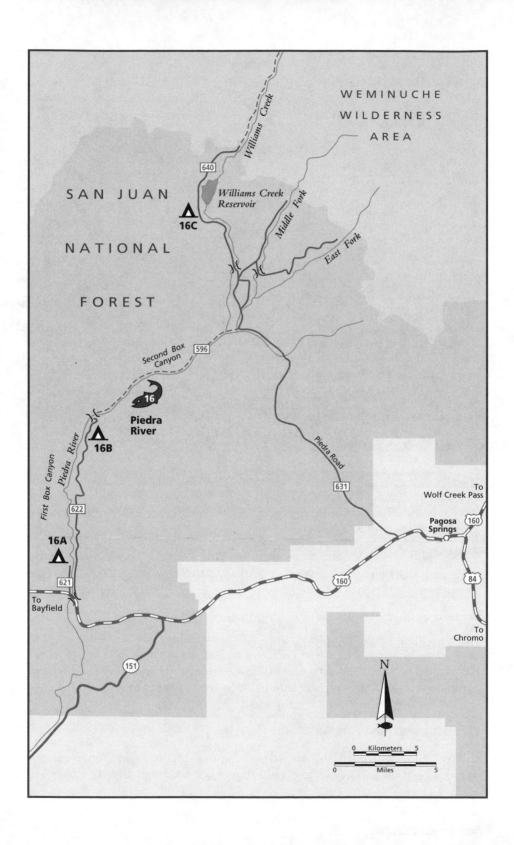

16C Camping: Williams Creek Area

This large, popular campground has good shade, drinking water, vault toilets, tables, and fire grates. From Pagosa Springs, take U.S. 160 west for 2.5 miles to FR 631 (Piedra Road) and go 22 miles to Forest Road 640, then turn north and go 0.5 mile.

17 San Juan River in Pagosa Springs

Key species: Brown trout, rainbow trout.

Description: The San Juan River drains the Continental Divide in the basin below spectacular Wolf Creek Pass and parallels U.S. Highway 160 into a scenic ranching valley for 20 miles until it reaches the bustling community of Pagosa Springs, where about 1 mile of extensive trout-habitat improvements have been created right through town.

Tips: Nymphs and flashy lures work well during periodic off-color water throughout the summer.

The fishing: Brown trout up to 20 inches, but averaging 14 to 16 inches, are being caught in this stretch, along with a growing population of rainbows up to 14 inches long. Worms, PowerBait, and salmon eggs are the baits of choice, but most people use flies and lures on this rehabilitated stretch of river. This stretch of the San Juan River offers every major hatch to be found on Rocky Mountain big rivers, beginning with midges and caddis flies pre-runoff and then mayflies, stoneflies, and terrestrials post-runoff. Use popular bead-head nymph imitations of the insects with good results. Hoppers and ants work well later in the summer, and streamers such as Woolly Buggers and large Muddler Minnows are effective both pre- and post-runoff. Mepps and Panther Martin natural color combinations during clear water and chrome or red and white combinations during off-color water should provoke strikes from big brown trout.

Whirling disease: Negative.

Directions: From Durango, take U.S. Highway 550 south for 5 miles to U.S. Highway 160 and drive 50 miles east to Pagosa Springs.

Additional information: A daily bag limit of two fish is enforced on the 1.2-mile stretch of river between the intersection of U.S. Highways 160 and 84 downstream to the Apache Street bridge. The improved-habitat section begins just north of the intersection of U.S. 160 and 84 east of Pagosa Springs and continues for 1 mile to the Apache Street bridge on the south side of town.

Contact: Colorado Division of Wildlife, Montrose; (970) 249–3431.

18 Ridgway Reservoir

Key species: Rainbow trout, brown trout, kokanee.

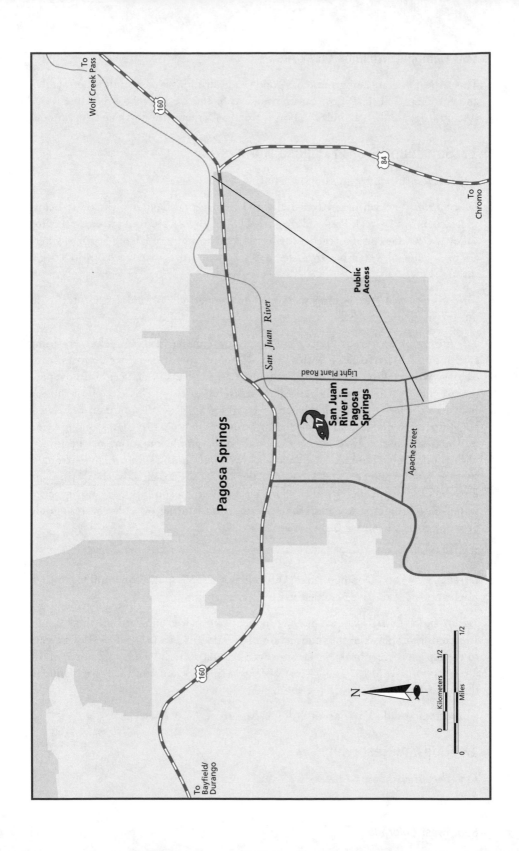

To
Wolf Creek Pass

160

84

To
Chromo

Public
Access

Pagosa Springs

San Juan River

Light Plant Road

San Juan
River in
Pagosa
Springs

17

Apache Street

160

To
Bayfield/
Durango

N

Kilometers
0   1/2

Miles
0   1/2

Description: Colorado's newest, and some would say prettiest, reservoir lies in the rolling red-stone hills of the upper Uncompahgre Valley.

Tips: Everything seems to work in this underfished reservoir.

The fishing: Bank-fishing with spinners, worms, PowerBait, and salmon eggs will take rainbows up to 16 inches all summerlong. Trolling downriggers or using spoons or jigs in deep water will haul in kokanees and browns in the heat of summer.

Directions: From Montrose, take U.S. Highway 550 south for 20 miles.

Additional information: A Colorado State Parks season pass or entry fee is required. Reservations are advised on weekends and holidays. About 85 percent of the reservoir's facilities are handicapped accessible. There is one four-lane concrete boat ramp.

Contact: Ridgway State Park; (970) 626–5822.

18A Camping: Elk Ridge Area

With modern facilities, including hot showers, flush toilets, and utility hookups, this lakeside campground can accommodate tent campers and full-size RVs. From Montrose, take U.S. 550 south for 22 miles.

18B Camping: Dakota Terraces Area

With modern facilities, including hot showers, flush toilets, and utility hookups, this campground, situated in a piñon and juniper forest, can accommodate tent campers and full-size RVs. From Montrose, take U.S. 550 south for 22 miles.

18C Camping: Pa-Co-Chu-Puk Area

On the river beneath Ridgway Reservoir Dam, this campground has full facilities available. From Montrose, take U.S. 550 south for 22 miles.

19 Uncompahgre River

Key species: Brown trout, rainbow trout.

Description: A $100,000 stream habitat and trail project on the tailwater below the Ridgway Reservoir Dam has turned this section into a productive, hassle-free fishing experience.

Tips: A chamois strip-leach is consistently successful.

The fishing: Flies-and-lures-only and catch-and-release regulations have produced an outstanding trout fishery, with fish ranging from 12 to 16 inches, but it has been overshadowed by the reservoir angling. The fish will take attractor and natural dry flies and standard nymphs like Hare's Ears, Pheasant Tails, and bead-head Princes. Look for big fish from the reservoir to run upstream to spawn. Use streamers and

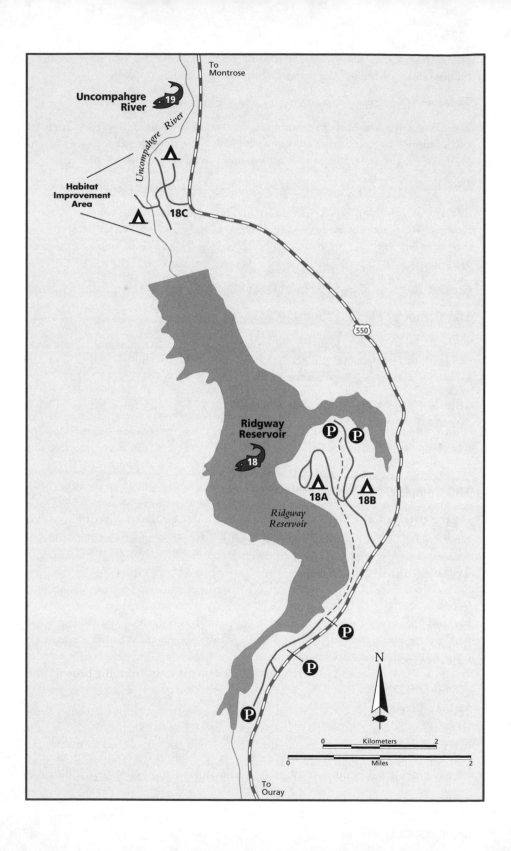

spoons, as well as salmon eggs and salmon-egg patterns, as big fish often position themselves downstream from spawning beds to gobble up loose eggs.

Whirling disease: Negative.

Directions: From Montrose, take U.S. Highway 550 south for 22 miles. Turn west into Pa-Co-Chu-Puk Campground.

Additional information: The habitat-improvement area extends about 2 miles downstream to the state park boundary. A Colorado State Parks season pass or daily use fee is required.

Contact: Ridgway State Park; (970) 626–5822.

20 Upper Gunnison River

Key species: Brown trout, rainbow trout, kokanee, Snake River cutthroat trout.

Description: The Gunnison River is formed by the confluence of the Taylor and East Rivers at the town of Almont. It joins the Colorado River south of Grand Junction about 100 miles to the west. The middle section of the river is dammed into three reservoirs before flowing through the spectacular Black Canyon of the Gunnison and Gunnison Gorge, joining the silt-laden North Fork of the Gunnison at the 76-mile point.

Tips: Nothing fancy is required to fish the upper Gunnison River. Concentrate on presentation.

The fishing: The upper Gunnison River, from Almont to Blue Mesa Reservoir, is very likely the best overall trout-fishing river in Colorado. The entire stretch exceeds Gold Medal standards for both size and numbers of rainbows and browns, in some areas by double. Spring on the upper Gunnison is primarily nymph, streamer, and spinner fishing, with old standards such as large bead-head Prince, Pheasant Tail, and Hare's Ear nymphs recommended for fly-fishing. By mid-July dry-fly patterns for stoneflies and several species of mayfly—particularly medium to small parachute Adams—are effective. Later in the summer terrestrials such as grasshoppers, ants, crickets, and beetles become an important part of the trout's diet, and flies corresponding to these insects can be effective if fishing along the bank, particularly beneath overhanging vegetation. In the fall the upper Gunnison is the spawning route for many thousands of kokanee salmon from Blue Mesa Reservoir to the Roaring Judy Hatchery, 3 miles up the East River. Big brown trout run up the Gunnison from Blue Mesa during the same period. Muddler Minnows, dark Woolly Buggers, Zonkers, and Platte River Specials can be effective during spawning runs and on hot summer days to tempt big fish out of cool deep holes. Spin fishers report success with Mepps #2 and #3, bucktails, gold Rooster Tails, Blue Foxes #2, and Panther Martins. Use gold or silver lures in the spring and summer and black in the fall. A quick retrieval over deep holes is most effective. While there

The Gunnison River above Blue Mesa Reservoir

are five public access points on the river above Blue Mesa Reservoir, floating is the best way to fish the river.

Stream census data: Fish censusing on some areas of the upper Gunnison has produced 126 pounds per acre, with thirty-four fish larger than 14 inches. One of the best stretches is the wildlife area just west of the town of Gunnison near the Palisades Park subdivision.

Whirling disease: Positive, but the upper Gunnison is restocked naturally by rainbows and Snake River cutthroat from Blue Mesa Reservoir and by local fishing groups.

Directions: From the town of Gunnison, upstream wading access can be reached by taking Colorado Highway 135 north about 2 miles to the bridge crossing the river. About a half mile downstream is public access. Or continue north on the highway to Almont. About 2 miles downstream from Almont is public access. Downstream from Gunnison, take U.S. Highway 50 about 3 miles west to the Neversink Day-Use Area or 6 miles west to the Cooper Ranch Day-Use Area.

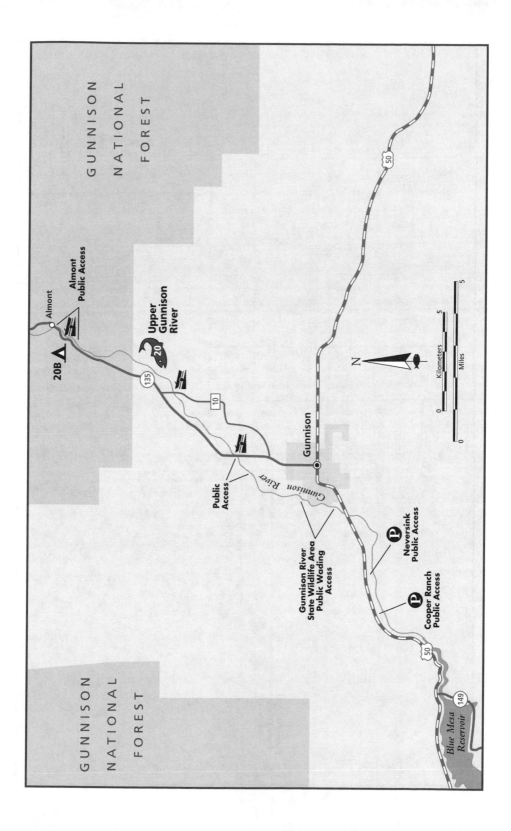

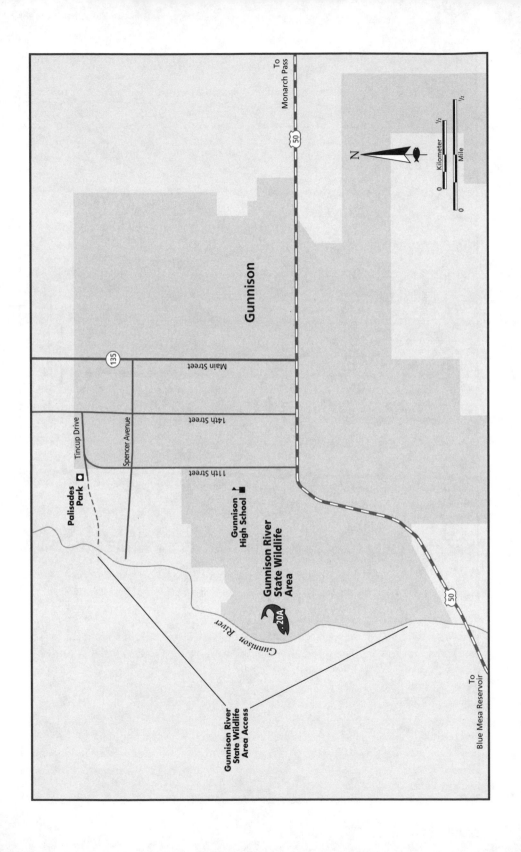

Additional information: All kokanees must be returned immediately to the water from August 1 to October 31. (Rainbows must be returned immediately to the water year-round.) Fishing is restricted to flies and lures only from Almont to Blue Mesa Reservoir. Two brown trout larger than 16 inches can be kept per day. Public wading access is found in a 1.5-mile stretch below Almont, a 0.5-mile stretch on the south bank west of Colorado Highway 135, a 1.5-mile stretch in the Gunnison River State Wildlife Area west of Gunnison, and at the Neversink and Cooper Ranch Day-Use Areas west of Gunnison at the entrance to the Curecanti National Recreation Area. Boats can be launched at the upper two access points.

Contact: Colorado Division of Wildlife, Montrose; (970) 249–3431.

20A Access: Palisades Park Area

This access is at the northwest corner of the town of Gunnison and opens up wading access to 1.5 miles on the south bank of the river. Take U.S. 50 west through Gunnison, then turn right on Eleventh Street and go north to Tincup Drive, then turn west to Palisades Park. The trail begins at the northwest corner of the park, and it is about 0.5 mile to the river.

20B Camping: Almont Area

This small campground on the river is primarily for tents and offers rest rooms, tables, cooking grates, and drinking water. From Gunnison, take CO 135 north for 9 miles.

21 Taylor River

Key species: Rainbow trout, brown trout.

Description: This river drains Taylor Park Reservoir in the upper Gunnison Basin and runs 20 clear and cool miles to its confluence with the East River at Almont, where it becomes the Gunnison River.

Tips: Mysis shrimp patterns and tiny nymphs matching the hatches are necessary to catch the picky fish on the upper river.

The fishing: The tailwater below Taylor Reservoir is still producing monster rainbows, with several fish larger than 30 inches and 20 pounds reported caught since 1997. Mysis shrimp and midges are the most common forage food. Green drakes hatch in July and August, heavily in the lower river, and caddis flies hatch from afternoon to evening nearly all summerlong. Realistic patterns are important in the upper river. High-floating attractor patterns work best in the choppy water downstream. The lower Taylor, just above Almont, is producing browns and a smaller number of rainbows for lure and bait anglers. Below the tailwater and private stretch, brown trout predominate and have been heavily fished. Fish as early or as late in the day as possible, or look for cloudy weather, which will draw the browns out of their cover. Spinners and streamers, as well as grasshopper and ant patterns, are effective in the fall.

The Taylor River below Taylor Park Reservoir holds Colorado's largest trout.

Whirling disease: Whirling disease has invaded the lower Taylor River, but lack of stocking and heavy fishing pressure is responsible for the low numbers of rainbows throughout most of this stretch.

Directions: From Gunnison, take Colorado Highway 135 north to Almont, then take the right fork onto Forest Road 742 (Taylor Canyon Road) upstream to the reservoir.

Additional information: The tailwater below the dam to the well-marked private property 0.4 mile downstream is flies-and-lures-only, catch-and-release water. There are several well-marked, patrolled areas of private property along the river totaling about 6 miles.

Contact: Colorado Division of Wildlife, Montrose; (970) 249–3431.

21A Camping: One Mile Area

This campground sits above the river in an aspen and pine grove and offers picnic tables, vault toilet, fire grates, and drinking water. From Gunnison, take CO 135 north for 10 miles, then turn northeast on FR 742 (Taylor Canyon Road) and go 8 miles.

21B Camping: North Bank Area

On the north bank of the river well away from traffic, this campground offers tables, fire grates, vault toilets, and hand-pumped water. From Gunnison, take CO 135 north for 10 miles, then turn northeast on FR 742 and go 8 miles.

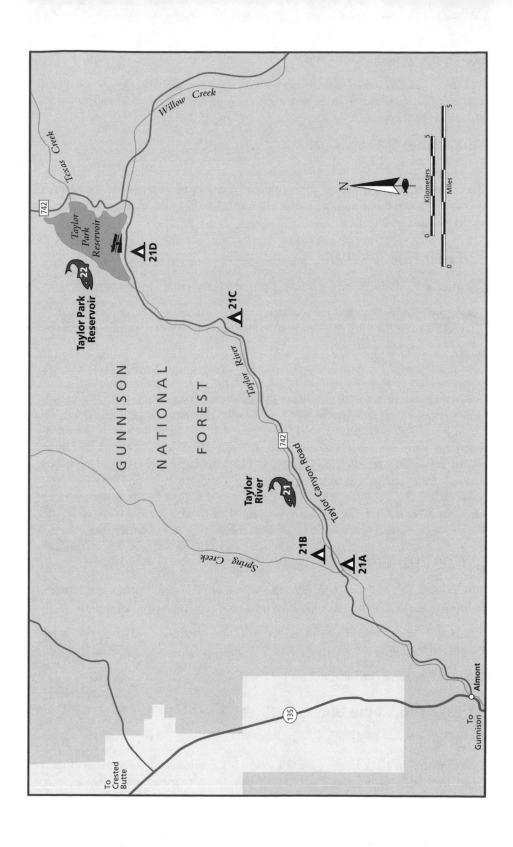

21C Camping: Lottis Creek Area

This large campground accommodates both RVs and tents in shaded sites and offers tables, vault toilets, and drinking water. From Gunnison, take CO 135 north for 10 miles, then turn northeast on FR 742 and go 17 miles.

21D Camping: Lakeview Area

On a hill about 100 feet above the south shore of Taylor Park Reservoir, this popular campground offers picnic tables, fire grates, drinking water, vault toilets, and a boat ramp. From Gunnison, take CO 135 north for 10 miles, then turn northeast on FR 742 and go 23 miles.

22 Taylor Park Reservoir

Key species: Rainbow trout, lake trout, northern pike, cutthroat trout.

Description: Taylor Park is a high-altitude reservoir covering 2,000 acres, located 30 miles northeast of the town of Gunnison on the western slope of the Collegiate Range.

Tips: Good fishing action for rainbow trout and northern pike can be had along the northern shore or at inlets by wading or using a float tube.

The fishing: Rainbows up to 16 inches can be caught from shore using PowerBait, salmon eggs, silver Kastmaster lures, or Woolly Buggers with a casting bubble. Trolling along the west shoreline with pop gear trailing a night crawler is also effective. Lake trout, somewhat smaller than their low-elevation counterparts, can be caught by trolling large spoons or lures in deeper areas. Northern pike are fished successfully in shallow areas using large crankbait, jerk bait, or Panther Martin lures. Two feeder streams running into the reservoir, Willow Creek at the southeast corner and Texas Creek at the northeast corner, offer classic small-stream dry-fly fishing. Big reservoir fish will congregate at these inlets in the spring. Some larger cutthroat will drop into the lake at the inlet from Willow Creek. Use streamers, spinners, or salmon eggs on these fish.

Directions: Take Colorado Highway 135 north out of Gunnison 10 miles to Almont, then turn west onto Forest Road 742. Drive 20 miles to Taylor Park Reservoir.

Additional information: There is a three-fish limit, including only one fish larger than 26 inches, on lake trout.

Contact: Gunnison National Forest; (970) 641–0471.

23 Lake Fork of the Gunnison River

Key species: Brown trout, rainbow trout.

Description: The Lake Fork of the Gunnison River's headwaters are south of Lake City near Redcloud and Handies Peaks. It flows north through canyons and steep valleys on the upper half, then through rolling ranch country below to Blue Mesa Reservoir.

Tips: A stealthy approach and natural presentation are the keys to success.

The fishing: Rainbow and brown trout from 10 to 18 inches are common the length of the river. About 35 miles of the Lake Fork parallel a public road, with eleven stretches of public access varying from a few hundred yards to 5 miles long. The access points are generally not well marked, and locals and government agencies use different names to describe them. Stop in a local fishing store and ask for a map. Two new public access areas are particularly promising. A 3-mile stretch of river upstream from the Red Bridge Campground, on Forest Road 25, has received extensive stream restoration work and has yearly reports of rapid population growth for both browns and rainbows. Another new area is the 2-mile public access upstream of the Gate Campground. Access can be gained by parking at the campground and hiking upstream. Browns and rainbows up to 20 inches are not uncommon at both of these access areas. On the upper river dry flies in popular attractor patterns like Stimulators, Humpies, and Royal Wulffs work well for small rainbows, browns, and brook trout. Downstream the river has a golden stonefly hatch as the runoff abates in late June to early July, followed by a green drake hatch. Any stonefly pattern, such as a large yellow stonefly nymph fished deep or a yellow or orange Stimulator fished on top, will pull big browns and rainbows out of holding lies during high water. Hit the area downstream of Gateview Campground to Blue Mesa

Habitat improvements on the Lake Fork of the Gunnison River

Reservoir during the end of runoff and again in late September and October for the brown trout spawning run, with fish up to 6 pounds. Spin fishers should have a selection of small- to medium-size Mepps and Panther Martin spinners, silver and gold Kastmasters, Rooster Tails with brown, yellow, and black color combinations, and chrome and blue Mirrolures. Of course, weighted worms and PowerBait, dropped into deep holes, are perennial favorites in the no-restriction areas.

Stream census data: In 1999 a survey 2 miles above Red Bridge Campground found 223 fish, totaling 107 pounds per acre, with 44 fish per acre larger than 14 inches (85 percent browns, 15 percent rainbows).

Whirling disease: Negative.

Directions: From Gunnison, drive 10 miles west on U.S. Highway 50, then go south on Colorado Highway 149 for 35 miles.

Additional information: From the Red Bridge Campground for 15 miles upstream to the upper end of the Devil's Creek access, fishing is flies and lures only, there is a limit of two brown trout larger than 16 inches, and all rainbows must be returned immediately to the water. From Red Bridge downstream to Gateview Campground, the daily bag limit is two trout (any species), and there are no restrictions on the type of fishing.

Contact: Colorado Division of Wildlife, Montrose; (970) 249–3431.

23A Camping: Gateview Campground

This remote National Park Service campground is free and has seven sites for tents and small RVs, with drinking water, tables, fire grates, and vault toilets. From Gunnison, drive 10 miles west on U.S. 50, then go south on CO 149 for 35 miles to the river, then north for 6 miles along the river on Forest Road 25.

23B Camping: Red Bridge Campground

This rustic Bureau of Land Management (BLM) campground, upstream of the Gateview Campground, has eight sites for tents and small RVs, with tables, fire grates, and a vault toilet, but no drinking water. From Gunnison, drive 10 miles west on U.S. 50, then go south on CO 149 for 35 miles to the river, then north for 2 miles on FR 25.

23C Camping: Gate Campground

This BLM campground has vault toilets, tables, and fire grates, but no drinking water. From Gunnison, drive 10 miles west on U.S. 50, then go south on CO 149 for 39 miles.

24 Cochetopa Creek

Key species: Rainbow trout.

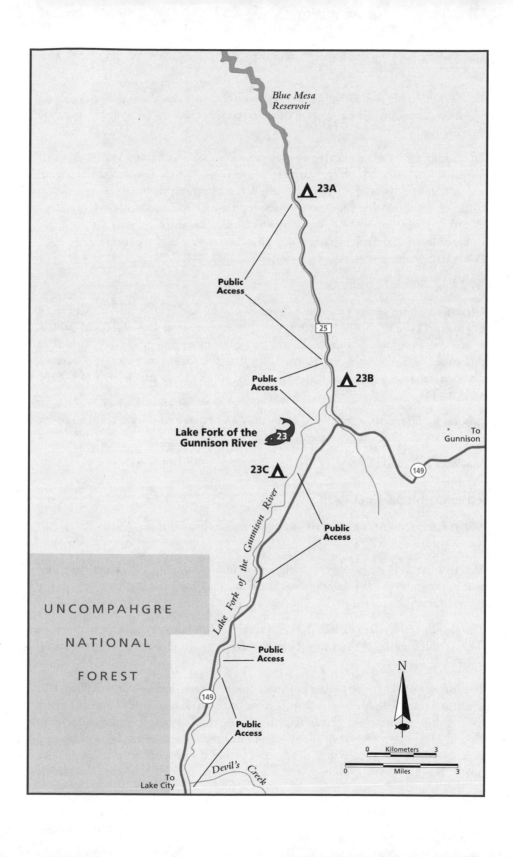

Blue Mesa
Reservoir

△ 23A

Public
Access

[25]

Public
Access   △ 23B

Lake Fork of the
Gunnison River   23

23C △

To
Gunnison

[149]

Public
Access

UNCOMPAHGRE

NATIONAL

FOREST

Public
Access

[149]

Public
Access

To
Lake City   Devil's Creek

N

0   Kilometers   3

0   Miles   3

Description: This is a small stream draining a high, sage-covered valley on the west side of the Cochetopa Hills.

Tips: While highly touted, only one stretch of the upper creek and two stretches on private ranches in the lower section that are state-stocked waters seem consistently worthwhile.

The fishing: The Coleman easement below Dome Lakes is heavily grazed and suffers from low water, but you can drive to it, and this stretch is designated Wild Trout water. Rainbow trout up to 15 inches can be caught using small-stream tactics and common attractor dry flies. Streambed vegetation precludes spinners or heavy nymphs, except during high water. Stocked rainbows in the private stretches are susceptible to standard attractor dry flies and nymphs, worms, salmon eggs, PowerBait, and spinners. Ask for permission.

Whirling disease: Negative.

Directions: From Gunnison, take U.S. Highway 50 east for 11 miles to Colorado Highway 114 and go southeast for 19 miles to Saguache County Road NN14, which is the beginning of the well-marked Coleman easement. The best fishing in this stretch is 3 to 4 miles up the road to where the road comes closest to stream. The private ranches with public access are just south of the intersection of U.S. 50 and CO 114.

Additional Information: Flies-and-lures-only and catch-and-release regulations are in effect on the Coleman easement.

Contact: Colorado Division of Wildlife, Montrose; (970) 249–3431.

25 Blue Mesa Reservoir

Key species: Lake trout, rainbow trout, kokanee, brown trout, Snake River cutthroat trout.

Description: A 15-mile-long crystalline blue impoundment, Blue Mesa Reservoir snakes through the sand-colored, sagebrush-studded mesas of the lower Gunnison Basin beneath the jagged peaks of the West Elk Wilderness.

Tips: In the spring and fall, fish the various inlets with salmon eggs or imitations, as big fish will congregate there to gobble dislodged eggs from the spawning occurring upstream.

The fishing: While rainbows and kokanees are the reservoirs most popular fish, lake trout can reach 30-plus pounds. Springtime is the best lake trout and big brown trout fishing. Lake trout can be taken on deep-trolled heavy jigging lures with chunks of sucker meat. From about July 4 until the fall spawning, browns up to 7 pounds will only be caught in shallow water before the sun comes up or after it goes down. Use big spoons, spinners, and flies that imitate small fish, mice, and frogs.

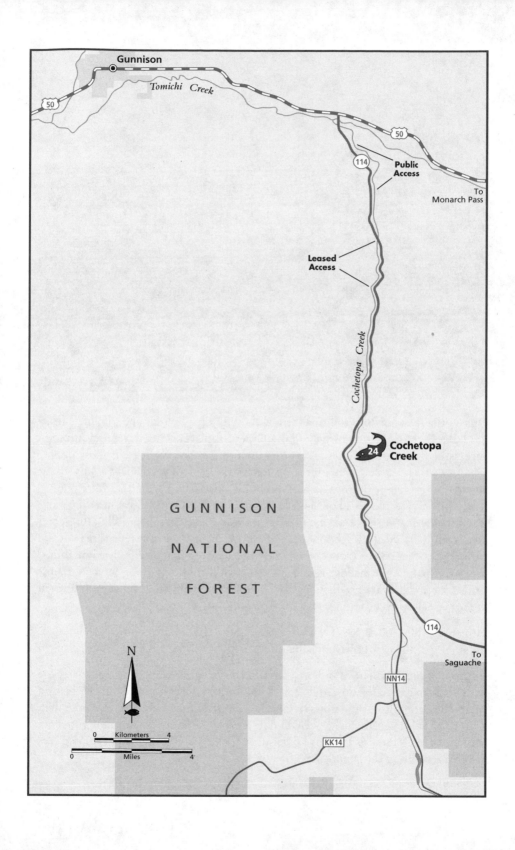

Gunnison

Tomichi Creek

50

50

114

**Public
Access**

To
Monarch Pass

**Leased
Access**

Cochetopa Creek

24 **Cochetopa
Creek**

G U N N I S O N

N A T I O N A L

F O R E S T

N

0   Kilometers   4

0   Miles   4

114

To
Saguache

NN14

KK14

Blue Mesa Reservoir is known for Kokanee salmon and huge lake trout.

During the spawning big and small fish will cruise the shallows and the inlets from the Lake Fork of the Gunnison and the Gunnison Rivers. Streamers and lures are successful at this time. Kokanees up to 4 pounds can be caught by trolling down-riggers or tiny red and green lures on long strings of tiny cowbells or by using spoons or jigs under patches of blue-green plankton. Two areas that have consistently produced kokanees are the Iola Basin and Soap Creek Cove near the dam. Rainbow trout and Snake River cutthroat are vulnerable to standard flies, lures, and bait from the bank throughout the year but particularly at the inlet areas in the spring. Some big brown trout surface along the dam at night. Big mouse imitations, top-water plugs, and shallow-running spoons will haul in up to 8 pounders. Bank-fishing and wading are productive at the inlet east of Colorado Highway 149 when the water is low in the spring.

Directions: Blue Mesa Reservoir runs parallel to U.S. Highway 50, beginning 10 miles west of the town of Gunnison.

Additional information: In order to control lake trout predation on kokanees, the daily bag limit is eight lake trout. Know and follow the rules inside the recreation area—they are diligently enforced. Check for restrictions on kokanee at the inlet area in the fall. They are being beefed up to protect the kokanee spawning run, now the largest in Colorado. There is no entrance fee or daily use fee, but camping fees are charged during the summer. Six boat ramps are available.

Contact: Curecanti National Recreation Area; (970) 641–2337.

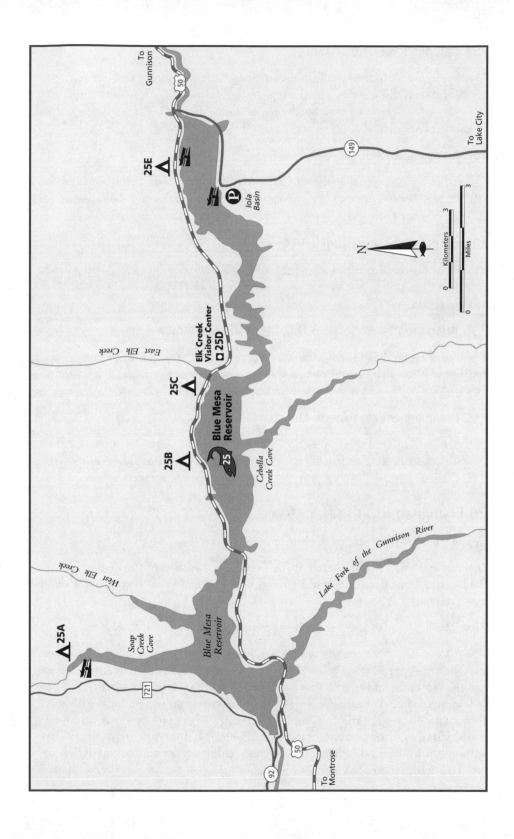

25A Camping: Ponderosa Area

This campground, located at the mouth of Soap Creek Cove, has tables, fire grates, vault toilets, drinking water, a boat ramp, and a horse corral. From Gunnison, take U.S. 50 west for 26 miles, turn north on Colorado Highway 92 for 1.5 miles, then go east on Forest Road 721. Follow the lakeshore for 7.5 miles.

25B Camping: Dry Gulch Area

Located in a cottonwood-sheltered gulch away from the lake, this quiet campsite offers tables, toilets, fire grates, drinking water, and a corral. From Gunnison, take U.S. 50 west for 17 miles.

25C Camping: East Elk Creek Area

Close to a marina, a restaurant, and the lake, this deluxe campsite offers the basics as well as flush toilets, hot showers, and a dump station. From Gunnison, take U.S. 50 west for 16 miles.

25D Information and Services: Elk Creek Visitor Center

The visitor center is the headquarters for the recreation area and offers information and services for visitors and campers. From Gunnison, take U.S. 50 west for 15 miles.

25E Camping: Stevens Creek Area

This campsite offers full services for RVs, except electrical hookups, and is often crowded. It's also a major launch site for boats. From Gunnison, take U.S. 50 west for 12 miles.

26 Fryingpan River

Key species: Brown trout, rainbow trout.

Description: The 14-mile stretch of the Fryingpan River from Ruedi Reservoir to the Roaring Fork River is a world-famous tailwater fishery cutting through a redstone canyon.

Tips: The biggest fish are in the half-mile section just below the dam.

The fishing: The Fryingpan River, for angling purposes, can be divided into three stretches: the upper 2 miles below the dam, the lower 5 miles down to Taylor Creek, and the remainder of the river down to its confluence with the Roaring Fork River in Basalt. The upper stretch holds rainbows and browns up to 8 pounds, who gorge themselves on mysis shrimp from the reservoir. This is one of the most heavily fished stretches of trout water in the United States, and the fish are described, not without justification, as "Ph.D." fish. Success requires exact duplication of the current fare, with expert placement of flies right to the fish. Some have been caught so

The Fryingpan River has lots of big rainbows and browns.

many times that they don't even put up much of a fight, knowing they will just be returned to the water. Some anglers have suggested that the use of a strike indicator on a fly line will cause fish to ignore an otherwise perfect presentation. From the lower boundary of the catch-and-release section to Taylor Creek, there are still good populations of rainbows and browns up to 5 pounds. This stretch offers better chances for success to the nonexpert angler, as the fish are more tuned to a variety of insect hatches throughout the year and are not so heavily fished. Below Taylor Creek the ratio of browns to rainbows is increasing, and the browns, for the most part, are more difficult to catch than the rainbows. Brown trout are active early and late in the day, unless a major hatch is going on. A quickly retrieved red or gold spinner, as well as a brightly colored streamer or Woolly Bugger, will occasionally move these trout out of holding water. However, some of the best fishing on the entire river is from November to April when midges are hatching, particularly on cloudy, rainy, or snowy days.

Stream census data: Stream fish surveys in 1998 for brown trout estimated an incredible 1,767 fish between two and seven years old at a site below Ruedi Reservoir Dam and 1,568 fish between two and six years old at the Old Faithful site. Rainbows, while fewer in numbers than browns, are holding steady in the upper reaches of the river, with an estimated 252 fish between two and eight years old at the dam, 56 of those between five and eight years old. One hundred and twenty rainbows between two and eight years old were estimated at the Old Faithful survey site, with 28 in the five- to eight-year-old range.

Whirling disease: The lower stretch of the Fryingpan River has seen a decline in rainbows due to whirling disease. The upper two-thirds of the river appears to be unaffected as of 1999.

Directions: From Glenwood Springs, drive 24 miles south on Colorado Highway 82 to Basalt, then take Forest Road 105 (Fryingpan Road) east for 13 miles to the reservoir.

Additional information: The entire river is Gold Medal water, and fishing is restricted to flies and lures, with a possession limit of two brown trout smaller than 14 inches except for the 2 miles below the dam, which requires immediate release of all fish. Much of the river is private, but the fishing accesses are well marked. There are no campgrounds along the Fryingpan River, but there are several National Forest campgrounds on Ruedi Reservoir.

Contact: Colorado Division of Wildlife, Montrose; (970) 249–3431.

27 Roaring Fork River

Key species: Brown trout, mountain whitefish, rainbow trout.

Description: With headwaters at 12,000 feet in the Hunter/Fryingpan Wilderness, the rivers flows 70 miles through alpine meadows, canyons, and the red-rock hills of the trendy and bustling Roaring Fork Valley to its confluence with the Colorado River at Glenwood Springs.

Tips: Get a local map to river access areas as they are difficult to locate and subject to change, and private property owners are strict about trespassing.

The fishing: The 6-mile stretch of the Roaring Fork River from Aspen to the Upper Woody Creek Bridge is Wild Trout water and is accessible on the north side of the river by the Rio Grande hiking/biking trail. The steep gradient of the river in this stretch causes blowout during runoff, and it freezes much of the winter. The primary fish in this stretch is brown trout, as whirling disease has caused population declines of rainbow trout. In the spring and fall, before and after runoff, patterns imitating stonefly nymphs are too tasty to resist for the cautious fish. Key into hatches the rest of the time and fish close imitations. When no insect activity is apparent, try the pools with streamers or big bead-head nymphs. The stretch from Basalt, where the Fryingpan joins the river, 8 miles down to Carbondale has a lower gradient and is fishable most of the year. Brown trout and whitefish are the predominant species and are vulnerable. The same fly selection as in the upper stretch will work, but midges, which hatch from November to April, are the main food source during that time. Mountain whitefish are abundant in this stretch and are easily caught in the winter by drifting midge nymphs into deep holes. The river from Carbondale to Glenwood Springs is ranked as Gold Medal water and is dominated by big browns, whitefish, and some big rainbow trout. The high volume of water and limited access in this stretch make this a floating trip for the most part.

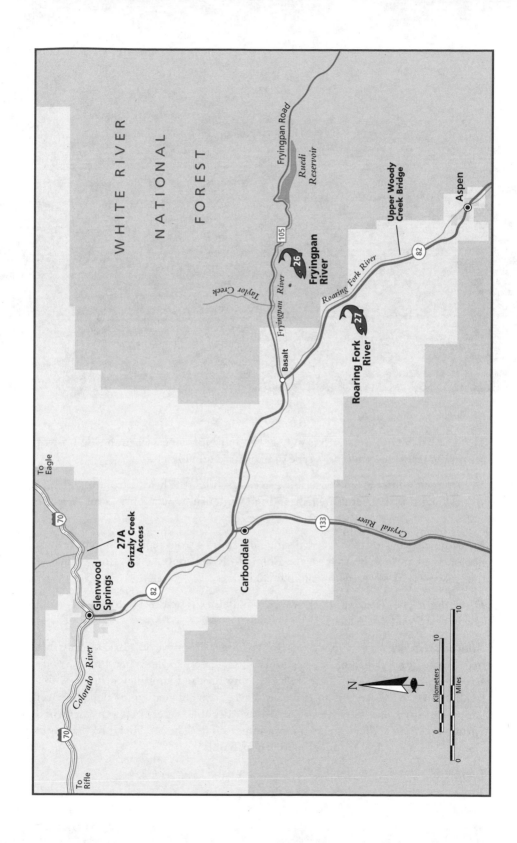

The best fishing in this stretch is in October and November, when the big browns are on the prowl for sculpins, a type of big native minnow.

Stream census data: From Basalt downriver 2.5 miles, the brown trout population was estimated in 1997 at 2,300 fish, and the whitefish population was estimated at 3,000.

Whirling disease: Positive. Severe declines in rainbow trout reproduction have been documented, but rainbows from the Colorado River continue to restock much of the Roaring Fork River, with fish up to 20 inches.

Directions: The Roaring Fork River parallels Colorado Highway 82 from Glenwood Springs to Aspen.

Additional information: From Aspen to the Upper Woody Creek Bridge, only flies may be used, and all fish must be returned immediately to the water. From Woody Creek downstream to the Colorado River, only flies and lures may be used, with a bag limit of two fish larger than 16 inches. There are eight boat ramps along the river and twenty-two short stretches of well-marked public access between Glenwood Springs and Aspen. There are no public campgrounds. The Mt. Sopris RV Park is in Carbondale, and a KOA campground is near Basalt.

Contact: Colorado Division of Wildlife, Montrose; (970) 249–3431.

27A Access: Grizzly Creek Rest Area on the Colorado River

The Colorado River east of Glenwood Springs holds some rainbows and browns up to 18 inches, but the steep gradient and high water make the river unfishable except in early spring and fall. Try drifting heavily weighted Prince nymphs, Woolly Buggers, or big spinners into deep holes to catch these fish. A hiking/biking trail parallels the entire river, but the best access to fishable water is the Grizzly Creek Rest Area 6 miles east of Glenwood Springs on I–70.

28 Sylvan Lake

Key species: Rainbow trout, brook trout, brown trout.

Description: This 45-acre reservoir is nestled at 8,500 feet amid hills dotted with pine and aspen and offers panoramic views of surrounding peaks.

Tips: In the fall big brook trout move into the shallows to feed on surface insects.

The fishing: Rainbow trout averaging 15 inches are plentiful and are taken on mayfly and caddis fly patterns, as well as on standard attractor patterns. A 20-inch fish isn't unusual. Flies, whether delivered on a fly rod or a spinning outfit using a bubble, seem to work best. Scuds and midges are the most consistent food sources, with caddis fly and mayfly hatches later in the season. When the fish aren't on the surface, use leech or streamer patterns, and use small red-and-white spinners trolled deep for the big browns and brookies, up to 5 pounds, that stay in deep water. Worms and salmon eggs fished just off the bottom are also effective. The best fishing can be done by belly boat.

Directions: From the town of Eagle, take Forest Road 400 (Brush Creek Road) south for 15 miles to the lake.

Additional information: A Colorado State Parks season pass or daily entry fee is required. Only boats with electric motors and hand-propelled craft are allowed on the lake. One boat ramp is available. The creel limit is four fish.

Contact: Sylvan State Park; (970) 625–1607.

28A, B Camping: Elk Run and Fisherman's Paradise Areas

These side-by-side campgrounds are on the north side of the lake, with Elk Run below the dam and Fisherman's Paradise at lakeside. Full modern facilities are available, as are nine rental cabins. From the town of Eagle, take FR 400 (Brush Creek Road) south for 15 miles to the lake.

29 Eagle River

Key species: Brown trout, rainbow trout.

Description: The river begins at the Tennessee Pass between the towns of Minturn

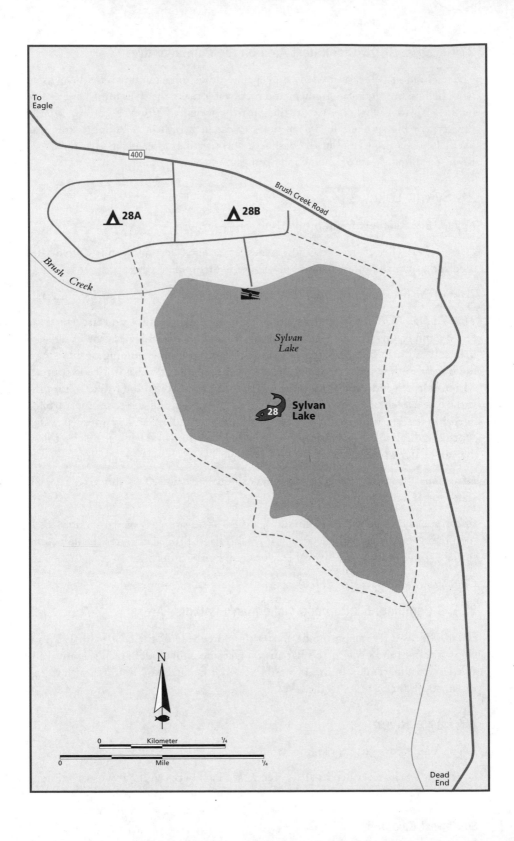

and Leadville and flows northwest to its confluence with Gore Creek near I–70. It then parallels the interstate west for 35 miles through the highly developed Eagle Valley to its confluence with the Colorado River at Dotsero.

Tips: The bottom is very slippery; a walking stick is advised.

The fishing: Rainbow trout have bounced back in the lower section as mining pollution has abated. From its confluence with Gore Creek at Dowds Junction downstream to Avon, the Eagle River predominantly holds small brown trout. From Avon to Wolcott rainbows share the river with the browns, and below Wolcott the Eagle is primarily a rainbow fishery, with fish averaging between 12 and 16 inches and occasionally running up to 18 inches. Gore Creek upstream 3 miles to Red Sandstone Creek holds rainbows, browns, and cutthroat up to 16 inches. Caddis flies and green drakes hatch after runoff. Dry flies are effective all summerlong. The best fishing on the Eagle River is from March to April and from October to November, in the lulls, probably coincidentally, between ski season and tourist season. Midges and blue-winged olives are the mainstays of the trout's diet during both of these periods, and small imitations, nymphs or dries, will catch fish. After runoff look for the fish to key in on stonefly imitations like large to medium Stimulators and Renegades. Later in the summer the green drake hatch is followed by terrestrials like ants and hoppers. Spinners and streamers can be effective if fished over holes and behind boulders, especially in the fall in the stretch of the Eagle River above its confluence with the Colorado, where the big browns run up into the Eagle to spawn.

Whirling disease: Negative.

Directions: From Vail, take I–70 west to Dowds Junction and exit to U.S. Highway 6 west, which parallels the river downstream to Gypsum.

Additional information: There are four fishing access points along U.S. 6, as well as one between Gypsum and the Eagle's confluence with the Colorado River. Pay attention to the no-trespassing signs. Wading can be treacherous, even in low-water conditions—felt soles with cleats are recommended. Gore Creek upstream 2 miles from its confluence with the Eagle River is Gold Medal water and has public access on the north side of the river. From Red Sandstone Creek downstream to Dowds Junction, Gore Creek is limited to flies and lures only, with a bag limit of two fish larger than 16 inches. The Eagle River also has a bag limit of two fish larger than 16 inches. No public campsites are available along the river from Dowds Junction to Glenwood Canyon, though several private campgrounds are available.

Contact: Colorado Division of Wildlife, Montrose; (970) 249–3431.

30 Vega Reservoir

Key species: Rainbow trout, brown trout.

Description: Vega Reservoir covers 900 acres in a sagebrush- and aspen-filled bowl

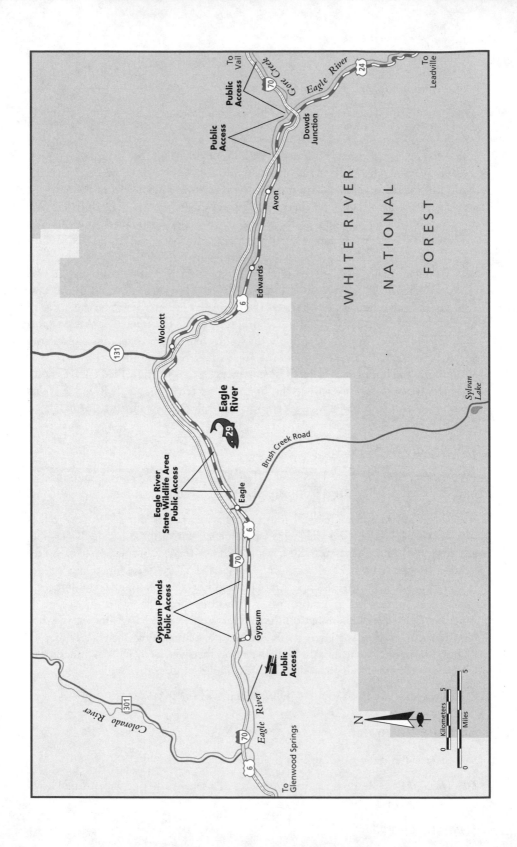

on the northeast corner of Grand Mesa, a high plateau comprising thousands of acres and more than a hundred lakes and streams.

Tips: Bring mosquito repellent.

The fishing: Built in a wide, shallow meadow, this mid-altitude reservoir is one of the most productive rainbow trout fisheries in the state. Once producing a surfeit of large fish, three years of heavy drawdowns seem to have reduced the big-fish catches. However, the reservoir, which is heavily fished in the winter and summer, still produces four-fish bag limits of 16 to 18 inchers from shore or boat, using every possible fishing method from bait to flies and lures.

Directions: From Grand Junction, go 5 miles east on I–70 to Colorado Highway 65, then go east 8 miles to Colorado Highway 330. Stay on CO 330 through the town of Collbran, then go east 8 miles to the reservoir.

Additional information: A Colorado State Parks season pass or daily use fee is required, and camping fees are charged. Two boat ramps are available.

Contact: Vega State Parks; (970) 487–3407.

30A Camping: Vega Coves Area

Situated on a peninsula on the north side of the lake, this campground offers RV and tent camping with tables, drinking water, rest rooms, and a boat ramp. From Grand Junction, go 5 miles east on I–70 to CO 65, then go east 8 miles to CO 330. Stay on CO 330 through the town of Collbran, then go east 8 miles to Vega Reservoir and proceed 1 mile.

30B Camping: Oak Point Area

Primarily for RVs, this campground offers the basics plus a dump station, flush toilets, and a boat ramp. From Grand Junction, go 5 miles east on I–70 to CO 65, then go east 8 miles to CO 330. Stay on CO 330 through the town of Collbran, then go east 8 miles to Vega Reservoir and proceed 2 miles.

30C Camping: Aspen Groves Area

Primarily for tents, this campground on the southeast corner of the reservoir has drinking water, rest rooms, fire grates, tables, and water. From Grand Junction, go 5 miles east on I–70 to CO 65, then go east 8 miles to CO 330. Stay on CO 330 through the town of Collbran, then go east 8 miles to Vega Reservoir and proceed 4 miles.

30D Camping: Early Settlers Area

This is a new campsite designed and equipped for RVs, with flush toilets, showers, water, electrical hookups, and a playground. From Grand Junction, go 5 miles east on I–70 to CO 65, then go east 8 miles to CO 330. Stay on CO 330 through the town of Collbran, then go east 8 miles to Vega Reservoir. Turn south and cross the dam.

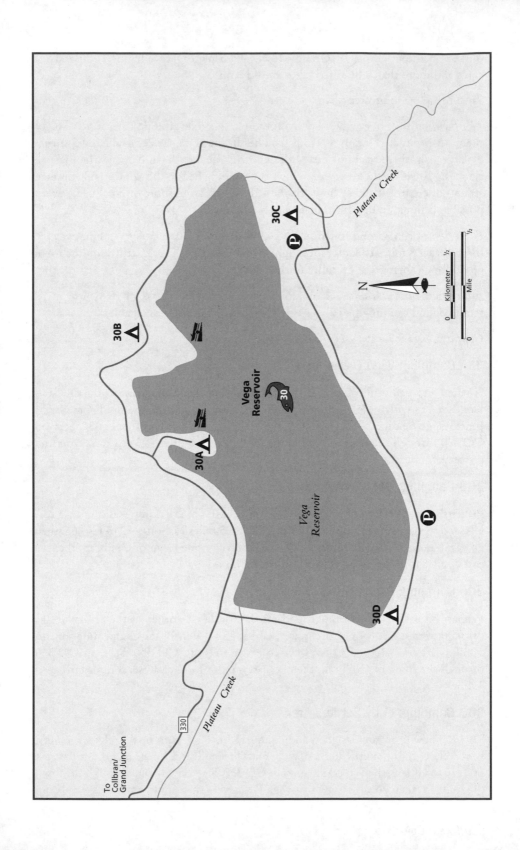

31 Crawford Reservoir

Key species: Northern pike, largemouth bass, yellow perch, crappie, catfish.

Description: Located in a state park, Crawford Reservoir's 397 acres lie in the piñon and juniper scrub foothills beneath the Elk Mountains.

The fishing: The reservoir is stocked annually with brood largemouth bass up to 20 inches and has a growing population of illegally stocked northern pike, which is seriously impacting the yellow perch population. Anglers are encouraged to catch and keep as many pike as they are able. Look for bass morning and evening around vegetation. Cast top-water plugs into these areas; late morning to late afternoon go deep with buzz bait lures, rubber worms, or tube jigs. Pike lying in ambush in shallow water will also hit lead-head tube jigs, using either a slow or jerky retrieval. The panfish love night crawlers and popper flies.

Directions: From Delta, go east for 30 miles on Colorado Highway 92 to Crawford. The reservoir is 1 mile south of town on CO 92.

Additional information: The bag limit on crappies and catfish is ten fish. There is no limit on pike. Bass must be 15 inches or larger to be kept. A Colorado State Parks season pass or daily use fee and camping fees are required. Two boat ramps are available.

Contact: Crawford State Park; (970) 921–5721.

31A Camping: Clear Fork Area

This is a sunny campground at water's edge with flush and vault toilets, showers, and drinking water. From Delta, go east for 30 miles on CO 92 to Crawford. Drive 1 mile south of town on CO 92 to the reservoir, then proceed 1 mile.

31B Camping: Iron Creek Area

This lakeside campground has electrical and water hookups, drinking water, flush toilets, hot showers, and a boat ramp. From Delta, go east for 30 miles on CO 92 to Crawford. Drive 1 mile south of town on CO 92 to the reservoir, then proceed 2 miles.

32 Corn Lake

Key species: Rainbow trout.

Description: This medium-size urban lake adjacent to the Colorado River on the south side of Grand Junction provides a launching site for boaters and rafters to the river.

Tips: Anything goes with the fish in Corn Lake.

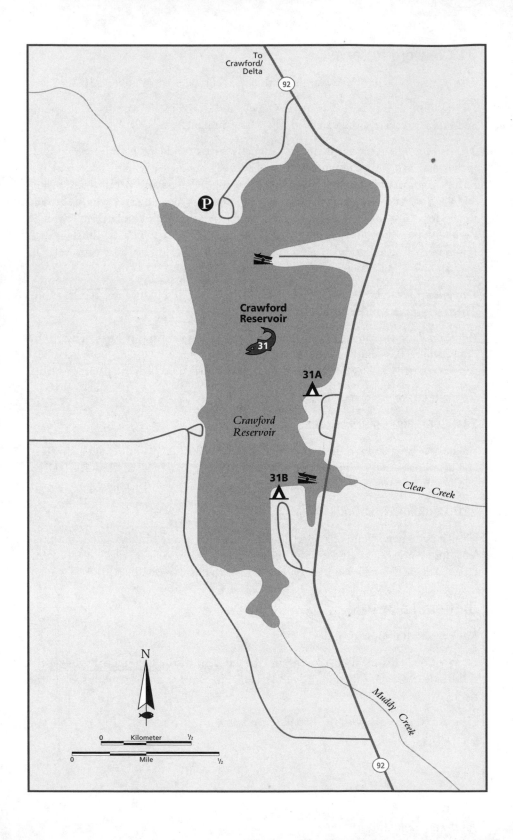

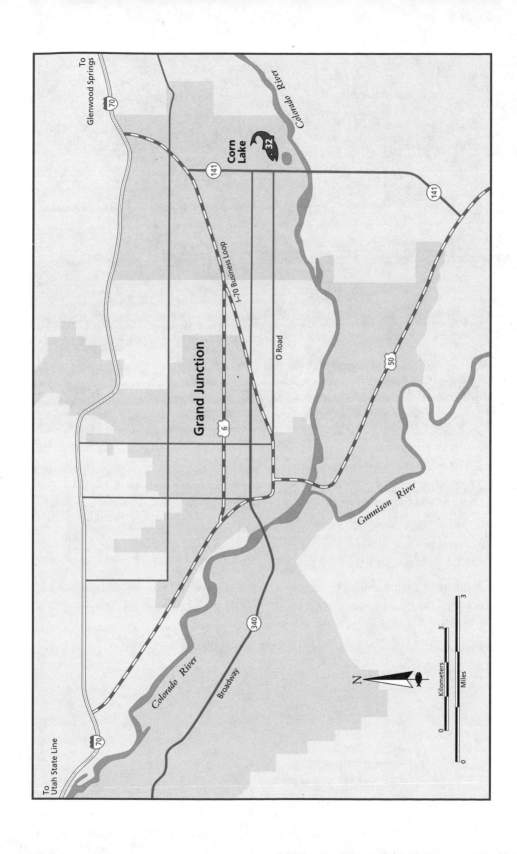

The author hooks one of the many nice rainbows.

The fishing: One of the few West Slope impoundments to receive stocked 10-inch rainbow trout (approximately 32,000 annually), fishing for them with worms and lures will be furious each spring. Some may survive and grow into even bigger fish.

Directions: From the I–70 business loop through Grand Junction, go south on CO 141 for 2 miles to reach the lake.

Additional information: A Colorado State Parks season pass or daily use fee is required for vehicles, but there is no fee for bicycles or pedestrians. No camping is allowed.

Contact: Colorado River State Park; (970) 434–3388.

Northwest Colorado

33 Rio Blanco Reservoir

Key species: Northern pike, largemouth bass, channel catfish, black crappie, yellow perch, bluegill.

Description: Rio Blanco Reservoir is a 120-acre warm-water impoundment of the White River in the sage-covered hills west of Meeker.

Tips: This is a very popular bait and bobber panfish fishery.

The fishing: Fish for pike as large as 20 pounds using bait fish, bait-fish imitation streamers such as rabbit-fur Zonkers, or top-water plugs in the shallows by sighting the fish, casting over and in front of it, and retrieving the line across the fish's line of sight. In the morning and evening, cast plugs that imitate mice or frogs, or popping bugs, over weed beds or subsurface snags to catch bigmouth bass. Channel

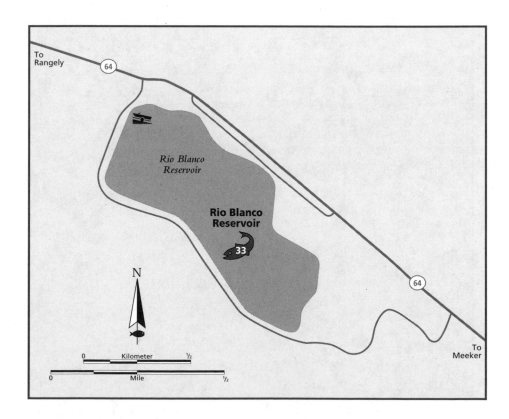

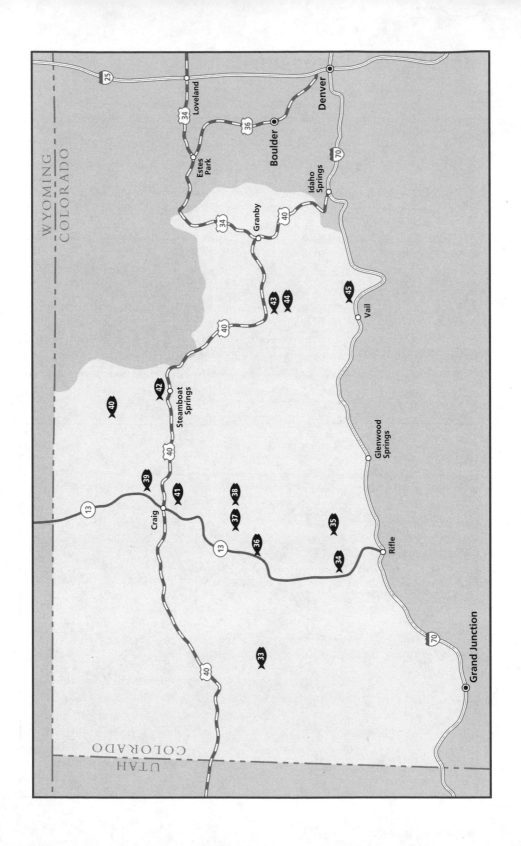

cats can be taken at night by fishing stink bait in deep water near the dam. The reservoir's multitude of black crappies, perch, and bluegills can be caught on night crawlers beneath a bobber fished off the bottom.

Directions: From Meeker, go west 20 miles on Colorado Highway 64 to the Rio Blanco State Wildlife Area.

Additional information: The White River below the reservoir is a decent trout fishery.

Contact: Colorado Division of Wildlife, Grand Junction; (970) 248–7175.

34 Rifle Gap Reservoir

Key species: Walleye, yellow perch, smallmouth bass, largemouth bass, rainbow trout.

Description: Rifle Gap Reservoir is a 300-acre impoundment in sagebrush and juniper high-desert mountains.

Tips: About 350 3- to 5-pound rainbow trout brood fish are stocked in the lake periodically.

The fishing: Walleye as large as 10 pounds can be taken by fishing spinner bait lures slowly along the bottom in deep water. Smallmouth bass can be caught with crayfish imitations and lures resembling small bait fish along subsurface structures and in coves. Look for largemouth bass near cover such as weed beds and snags, and cast popping bugs, mice or frog imitations, or spinners with rubber worms. As many as 75,000 10-inch rainbows are stocked annually and can be taken on worms, spinners, and flies from shore or from water craft working the shallows.

Directions: From Glenwood Springs, take I–70 west for 45 miles to the Rifle exit, then take Colorado Highway 13 north for 3 miles, turn right on Colorado Highway 325, and drive 9 miles to the park entrance.

Additional information: A Colorado State Parks season pass or daily use fee is required. Camping fees are charged.

Contact: Rifle Gap State Park; (970) 625–1607.

34A–D Camping: Rifle Gap Reservoir Area

Four basic campgrounds are within a half mile of one another on the north shore of Rifle Gap Reservoir, totaling forty-six campsites that can accommodate tents, pickup campers, and small motor homes. Drinking water, tables, fire grates, a vault toilet, and an RV dump station are available. There is no shade and electric hookups aren't available. A Colorado State Parks season pass or daily use fee is required, and camping fees are charged. Campgrounds begin about three-fourths of a mile from the park entrance.

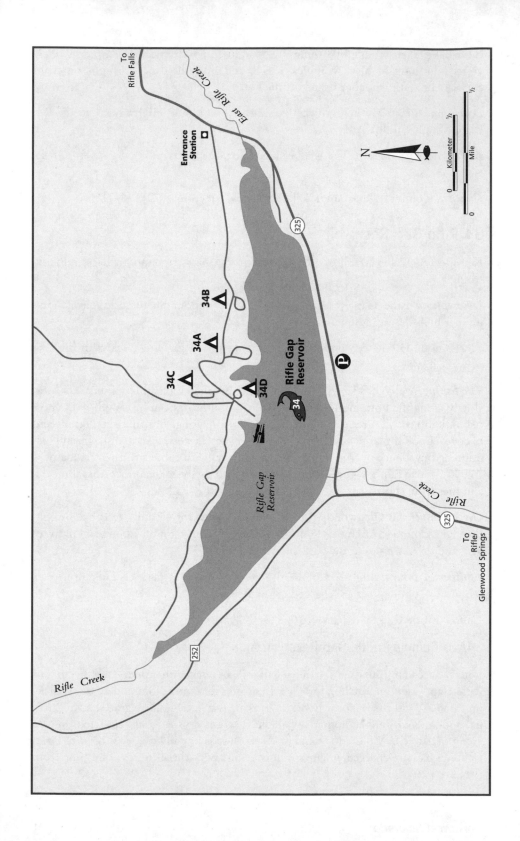

35 Harvey Gap Reservoir

Key species: Northern pike, tiger muskie, channel catfish, smallmouth bass, large-mouth bass, bluegill, black crappie, rainbow trout.

Description: Harvey Gap Reservoir is an isolated 160-acre impoundment in sage-brush and juniper high-desert mountains.

Tips: Some of the fattest channel catfish in the state can be caught near the dam using cut bait on the bottom.

The fishing: In the spring and fall and during warm summer mornings and evenings, northern pike up to 24 inches will prowl the shallows, looking for bait fish. Sight one and drop a small fish-imitation plug in its path, and jig the plug in starts and stops. Tiger muskies can be caught from shore or boat with big floating plugs baited with sucker meat. Be ready for an explosive strike. Work largemouth bass near banks or vegetation with buzz bait lures, rubber worms, or top-water plugs. Bluegills and black crappies are susceptible to worms and bobber fish. Rainbows, which are primarily stocked (25,000 10-inch fish annually), are taken on simple lures, worms, salmon eggs, and common fly patterns.

Directions: From Glenwood Springs, take I–70 west for 20 miles to the town of Silt, then take Main Street west to First Street and go north 1 mile to Garfield County Road 233, turn west, and then go north on Garfield County Road 237 and follow the signs to the reservoir.

Additional information: Camping at the reservoir is not allowed. There are thirty picnic sites and one boat ramp. A Colorado State Parks season pass or daily use fee is required.

Contact: Harvey Gap State Park; (970) 625–1607.

36 White River

Key species: Rainbow trout, brown trout, cutthroat trout hybrid.

Description: The North Fork of the White River flows out of Trapper's Lake on the west side of the Flat Tops Wilderness and joins the South Fork 32 miles downstream in the open ranch lands of the White River Valley. From there the river flows another 18 miles to the town of Meeker.

Tips: Black beetle fly patterns are deadly in the late summer and fall.

The fishing: The North Fork of the White River from the confluence upstream to Trapper's Lake is easily accessible and holds cutthroat hybrids, rainbows, and brookies, all relatively small. An exception is at the Lost Creek Ranger Station access, 30 miles from Meeker. Stream improvements at that access have allowed rainbows and browns to achieve a decent size, 12 to 14 inches on average. Below the confluence, just above Lake Avery, the fishing improves, and the fish are larger the

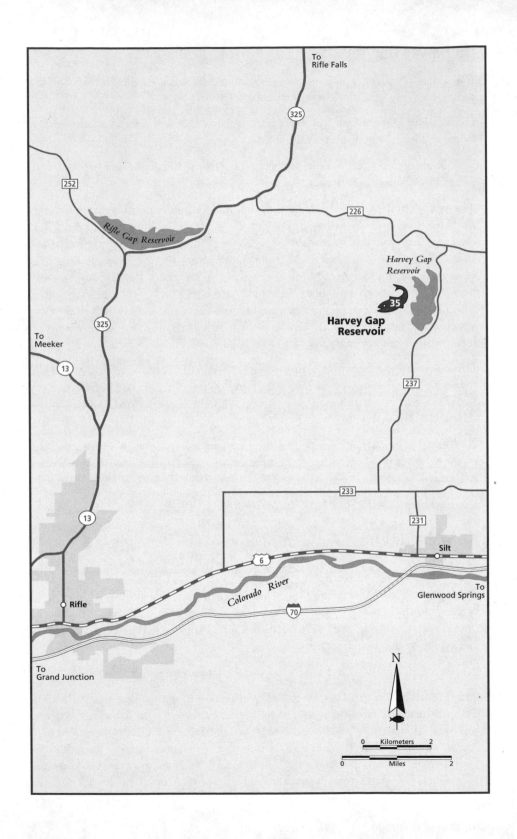

To
Rifle Falls

325

252

Rifle Gap Reservoir

226

Harvey Gap Reservoir

35

Harvey Gap Reservoir

325

To
Meeker

13

237

13

233

231

Silt

6

Colorado River

70

To
Glenwood Springs

Rifle

To
Grand Junction

N

0   Kilometers   2

0   Miles   2

The White River near Meeker

closer you get to Meeker. A 6-pound rainbow was caught a few miles above Meeker in 1997. In 1995 a 10-pound brown was caught within the town limits. Light fishing pressure in this remote area has allowed fish populations to stay healthy, even with bait-, lure-, and fly-fishing allowed. Worms and salmon eggs fished on the bottom will take trout, as will common lures like Panther Martins and Mirrolures. Fly anglers will be successful using caddis imitations such as Elk Hair Caddis, nymphs, and sparkling Caddis emergers, both before and after runoff. Midges and mayflies emerge sporadically throughout the season. Terrestrial imitations like parachute hoppers, as well as Renegades, Woolly Buggers, and Muddler Minnows are effective in late summer and early fall.

Whirling disease: Negative.

Directions: From Denver, take I–70 west for 190 miles to Rifle, then take Colorado Highway 13 north for 42 miles through Meeker to Rio Blanco County Road 8 (Trapper's Lake Road) and go 45 miles to Trapper's Lake from Meeker. While the lower section is interspersed with private property, there are more than a dozen sections of well-marked public access. From Grand Junction, take I–70 east for 50 miles to Rifle.

Additional information: At the Nelson Prather, Wakara, and Sleepy Cat accesses east of Meeker, only flies and lures may be used, and all trout must be returned immediately to the water.

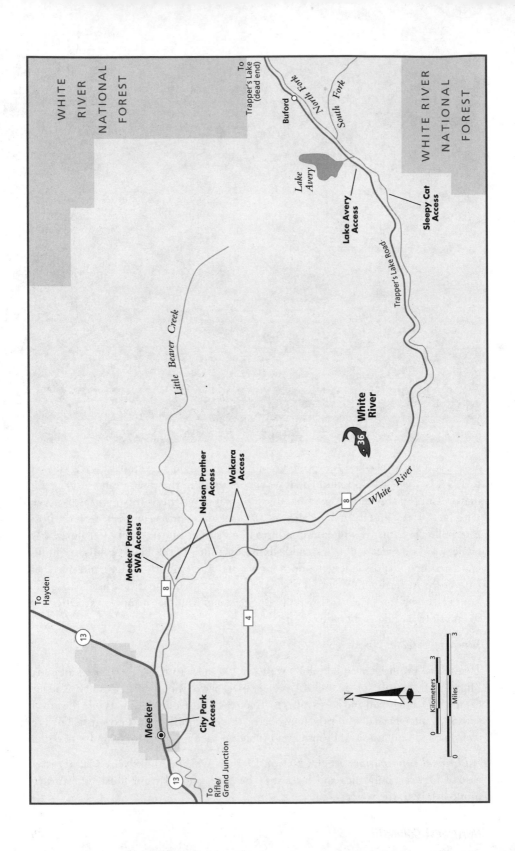

Contact: Colorado Division of Wildlife, Grand Junction; (970) 248–7175.

36A Camping: North Fork Campground

This campground has forty tent and small RV sites nestled in the pines along the White River. It offers tables, fire grates, drinking water, and vault toilets. From Meeker drive 31 miles east on Rio Blanco CR 8 (Trapper's Lake Road).

36B Camping: Himes Peak Campground

With eleven tent and small RV sites along the White River, this campground offers tables, fire grates, drinking water, and vault toilets. From Meeker drive 42 miles west on Rio Blanco CR 8.

37 Trapper's Lake

Key species: Colorado River cutthroat trout, brook trout.

Description: Trapper's Lake is a natural 200-acre, 180-foot-deep lake nestled among dense fir, pine, and spruce at an elevation of 9,600 feet on the western edge of the Flat Tops Wilderness. Immense lava walls tower 1,500 feet above the lake's eastern edge.

Tips: The best fishing occurs when the water temperature is between 50 and 60 degrees, in the morning or evening and on overcast days.

The fishing: Cutthroat trout in Trapper's Lake average 12 to 14 inches and occasionally will grow to 18 inches. The best fishing is on the north side of the lake, where a shelf less than 20 feet deep grows thick underwater vegetation that produces most of the aquatic insects on the lake. Wading is fairly easy in this area, but anglers often position float tubes, canoes, and rowboats farther out on the lake and fish back toward the shore. Since cutthroat trout are not particularly carnivorous, spinning lures are not particularly effective in this lake, but spin anglers can use the fly-and-bubble setup to great advantage because these fish will hit dry flies and nymphs retrieved vigorously. Both gold-ribbed Hare's Ears and Elk Hair Caddis are effective using this technique, even during choppy water conditions. When fish are hitting the surface, try a black midge, Irresistible, Royal Wulff, or Humpy. If the fish's fins are breaking the surface, try a Pheasant Tail nymph and strip your line vigorously. During late July and August, the fish will take flying ant imitations.

Directions: From Denver, take I–70 west for 190 miles to Rifle, then take Colorado Highway 13 north for 42 miles through Meeker to Rio Blanco County Road 8 (Trapper's Lake Road) and go 45 miles to the lake.

Additional information: Fishing is restricted to flies and lures only, with a daily bag limit of eight fish smaller than 10 inches.

Contact: Colorado Division of Wildlife, Grand Junction; (970) 248–7175.

Ron Baird fights a 15-inch cutthroat trout at Trapper's Lake.

37A Camping: Trapper's Lake Campground

This campground has fifty-two tent and small RV sites along the northwest side of Trapper's Lake. Tables, fire grates, drinking water, and vault toilets are available. From Meeker drive 46 miles west on Rio Blanco CR 8.

38 Flat Tops Wilderness Lakes

Key species: Brook trout, rainbow trout, brown trout, cutthroat trout, lake trout.

Tips: This is hike-in fishing, and the waters are for the most part small, so keep gear light.

Description: The Flat Tops Wilderness is a several-hundred-square-mile high plateau formed by glaciers 10,000 years ago. The area is covered with glacial vents and deep valleys, holding dozens of small lakes, beaver ponds, small streams, and rivers.

The fishing: The hardy angler can hike to fifty lakes and small streams holding brookies, rainbows, browns, cutthroat, and even some lake trout. These productive waters have produced 30-pound lake trout and 5-pound brookies and cutthroat,

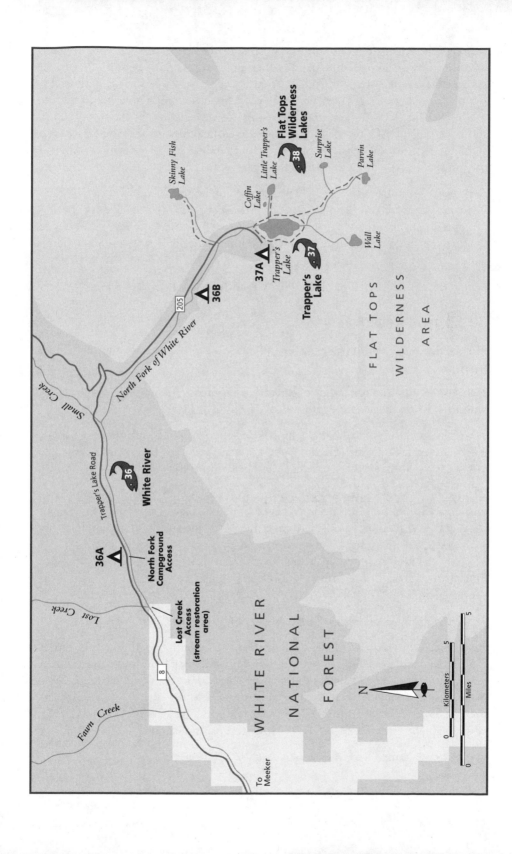

although these fish are rare occurrences. Most of the fish in the Flat Tops are relatively small. Just take the old-standby flies and lures, salmon eggs, or PowerBait because these waters see light fishing pressure, and the fish aren't particularly picky. If you make it to Trapper's Lake and decide to make the 1-mile hike to Little Trapper's Lake, look for Coffin Lake along the way, hidden in the trees, with a shoreline littered with deadfall. Backcasting is difficult due to the timber, so use a spinning outfit with a fly and bubble to get out into the lake. Retrieving a weighted nymph slowly, followed by short pauses to let it sink, can be effective.

Directions: From Denver, take I–70 west for 190 miles to Rifle, then take Colorado Highway 13 north for 42 miles through Meeker to Rio Blanco County Road 8 (Trapper's Lake Road) and go 45 miles to Trapper's Lake, where the trailheads into the Flat Tops Wilderness begin. From Grand Junction, take I–70 east for 50 miles to Rifle.

Contact: Colorado Division of Wildlife, Grand Junction; (970) 248–7175.

39 Elkhead Reservoir

Key species: Largemouth bass, smallmouth bass, black crappie, northern pike, lake trout.

Description: Elkhead Reservoir is a 450-acre irrigation impoundment in the rolling wheat fields and rangelands northwest of the town of Hayden.

Tips: The locals are tight-lipped about this lake, especially about the bass fishing, which makes it seem worth checking out if you are going to be in the area. You may also want to check out the creek above and below the reservoir.

The fishing: This lake has good populations of largemouth and smallmouth bass, with many fish of both species in excess of 15 inches, black crappies up to 12 inches, and a good number of northern pike. Look for the smallmouth bass in rocky subsurface areas foraging for crayfish, then drop a crayfish pattern or a Clouser's Minnow and hop it along the bottom. Rubber worms tossed around tree stumps or other surface structures will draw out the largemouth bass. Weighted whole suckers fished deep can be effective for lake trout, some as large as 30 inches.

Directions: From Hayden, go 8 miles northwest on Routt County Road 78.

Additional information: Only largemouth and smallmouth bass 15 inches or longer can be kept, with a bag limit of two fish. The lake trout bag limit is one fish. All lake trout between 22 and 34 inches must be returned immediately to the water. Two primitive campgrounds are located on the south side of the lake. Boating is prohibited if it creates a wake north of the buoy line or within 100 yards of the boat ramp. A Colorado State Parks season pass or daily use fee and camping fees are required.

Contact: The Yampa River Legacy Project; (970) 276–2061.

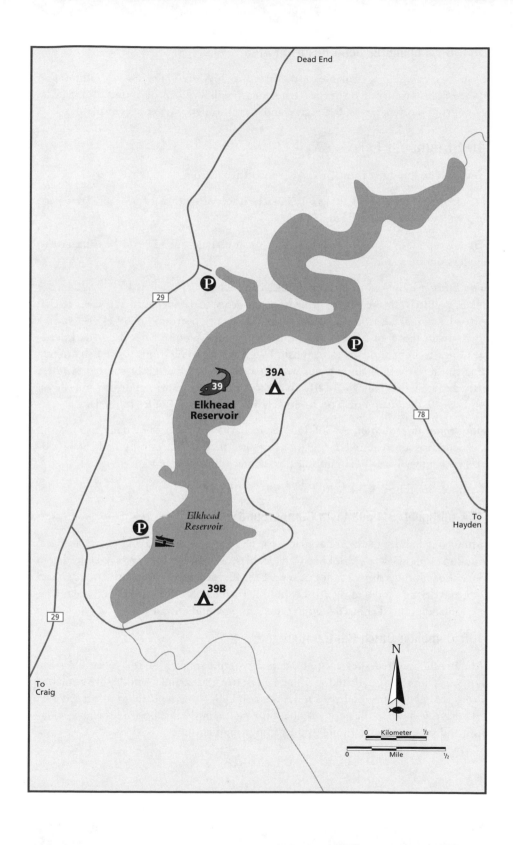

Dead End

P

29

P

39
Elkhead
Reservoir

39A
Λ

78

Elkhead
Reservoir

P

39B
Λ

To
Hayden

29

To
Craig

N

0   Kilometer   ¹/₂
0   Mile   ¹/₂

39A, B Camping: Elkhead Reservoir Area

Dispersed camping is available on the East Beach Area. There are no facilities and no services. Twenty-five sites for tents and small RVs can be found at 39B. The campground offers tables, fire grates, and a vault toilet. No water is available.

40 Steamboat Lake

Key species: Rainbow trout, Snake River cutthroat trout.

Description: Steamboat Lake is a 1,000-acre reservoir within a 1,500-acre state park in a valley at the base of Hahn's Peak.

Tips: Keep an eye on the weather, which can change quickly and be a hazard to anglers on the water.

The fishing: Rainbow trout average 14 to 16 inches, with fish as large as 20 inches taken regularly. Snake River cutthroat trout grow to 18 inches in this lake, one of three lakes ranked as Gold Medal waters. Fish the bottoms of coves and stream inlets from shore, or boat or float-tube using large Woolly Buggers or dark lead-head jigs to imitate the lake's crayfish. Use damselfly imitations if the fish are hitting the surface. In shallow water weighted streamers or brightly colored spinners fished to imitate small fish are effective. From Steamboat Springs, drive 2 miles west on U.S. 40, then turn north on Routt CR 129 and drive 24 miles to the lake.

Additional information: A Colorado State Parks season pass or daily use fee and camping fees are required. Regulations require flies and lures only and catch-and-release fishing. Three boat ramps are available, as are boat rentals.

Contact: Steamboat Lake State Park; (970) 879–3922.

40A Camping: Sunrise Vista Campground

About one hundred sites are available for large and small RVs and tents; electrical hookups, hot showers, drinking water, tables, and fire grates are available. From Steamboat Springs drive 2 miles west on U.S. 40, turn north on Routt County Road 129, and drive 24 miles to the park entrance. Turn left (south) just beyond the ranger station and proceed about 0.5 mile to the campground entrance.

40B Camping: Dutch Hill Campground

About one hundred sites accommodate large and small RVs and tents; electrical hookups, hot showers, drinking water, tables, fire grates, and a laundry are available. From Steamboat Springs drive 2 miles west on U.S. 40, turn north on Routt CR 129, and drive 24 miles to the park entrance. Turn left (south) just beyond the ranger station and proceed about 1 mile to the campground entrance.

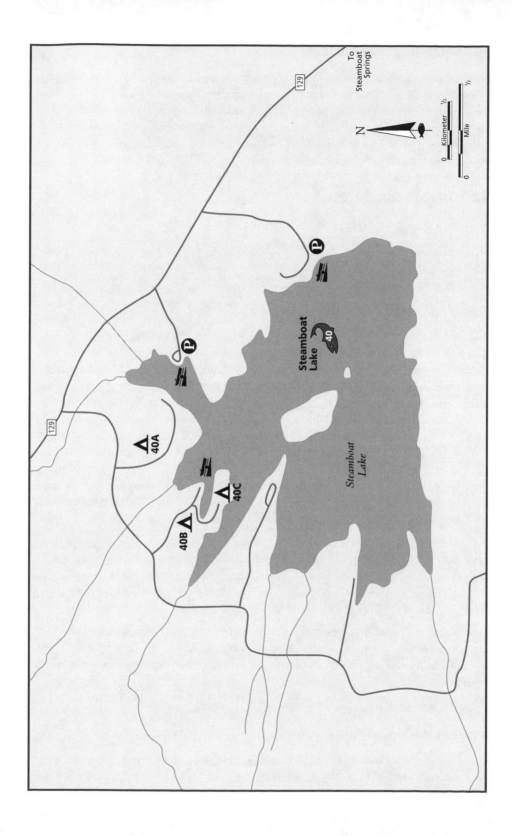

Steamboat Lake

Steamboat Lake

40

40A

40B

40C

P

P

129

129

To
Steamboat
Springs

N

0   Kilometer   ½

0   Mile   ½

40C Camping: Bridge Island

This campground offers nineteen walk-in sites with fire grates and tables for tent camping on an island on the north side of the lake. Showers, drinking water, and flush toilets are available at nearby Dutch Hill Campground. From Steamboat Springs drive 2 miles west on U.S. 40, turn north on Routt CR 129, and drive 24 miles to the park entrance. Turn left (south) just beyond the ranger station and proceed through the Dutch Hill Campground.

41 Lower Yampa River

Key species: Northern pike, smallmouth bass, channel catfish.

Description: This section begins, unofficially, at the town of Hayden, as the Yampa River widens and winds through sagebrush-studded foothills, expansive cottonwood groves, and high-desert canyons to the Utah border.

Tips: Most of the fishing along this section is done from small boats, as the river is surrounded by private land.

The fishing: In the stretch of the lower Yampa River between Hayden and the town of Craig, northern pike grow to 20 pounds, and smallmouth bass 15 to 17 inches long are common. For pike, throw top-water lures, bunny flies, or brightly colored streamers into slow backwater areas along the bank. The river is full of debris in this stretch, so heavy lures are easily snagged. Smallmouth bass can be taken on crayfish bait, crayfish streamers, small spinners, or minnows cast into slow, deep areas around rock formations. Below Craig giant channel cats lurk in the usually off-colored water, and anglers will want to anchor their boats over deep water and drop heavily weighted hooks with night crawlers, stink bait, or liver to pull these monsters up. Remember that once you hook any of these fish, they'll go for the current to escape, so heavier tackle than you would use on lakes will be required to boat them.

Whirling disease: Negative.

Directions: From Steamboat Springs, take U.S. Highway 40 west approximately 25 miles to Hayden. The first boat ramp is at the power plant 5 miles east of Hayden.

Additional information: Bag limits on pike, walleye, smallmouth bass, and channel catfish have been removed downstream of Hayden because these populations are doing so well that they may be threatening the endangered native fish they share the river with.

Contact: Yampa River Legacy Project; (970) 276–2061.

41A Loudy Simpson Park

Camping and river access are available at this area located on the south side of Craig on Colorado Highway 13. No accommodations are available and there is no fee. In

Sunset on the lower Yampa River

Craig proceed west on Victory Way to Ranney Street; turn south and drive 1 mile to the park. Craig is 42 miles west of Steamboat Springs.

41B Double Bridges Access

Proceed about 2 miles west of the town of Hayden on U.S. 40 and turn south at the river access site. Hayden is 25 miles west of Steamboat Springs.

42 Upper Yampa River in Steamboat Springs

Key species: Rainbow trout, brown trout, Snake River cutthroat trout, steelhead trout.

Description: The Yampa River begins in the aptly named Flat Tops Wilderness and flows through a beautiful ranching and farming valley before entering the resort community of Steamboat Springs.

Tips: Expect to share the river with tubers, kayakers, rafters, and lots of anglers, but fish it anyway. It's worth it.

The fishing: Thanks to a half-million-dollar stream-improvement project and lots of private stocking by public-spirited folks, the Yampa River for 5 miles above Steamboat Springs is an excellent place to fish. The river has been stocked with several age classes of fish and offers an unusual chance to hook up to 24-inch Snake River cutthroat trout, 3- to 5-pound steelhead trout, and rainbow and brown trout up to 20 inches. These trout are finicky, but Chernobyl Ants, red San Juan Worms,

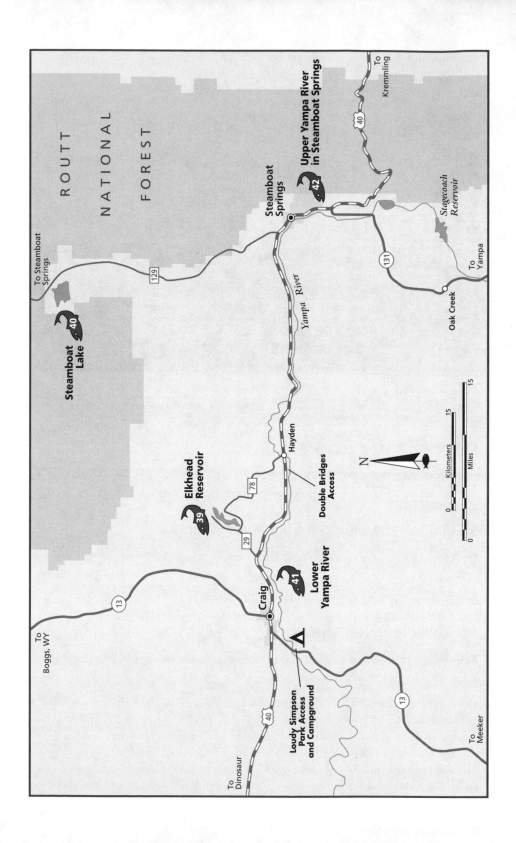

Pheasant Tail emergers, and midges are generally effective. When the water is high and off-color, try big shiny spoons and brightly colored spinners with Rooster Tails retrieved over slow areas, around rocks, and along the banks.

Whirling disease: Negative.

Directions: From downtown Steamboat Springs, cross the river at the James Brown Soul Center of the Universe Bridge (also known as the 5th Street Bridge) and go south for 2 miles on River Road to Treehouse Road, which is all public access with habitat improvements.

Additional information: The 5-mile stretch of river above Steamboat Springs is flies-and-lures-only, catch-and-release water.

42A Stagecoach Reservoir Tailwater

Description: This is a prime 0.6-mile stretch on the upper Yampa River below the dam at Stagecoach Reservoir.

The fishing: This is primarily a rainbow fishery with fish up to 18 inches, and it gets a lot of pressure. However, the river is free of ice and clear in the winter and early spring, and the fish are hungry enough to take standard fare like Prince nymphs, Pheasant Tail nymphs, bloodworms, and parachute Adams. Later in the season, match the hatch with appropriate natural imitations. Try small red-and-white, gold, or silver Mepps or Panther Martin lures in this stretch any time of the year.

Directions: From Steamboat Springs, take U.S. 40 south for about 4 miles and turn west on Colorado Highway 131, then continue south for 6 miles until its intersection with Forest Road 14, turn south, and drive 6 miles to Stagecoach Reservoir. At FR 14's intersection with Forest Road 18, turn east and follow the road 2 miles to the tailwater section below the dam.

Additional information: The 0.6 mile of the Yampa River below Stagecoach Reservoir is flies-and-lures-only, catch-and-release water. A Colorado State Parks season pass or daily use fee is required.

Contact: Stagecoach Reservoir State Park; (970) 736–2436.

43 Williams Fork Reservoir

Key species: Northern pike, rainbow trout, kokanee, brown trout, lake trout.

Description: Williams Fork Reservoir, with a rocky shoreline around its 1,800 glassy acres, sits in a high-altitude mountain valley.

Tips: The heaviest concentration of fish can be found along the shoreline on either side of the Williams Fork River inlet, particularly in the fall.

The fishing: This large mountain reservoir, while not stocked with 10-inch trout in the past few years, has healthy populations of large fish, which can be caught by

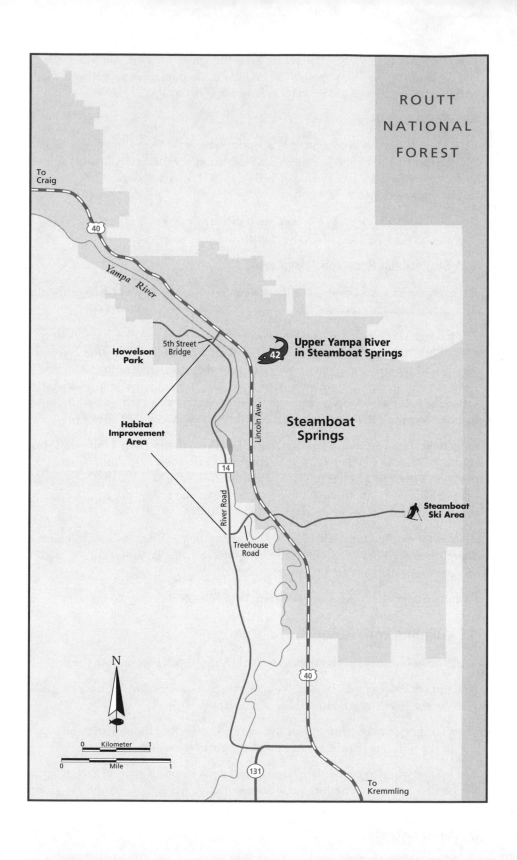

ROUTT

NATIONAL

FOREST

To
Craig

40

Yampa River

Howelson
Park

5th Street
Bridge

Upper Yampa River
in Steamboat Springs

42

Lincoln Ave.

Steamboat
Springs

Habitat
Improvement
Area

14

Steamboat
Ski Area

River Road

Treehouse
Road

40

N

0   Kilometer   1

0   Mile   1

131

To
Kremmling

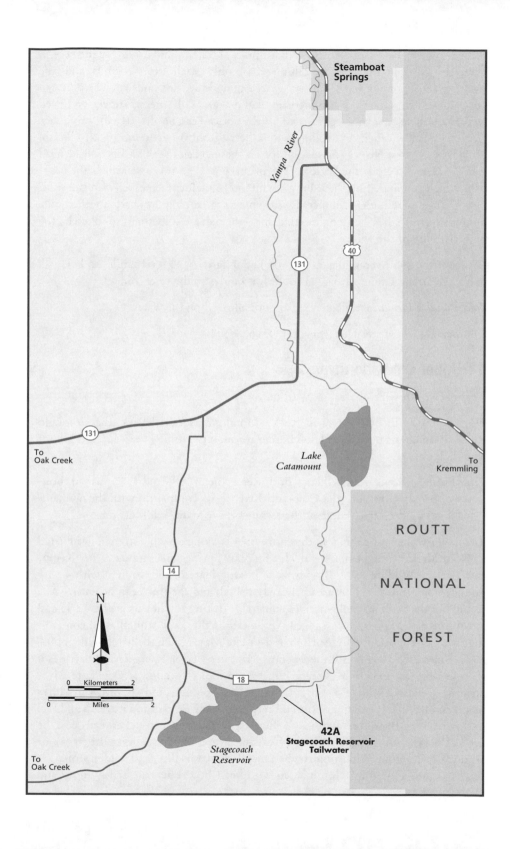

Steamboat
Springs

Yampa River

US 40

131

To
Oak Creek

131

Lake
Catamount

To
Kremmling

ROUTT

NATIONAL

FOREST

14

N

0   Kilometers   2

0   Miles   2

18

42A
Stagecoach Reservoir
Tailwater

Stagecoach
Reservoir

To
Oak Creek

skilled anglers. The state record northern pike, at 30.4 pounds, was caught here in 1996. Brown trout and kokanee salmon commonly reach 3 to 4 pounds, and lake trout up to 10 pounds and rainbows up to 2 pounds are not unusual. The pike can be caught with spoons or spinners in shallow areas. Large streamers retrieved behind a bubble or salmon eggs fished off the bottom can be effective for rainbows. Kokanees can be caught by trolling with Cherry Bobbers or Rainbow Needlefish. However, the best chance for success for all these species seems to be a lead-head tube jig bounced along the bottom. The primary prey in this reservoir is the crayfish, which is imitated by the tube jig, white in the fall and chartreuse in the summer. Using a wire leader will increase the chance of landing the sharp-toothed pike but will decrease the chance of hooking one—the fish are sometimes spooked by the high visibility of the wire.

Directions: From Kremmling, go east on U.S. Highway 40 for 12 miles to Parshall, then take Grand County Road 33 south for 3 miles to the reservoir.

Additional information: Float tubes are not allowed on the water.

Contact: Denver Water Department; (303) 628–6526.

44 Upper Colorado River

Key species: Brown trout, rainbow trout.

Description: With headwaters in Rocky Mountain National Park, the Colorado River continues its trek to the Utah border through the rolling sage-covered hills of Middle Park.

Tips: Flushing flows from Williams Fork Reservoir in 1996 and 1997 pushed thousands of brown trout into the Colorado River at its confluence with the Williams Fork River, right in the middle of the Kemp-Breeze State Wildlife Area.

The fishing: The best fishing on the entire river is along a 6-mile stretch, designated as Gold Metal water, beginning at Hot Sulphur Springs and ending at the Kemp-Breeze State Wildlife Area. Brown trout predominate in this stretch, with 4 to 5 pounders not unusual. This area is heavily fished, and the trout can be elusive as a result, but they still make themselves vulnerable during hatches, as well as early and late in the day. Midges, blue-winged olives, caddis flies, and stoneflies all come off the river pre-runoff, usually April to mid-or late May. Match the hatch with appropriate imitations—nymphs if there is no surface activity or emergers and dry flies if there is. Big streamers like Woolly Buggers, Muddler Minnows, and Platte River Specials are also effective pre-runoff, as are big spinners and spoons. Cast lures upstream over likely holding spots and reel in quickly or cast downstream and reel in slowly, using the rod to increase the lure's speed for short stretches. Lures can be used effectively during high water by casting into slow areas along the banks or around obstructions. After runoff when mayflies, caddis flies, and golden stoneflies hatch, anglers should match the hatch with bead-head Pheasant Tail nymphs and

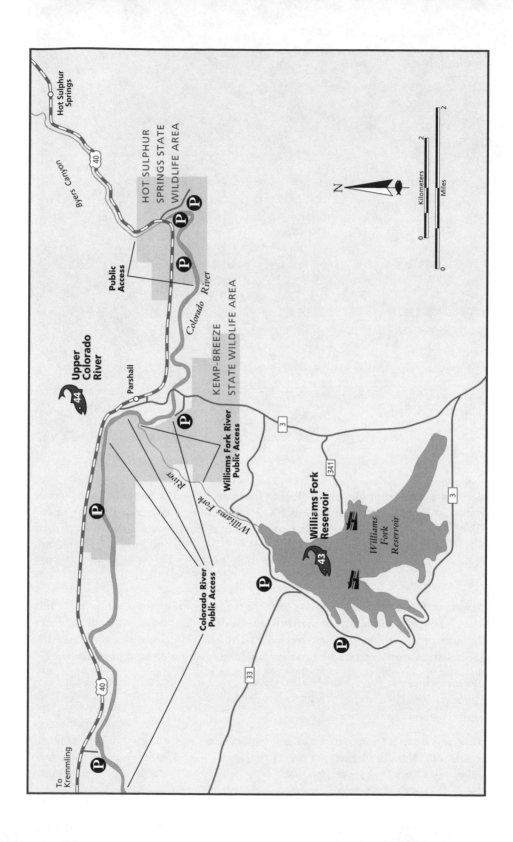

The Colorado River at Kemp-Breeze State Wildlife Area

parachute Adams for mayflies, Elk Hair Caddis and yellow Stimulators for caddis flies, and big golden stonefly nymphs and yellow or orange Stimulators for stoneflies. In late summer and early fall, plunk a big grasshopper into a slow area or drift a high-floating black ant pattern through it. The Williams Fork River through Kemp-Breeze also produces big browns and should be fished like the Colorado River.

Stream census data: The number of two- to six-year-old brown trout in the 2-mile stretch of the Colorado River downstream from its confluence with the Williams Fork River was estimated at about 4,500 fish in 1998. Creel surveys in recent years indicate that angler success on this stretch of river has increased significantly.

Whirling disease: There has been little natural reproduction of rainbow trout since the mid-1990s, but rainbow trout fingerlings have been stocked yearly, so there are some rainbows in the river.

Directions: From Denver, take I–70 west for 45 miles to the Silverthorne exit and go north on Colorado Highway 9 for 38 miles to Kremmling, then go east on U.S. Highway 40 for 11 miles to Parshall.

Additional information: From Byers Canyon 4 miles downstream to Kemp-Breeze, flies-and-lures-only and catch-and-release regulations are in place.

Contact: Colorado Division of Wildlife, Grand Junction; (970) 248–7175.

45 Blue River in Silverthorne

Key species: Rainbow trout, brown trout.

Description: The Blue River below Dillon Reservoir runs beneath I–70 and then through strip malls and outlet stores in the ski village of Silverthorne. Habitat improvements in the river and the addition of walkways and bridges have created an urban fishery with both spectators and anglers numerous during good weather. Some of the prime spots have earned nicknames such as the Big Gulp, due to its proximity to a 7-Eleven convenience store.

Tips: A suspected illegal chemical dump in 1998 into the river a few miles down from Silverthorne has impacted the fishery downriver.

The fishing: The 2-mile tailwater below Silverthorne is rated as Gold Medal water. Rainbow trout near the dam run up into the 10-pound range, with scarcer brown trout averaging 12 to 14 inches. These fish have become huge due to the presence of mysis shrimp in Dillon Reservoir, which are flushed downstream through the dam and provide a flow of food to the trout. The tiny fly patterns that imitate these shrimp can make the difference between a skunking and the fishing of a lifetime. Midges are another major food source—you'll want the smallest nymphs you can see and handle. The key to success is nymphing with a taut line and exact placement

Habitat improvements on the Blue River in Silverthorne

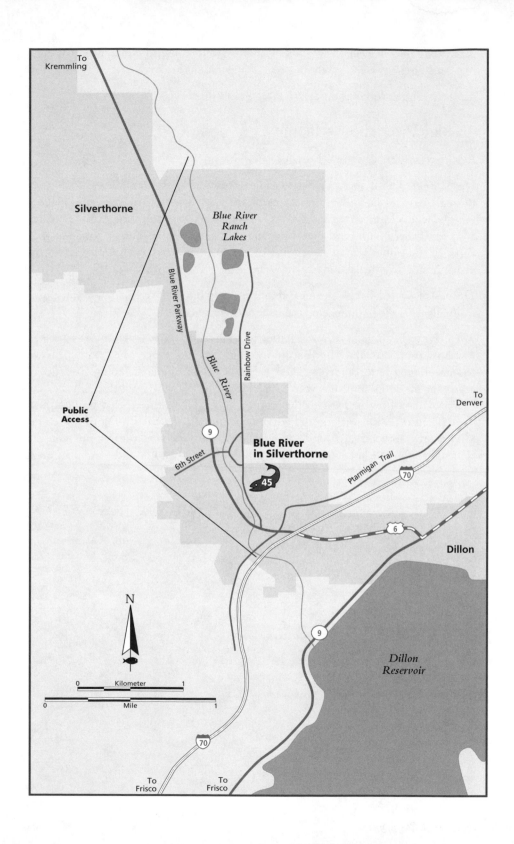

of the flies in front of the fish. This isn't as hard as it sounds because many of these fish can be seen in the crystalline water. The green drake hatch at the end of runoff is the best opportunity for dry-fly action. Use size 10 or 12 flies for these big mayflies. Getting information about hatches and advice on the proper flies is easy: Two fly shops are within short walking distance to the river. For whatever reason, lures are not often effective is this water.

Whirling disease: The Blue River is whirling-disease positive, but the disease's virulence appears to have lessened.

Directions: From Denver, take I–70 west for 40 miles and get off at the Silverthorne exit.

Additional information: Beginning in 2003 the stretch from the I–70 bridge upstream to the dam will have habitat improvements under construction and will be opened to the public. Thousands of 10-inch rainbows and 60,000 Colorado River rainbow fingerlings were stocked in 2002 along the 38-mile stretch from Silverthorne to Kremmling.

Contact: Colorado Division of Wildlife, Grand Junction; (970) 248–7175.

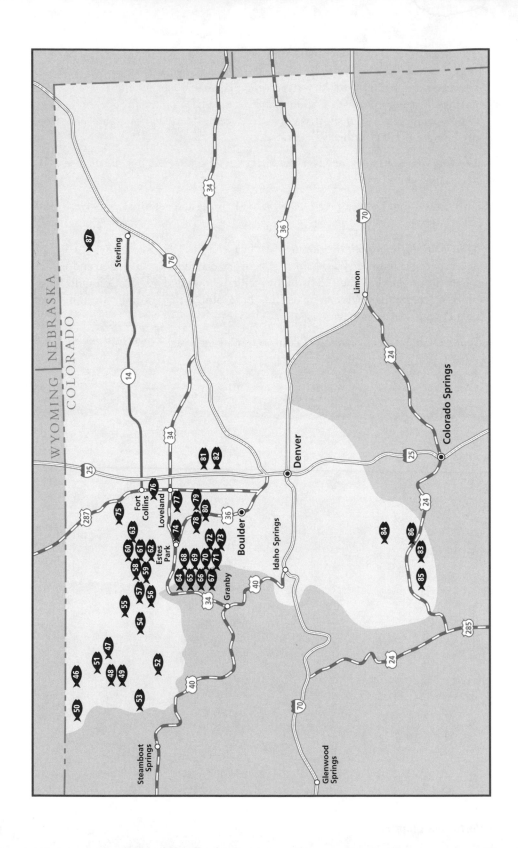

Northeast Colorado

46 North Platte River

Key species: Brown trout, rainbow trout.

Description: With headwaters along the east side of the Continental Divide bordering a vast basin known as North Park, the North Platte River meanders north through ranching country for 35 miles to the Wyoming border.

Tips: The best fishing is close to the Wyoming state line.

The fishing: Big rainbows and browns hold in pools at the lower end of the river called Northgate Canyon, but many decent-size fish can be found throughout this Gold Medal stretch until it gets low in the fall. Silver Panther Martins have a reputation for being effective in the pools and during high water, as do orange and red Woolly Worm patterns. Deep-fish Prince nymphs or streamers such as the Platte River Special in the canyon pools during low water and match the mayfly and caddis fly hatches during higher water. Elk Hair Caddis are consistent performers. Smaller lures, like gold or silver Mepps, spark the carnivorous nature of the browns, as do Woolly Buggers and Platte River Specials when cast into deep water against banks.

Whirling disease: The North Platte River is whirling-disease positive, and no rainbow trout fry were found in the river in summer 2000. However, many larger rainbows are found in the river, possibly migrating from side streams or the Encampment River in Wyoming.

Directions: Access to Northgate Canyon is found at the Routt launch site, 17 miles north of Walden on Colorado Highway 125.

Additional information: The river in Northgate Canyon is a Gold Medal water, and fishing is restricted to flies and lures only, with a two-fish bag limit. During medium to high water flows, the river in the canyon becomes unwadeable.

Contact: Colorado Division of Wildlife, Fort Collins; (970) 484–2836.

47 Michigan River

Key species: Brown trout.

Description: The Michigan River begins in the Colorado State Forest in the Medicine Bow Range on the east rim of North Park and flows through lush hay meadows and pastures in North Park before joining the North Platte River 12 miles north of Walden.

The North Platte River at the mouth of Northgate Canyon

Tips: Bring mosquito repellent. The irrigated meadows along the river produce swarms of mosquitoes, which are credited with keeping the fishing pressure light.

The fishing: This meandering off-color stream is classic brown trout water, holding some 4- to 5-pound fish, with the average in the 12- to 14-inch range. Work the pools against undercut banks with brightly colored spinners or streamers when the fish aren't rising. When they are rising the most likely prey will be caddis flies, and the Elk Hair Caddis is a proven pattern during this hatch. When the water is high, the fish will be holding in slower water, so use big attractor nymphs like bead-head Pheasant Tails or Princes. Heavy brush along the banks makes fishing difficult but also produces a lot of terrestrial insects in mid-to late summer, as do the surrounding hay fields. Try plopping grasshoppers into slow water or drifting black or red ant patterns into pools and undercut banks.

Whirling disease: Negative.

Directions: From Walden take Colorado Highway 125 north 1.2 miles to the first access or 4 miles to the second.

Additional information: The Diamond J State Wildlife Area opens up 10 miles of river north of Walden to fishing, but you must use one of the accesses on the highway to reach the river.

Contact: Colorado Division of Wildlife, Fort Collins; (970) 484–2836.

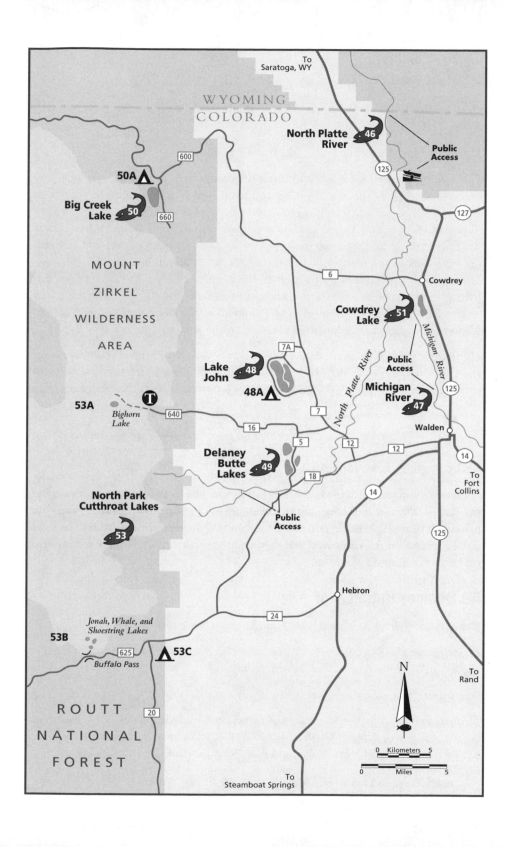

48 Lake John

Key species: Rainbow trout, Snake River cutthroat trout.

Description: This is a highly productive, shallow 565-acre lake in the sagebrush-covered hills of North Park.

Tips: Early spring and late fall are the best times to fish.

The fishing: Fingerlings stocked in the spring grow to 14 inches in their first year and to 20 inches by the end of their second summer. Nothing fancy is required at Lake John. The damselfly hatch in June and July is a highlight of fly angling, and an olive damselfly nymph fished just above the weeds and slowly pulled toward shore has proved to be deadly during this time. Trolling with spoons, casting brightly colored spinners from the bank or a float tube, casting nymphs and dry flies to cruising fish, or dropping Woolly Buggers to the bottom all seem to work. Prime bait fishing time is at night—best with a night crawler below a bubble or bobber, which works particularly well in spring and summer. In the fall a Zonker or Muddler Minnow on a sink-tip fly line draws big fish to the angler.

Directions: From Walden, drive 0.5 mile west on Colorado Highway 14, then turn right onto Jackson County Road 12 and proceed 8 miles west and then north to Jackson County Road 7. Go 7 miles north on Jackson CR 7 to Lake John.

Additional information: The bag limit is four fish.

Contact: Colorado Division of Wildlife, Fort Collins; (970) 484–2836.

48A Camping: Lake John Area

A private campground at the lake offers full services to RVs. Public camping around the lake is allowed in self-contained units and rest rooms and dump stations are provided. From Walden, drive 0.5 mile west on CO 14, then turn right onto Jackson CR 12 and proceed 8 miles west and then north to Jackson CR 7. Go 7 miles north on Jackson CR 7 to Lake John.

49 Delaney Butte Lakes

Key species: Brown trout, rainbow trout, Snake River cutthroat trout.

Description: This is a complex of three lakes ranging in size from 65 to 200 acres in the foothills on the west side of North Park.

The fishing: See individual lakes below.

Directions: From Walden, drive 0.5 mile west on Colorado Highway 14, then turn right onto Jackson County Road 12 and follow it 5.3 miles to Jackson County Road 18. Proceed 4.5 miles west on Jackson CR 18 to Jackson County Road 5, then go north 0.5 mile to lakes.

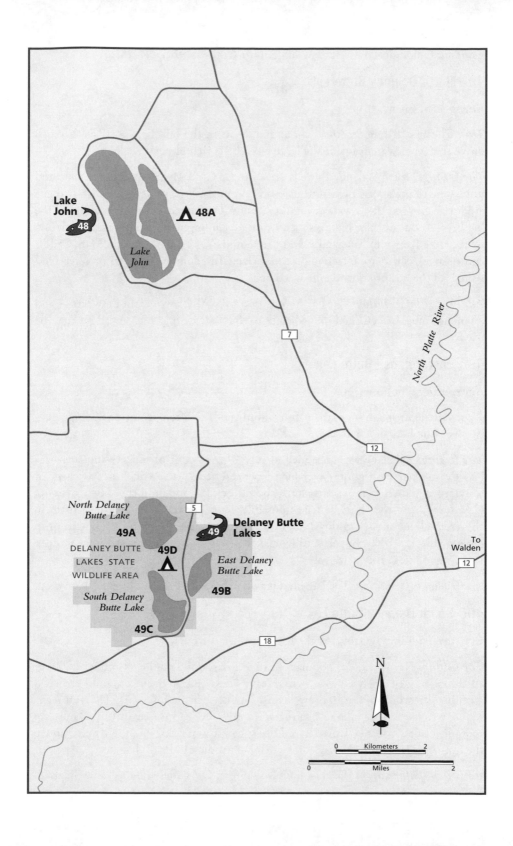

Lake
John

48

Lake
John

48A

7

North Platte River

12

North Delaney
Butte Lake

49A

5

Delaney Butte
Lakes

49

DELANEY BUTTE

49D

LAKES STATE

WILDLIFE AREA

East Delaney
Butte Lake

South Delaney
Butte Lake

49B

49C

18

12

To
Walden

N

0   Kilometers   2

0   Miles   2

Contact: Colorado Division of Wildlife, Fort Collins; (970) 484–2836.

49A North Delaney Butte Lake

Key species: Brown trout.

Tips: The best fishing is after ice-out and again in the fall. In warm weather fish move to deeper water outside the large weed beds that circle the lake.

The fishing: North Delaney Butte is one of three Gold Medal lakes in the state and holds one of the state's brown trout brood populations. Twenty-plus-inch browns are lurking in the lake's waters. Big Rapala and Tasmanian Devil lures will pull the big browns out of their hiding spots. Damselfly nymph and adult patterns, sizes 6 to 10, are effective in June and July. In June midsize dry flies like Elk Hair Caddis and orange Ashers are effective on the surface. In summer try a tan or olive scud fished on the bottom outside the weed beds.

Additional information: The bag limit is two fish. All brown trout between 14 and 20 inches must be returned immediately to the water. Only flies and lures may be used.

49B East Delaney Butte Lake

Key species: Rainbow trout.

Tips: Casting from shore at the south end of the lake often produces the biggest—if lower numbers of—fish.

The fishing: This lake was reclaimed in July 1999 to control suckers and then was heavily stocked with rainbows, which have reached 20 to 24 inches. A variety of standard dry flies, nymphs, and lures should be effective until these fish wise up. Cast lures from the shore as far as possible, let them sink, then retrieve them in short, quick bursts. From the shore or a belly boat, use a sink-tip fly line to drop olive or black Woolly Buggers, tube jigs, or streamers over the weed beds in deep water, then use a jerky retrieval.

Additional information: The bag limit is two fish. Only flies and lures may be used.

49C South Delaney Butte Lake

Key species: Rainbow trout, Snake River cutthroat trout.

The fishing: This lake holds populations of 4- to 5-pound rainbows and Snake River cutthroat, as well as a few big browns. Heavy weed beds in the lake should be fished with big lures and spoons to draw the fish out of their hiding spots. The best technique is to use a float tube to fish the weed beds in deep water. In July Damselfly nymphs can be effective from shore in July by slowly retrieving the fly just above the bottom. Use an Elk Hair Caddis during periodic caddis fly hatches.

Additional information: The bag limit is two fish. Only flies and lures may be used.

49D Camping: Delaney Butte Lakes Area

There is open camping available within the state wildlife area bordering all three lakes, with pit toilets and some shaded picnic tables. From Walden, go 0.5 mile west on CO 14, then turn right onto Jackson CR 12 and follow it 5.3 miles west to Jackson CR 18. Proceed 4.5 miles west on CR 18 to Jackson CR 5, then go north 0.5 mile to lakes.

50 Big Creek Lake

Key species: Arctic grayling, tiger muskie, lake trout.

Description: Big Creek Lake is a 450-acre reservoir in the sagebrush and pine-studded foothills on the northwest rim of North Park.

Tips: Arctic grayling are willing participants in creating fly-fishing enthusiasm in youngsters.

The fishing: Arctic grayling have been transplanted to Big Creek Lake in order to provide fishing opportunities that would be missed due to the lack of rainbows available for stocking. These fish, averaging 12 to 14 inches, fall willingly to flies, lures, and bait and can be great fun on light tackle. Tiger muskies up to 20 pounds are lurking in the lake and can be taken on top-water plugs stringing cut bait. The lake trout in the water's depths can be caught by deep trolling jig heads trailing a piece of sucker meat. These fish can be found in the shallows when the ice recedes in the springtime.

Directions: From Walden, take Colorado Highway 125 north for 9 miles to Cowdrey, then go west on Jackson County Road 6 for 16 miles to Jackson County Road 6A, which becomes Forest Road 600, and go 4 miles to Forest Road 660, turn left, and drive 0.25 mile to the lake.

Additional information: All lake trout between 22 and 34 inches must be returned immediately to the water. The bag limit for lake trout is one fish.

Contact: Colorado Division of Wildlife, Fort Collins; (970) 484–2836.

50A Camping: Big Creek Lake Area

This popular campsite on the edge of the Mt. Zirkel Wilderness Area has a boat ramp, rest rooms, drinking water, fire grates, and tables. From Walden, take CO 125 north for 9 miles to Cowdrey, then go west on Jackson CR 6 for 16 miles to Jackson CR 6A, which becomes FR 600, and go 4 miles to FR 660, turn left, and drive 0.25 mile to the lake.

51 Cowdrey Lake

Key species: Rainbow trout.

Description: Cowdrey Lake is an 80-acre reservoir surrounded by pastures and hay fields, located above the Michigan River in north-central North Park.

Tips: Favorite spots include the east side near the access area, the northwest corner, and the two large coves on the west side.

The fishing: The lake has received 34,000 10-inch rainbow trout annually to 2002 and will likely be stocked regularly for the next few years. Some bigger trout are present. The best fishing is just after ice-out and during the late fall, using flies, lures, and bait. Fishing is best from a float tube, using a jig tipped with meal or a wax worm over the weed beds. The best dry-fly fishing is done with a Rio Grande King, black ant pattern, or Adams.

Directions: From Walden, drive 7.5 miles north on Colorado Highway 125 and turn west into the reservoir at the sign.

Contact: Colorado Division of Wildlife, Fort Collins; (970) 484–2836.

52 Seymour Lake

Key species: Rainbow trout.

Description: This lake is small, 81 acres, and typical of the North Park area, but it is far enough off the beaten path to receive little fishing pressure.

Tips: Scheduled for full stockings for the next few years, small- to medium-size fish should be plentiful and not too wise. An estimated 28,000 fish have been stocked annually to 2002.

The fishing: There are no restrictions on bait at this lake, so try PowerBait or night crawlers beneath a bobber or on the bottom. Standard lures like Mepps and Panther Martins should be effective. Fly anglers should try black ant, Adams, and Rio Grande King dry-fly patterns or fish nymphs on the bottom along the edge of weed beds.

Directions: From Walden, go 14 miles southwest on Colorado 14 to Jackson County Road 28, turn left and go 1 mile south to Jackson County Road 11, proceed 3 miles south to Jackson County Road 288, then drive 0.5 mile west to the lake.

53 North Park Cutthroat Lakes

Key species: Greenback cutthroat trout.

Description: All the following cutthroat lakes are very high-altitude waters and tend to be covered with ice until July during normal-snow years. Weather at these altitudes can change very rapidly, and lightning presents a very real danger, especially to someone holding a graphite rod. Many of the lakes can only be reached by strenuous hiking. Take warm clothes, a first-aid kit, and food. Know your level of fitness, and time your fishing so you can reach your base camp or car before dark.

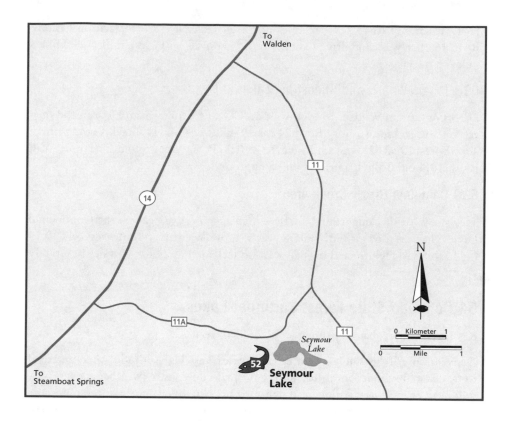

The fishing: These lakes are stocked every other year with cutthroat fry and finger-lings for recreational fishing because, due to their altitude and coldness, they cannot support natural reproduction. Nevertheless, these waters are capable of growing cut-throat trout to fairly large sizes, some reported up to 18 inches. Standard attractor dry-fly patterns like a Royal Wulff, Adams, Elk Hair Caddis, or a red Humpy work well on a fly rod or behind a bubble on a spinning outfit. Cast to fish cruising the lake's perimeter, let the fly sit for a few seconds, then retrieve it slowly. If there's no surface activity, cast a weighted natural nymph like a bead-head Hare's Ear, let it sink a little, then reel it in with short, slow retrievals to attract one of the big cutthroat. Small rainbow-hued, gold, or silver spinners can be effective here, as some of these big fish have likely become predators in order to grow to such large sizes.

Additional information: There is generally a four-fish bag limit for these waters. However, fish will often spoil during a long hike out, so consider releasing them.

Contact: Colorado Division of Wildlife, Fort Collins; (970) 484–2836.

53A Bighorn Lake

Directions: From Walden, drive 0.5 mile west on Colorado Highway 14, then turn right on Jackson County Road 12 and proceed 8 miles west and then north to

Jackson County Road 7. Go 2 miles north on Jackson CR 7 to Jackson County Road 16, turn west, and drive 10 miles to the trailhead for Forest Trail 1129. Hike 3 miles to the lake.

53B Jonah, Whale, and Shoestring Lakes

Directions: From Walden, go southwest on CO 14 for 10 miles to Hebron and then go west on Jackson County Road 24 for 10 miles to Grizzly Creek Campground. Take Forest Road 625 west for 5 miles to Buffalo Pass Campground. The three small lakes are about 0.5 mile north of the campground.

53C Camping: Grizzly Creek Area

This small, rustic campground, nestled in an aspen grove beneath the Continental Divide, has a rest room and drinking water. From Walden, go southwest on CO 14 for 10 miles to Hebron and then go west on Jackson CR 24 for 10 miles to Grizzly Creek Campground.

54 Colorado State Forest Cutthroat Lakes

Key species: Greenback cutthroat trout, golden trout.

Description: All the following cutthroat lakes are very high-altitude waters and tend to be covered with ice until July during normal-snow years. Weather at these altitudes can change very rapidly, and lightning presents a very real danger, especially to someone holding a graphite rod. Many of the lakes can only be reached by strenuous hiking. Take warm clothes, a first-aid kit, and food. Know your level of fitness, and time your fishing so you can reach your base camp or car before dark.

The fishing: These lakes are stocked every other year with cutthroat fry and fingerlings for recreational fishing because, due to their altitude and coldness, they cannot support natural reproduction. Nevertheless, these waters are capable of growing cutthroat trout to fairly large sizes, some reported up to 18 inches. Standard attractor dry-fly patterns like a Royal Wulff, Adams, Elk Hair Caddis, or red Humpy work well on a fly rod or behind a bubble on a spinning outfit. Cast to fish cruising the lake's perimeter, let the fly sit for a few seconds, then retrieve it slowly. If there's no surface activity, cast a weighted natural nymph like a bead-head Hare's Ear, let it sink a little, then reel it in with short, slow retrievals to attract one of the big cutthroat. Small rainbow-hued, gold, or silver spinners can be effective here, as some of these big fish have likely become predators in order to grow to such large sizes. Kelly Lake also holds golden trout up to 14 inches.

Directions: From Walden, drive 18 miles east on Colorado Highway 14 to North Michigan Reservoir, then take Jackson County Road 41 for 3 miles, passing the reservoir, until the road becomes a four-wheel-drive road.

Additional information: Fishing is restricted to flies and lures only, with a bag limit of two fish. However, fish will often spoil during a long hike out, so unless you're camping at the lakes (a good idea), consider releasing them. A Colorado State Parks season pass or daily use fee is required to gain admission to the area.

Contact: Colorado Division of Wildlife, Fort Collins; (970) 484–2836.

54A Ruby Jewell Lake

Directions: From the beginning of the four-wheel-drive road (see above), go northwest 1 mile to the Ruby Jewell Trailhead. The hike to the lake is a strenuous 4 miles.

54B Kelly Lake

Directions: From the beginning of the four-wheel-drive road (see above), go northwest 3.5 miles to the parking area for Kelly and Clear Lakes. The hike to the lake is a strenuous 8 miles.

54C Clear Lake

Directions: From the beginning of the four-wheel-drive road (see above), go northwest 3.5 miles to the parking area for Kelly and Clear Lakes. The hike to the lake is a very strenuous 10 miles.

54D Camping: North Michigan Reservoir Area

Excellent lakeside campsites with vault toilets, drinking water, tables, and fire grates are available for RVs and tents. From Walden, drive 18 miles east on CO 14 to North Michigan Reservoir, then take Jackson CR 41 for 1.5 miles to the campground.

54E Snow Lake, Upper Lake Agnes

Directions: From Walden, drive 27.5 miles east on CO 14 to the American Lakes turnoff to the south. Agnes Lake trailhead is 1 mile up the road on the south side of the Crags Campground. Hike 2 miles to Lake Agnes. Upper Lake Agnes is 0.25 mile above Lake Agnes. To access Snow Lake, stay on American Lakes Road another 2 miles to the American Lakes trailhead, then hike 5 miles to American Lakes. Snow Lake is a tough 600 feet above American Lakes.

54F Camping: Crags Area

Located on a steep, winding dirt road, the Crags Campground is recommended for tent camping and has rest rooms, drinking water, fire grates, and tables. From Walden, drive 27.5 miles east on CO 14 to the American Lakes turnoff to the south and go 1 mile.

55 Rawah Wilderness Cutthroat Lakes

Key species: Greenback cutthroat trout.

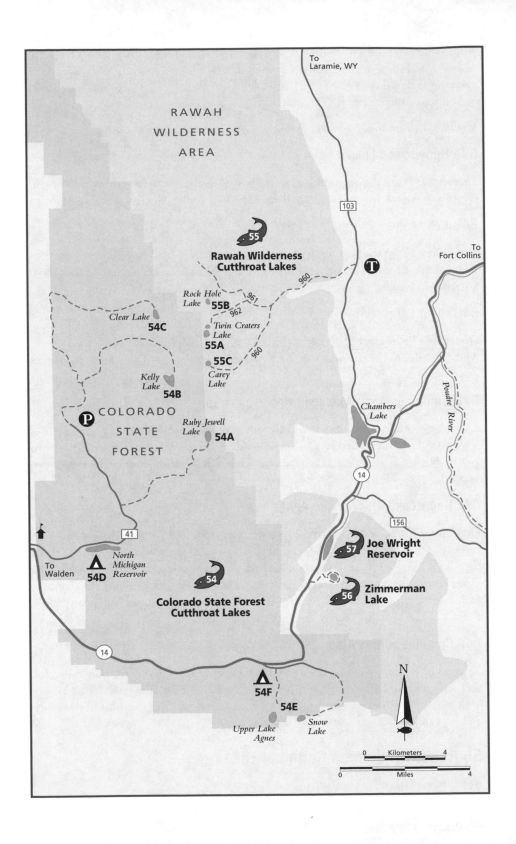

RAWAH
WILDERNESS
AREA

To
Laramie, WY

103

55

**Rawah Wilderness
Cutthroat Lakes**

Rock Hole
Lake **55B**
961
962
Twin Craters
Lake
55A
55C
Carey
Lake
960

960

To
Fort Collins

Clear Lake
54C

Kelly
Lake
54B

P **COLORADO
STATE
FOREST**

Ruby Jewell
Lake **54A**

Chambers
Lake

Poudre River

14

T

156

57 **Joe Wright
Reservoir**

56 **Zimmerman
Lake**

41

To
Walden

North
Michigan
Reservoir
54D

54 **Colorado State Forest
Cutthroat Lakes**

14

54F
54E
Upper Lake
Agnes
Snow
Lake

N

0   Kilometers   4

0   Miles   4

Description: All the following cutthroat lakes are very high-altitude waters and tend to be covered with ice until July during normal-snow years. Weather at these altitudes can change very rapidly, and lightning presents a very real danger, especially to someone holding a graphite rod. Many of the lakes can only be reached by strenuous hiking. Take warm clothes, a first-aid kit, and food. Know your level of fitness, and time your fishing so you can reach your base camp or car before dark.

The fishing: These lakes are stocked every other year with cutthroat fry and fingerlings for recreational fishing because, due to their altitude and coldness, they cannot support natural reproduction. Nevertheless, these waters are capable of growing cutthroat trout to fairly large sizes, some reported up to 18 inches. Standard attractor dry-fly patterns like a Royal Wulff, Adams, Elk Hair Caddis, or red Humpy work well on a fly rod or behind a bubble on a spinning outfit. Cast to fish cruising the lake's perimeter, let the fly sit for a few seconds, then retrieve it slowly. If there's no surface activity, cast a weighted natural nymph like a bead-head Hare's Ear, let it sink a little, then reel it in with short, slow retrievals to attract one of the big cutthroat. Small rainbow-hued, gold, or silver spinners can be effective here, as some of these big fish have likely become predators in order to grow to such large sizes.

Directions: From Fort Collins, drive 10 miles north on U.S. Highway 287, then turn west onto Colorado Highway 14 and proceed through Poudre Canyon. About 52 miles up the canyon, turn north on Larimer County Road 103, and drive 6 miles to the West Branch trailhead. Take Forest Trail 960 about 3.5 miles to its intersection with Forest Trail 961.

Additional information: There is generally a four-fish limit in these waters. However, fish will often spoil during a long hike out, so consider releasing them.

Contact: Colorado Division of Wildlife, Fort Collins; (970) 484–2836.

55A Twin Craters Lake

Directions: From the intersection of Forest Trails 960 and 961, take Forest Trail 961 about 1.5 miles west to Forest Trail 962 and hike 1 mile.

55B Rock Hole Lake

Directions: From the intersection of Forest Trails 960 and 961, take Forest Trail 961 about 2 miles to Bench Lake. Rock Hole Lake is just south of Bench Lake.

55C Carey Lake

Directions: From the intersection of Forest Trails 960 and 961, stay on Forest Trail 960 for 2 miles.

56 Zimmerman Lake

Key species: Greenback cutthroat trout.

Description: This 40-acre natural lake, just below the treeline at 9,500 feet, is surrounded by fir and spruce trees.

Tips: Fly-fishing from the bank is difficult. Take a belly boat or use a fly and bubble on a spinning rod.

The fishing: Zimmerman Lake is home to a brood population of pure greenback cutthroat trout that range up to 18 inches, with an average size of 12 inches. Since cutthroat trout are mainly insect eaters, spinners don't work well, but if used they should be small and colorful. These fish will surely hit anything once, usually as soon as it hits the water, but matching the hatch with dry flies and nymphs trailed slowly through the water will draw strikes. Small sizes work best.

Directions: From Fort Collins, drive 10 miles north on U.S. Highway 287, then turn west onto Colorado Highway 14 and proceed through Poudre Canyon. Joe Wright Reservoir is about 56 miles up the canyon. Two miles past the reservoir on the south side of the highway is the well-marked trailhead to Zimmerman Lake. The hike to the lake is about 1 mile and not too difficult.

Additional information: Only flies and lures may be used. All fish must be returned immediately to the water.

Contact: Colorado Division of Wildlife, Fort Collins; (970) 484–2836.

Zimmerman Lake holds a greenback cutthroat trout brood population.

FISHING COLORADO

57 Joe Wright Reservoir

Key species: Arctic grayling, Emerald Lake rainbow trout.

Description: Joe Wright Reservoir is a 160-acre impoundment just off of Colorado Highway 14, near Cameron Pass in the upper Poudre River watershed.

Tips: Anglers report catching forty to sixty fish on good days.

The fishing: The arctic grayling have overrun the wild Emerald Lake rainbow trout in this impoundment and comprise about 85 percent of the fish population found there, with fish as large as 17 inches reported being caught. Basic attractor dry-fly patterns should be used when fish are hitting the surface. Flashy bead-head nymphs fished deep work well along the lake's edge, which can be better accessed by a belly boat or canoe, except at the inlet of Joe Wright Creek, where the lake is shallow enough to wade. Small colorful lures fished deep are also extremely effective. These are not picky fish.

Directions: From Fort Collins, drive 10 miles north on U.S. Highway 287, then turn west onto Colorado Highway 14 and proceed through Poudre Canyon. Joe Wright Reservoir is about 56 miles up the canyon.

Additional information: The bag limit for rainbow trout is two fish larger than 16 inches. Only hand-propelled or electric motorized boats are allowed. Only flies and lures may be used.

Contact: Colorado Division of Wildlife, Fort Collins; (970) 484–2836.

58 Cache La Poudre River

Key species: Brown trout, rainbow trout, cutbows, greenback cutthroat trout, brook trout.

Description: Named for a secret site along the river where early French trappers stashed their gunpowder for fighting off Arapaho and Cheyenne raiding parties, the Cache la Poudre River runs 70 miles west to east from the north side of Rocky Mountain National Park through one of the most beautiful valleys in Colorado. One of the few undammed rivers in the state, the Poudre is rightfully designated a Wild and Scenic River until it reaches the foothills northwest of Fort Collins.

Tips: Nearly the entire river has public access to at least one section of bank.

The fishing: Seventy thousand 3- to 4-inch rainbow trout were stocked throughout the Cache la Poudre River from Chambers Lake down to Mishiwaka in 2002. There has been heavy stocking of 10-inch fish in the lower section—below Indian Meadows to the mouth of the canyon. Pods of large, healthy cutbows, some to 16 inches, can be found in riffle water above Indian Meadows.

Stream census data: At Indian Meadows, 21 miles above the mouth of the canyon along the meadow, 492 brown trout per surface acre, weighing an estimated 250 pounds, were captured in 1998. An estimated 103 of those were larger than 14 inches. Captures in recent years have been similar.

Whirling disease: Due to the high concentrations of whirling-disease organisms in the effluent from the Poudre fish-rearing unit, there has been virtually no natural reproduction of rainbows in the middle segment of the Poudre River since 1990, and this situation is unlikely to change in the near future. Brown trout have, however, maintained their populations and have even increased to some extent in many areas.

Directions: From Fort Collins, drive 10 miles north on U.S. Highway 287 to Ted's Place, then turn west on Colorado Highway 14. Public access begins about 2 miles west, where the river parallels the road, and continues for 49 miles.

Additional information: The river from the Pingree Park Bridge to the town of Rustic and from Black Hollow Creek to Big Bend Campground, along with the section paralleling Big South Trail are all designated Wild Trout waters. Fishing is restricted to flies and lures, with a bag limit of two trout larger than 16 inches. These areas are well marked.

Contact: Colorado Division of Wildlife, Fort Collins; (970) 484–2836.

59 Cache La Poudre River, Big South Trail Segment

Key species: Greenback cutthroat trout, brown trout, rainbow trout, brook trout.

Description: This section begins at the Big South trailhead, where Colorado Highway 14 diverges from paralleling the river, and the river runs for 16 miles to its headwaters in Rocky Mountain National Park. The lower section contains a series of cascades and plunge pools, which all but dictates that this stretch be fished well after runoff. The upper section is a classic small meadow stream.

Tips: The difficult access and short season have allowed the Big South section of the river to offer some good fishing for those willing to make the hike.

The fishing: This section offers some greenback cutthroat trout up to 16 inches in the upper meadow section, as well as brown, rainbow, and brook trout—the Grand Slam of Colorado trout fishing—in the steeper sections. The narrow river channel makes approach difficult, but while the fish are wary, they're less particular than their downstream counterparts and will take a variety of dry-fly attractor and general nymph patterns, as well as brightly colored spinners.

Whirling disease: Negative.

Directions: From Fort Collins, drive 10 miles north on U.S. Highway 287 to Ted's Place, then turn west onto Colorado Highway 14 and go 49 miles to the trailhead.

Additional information: As a Wild Trout water, fishing is limited to flies and lures.

Contact: Colorado Division of Wildlife, Fort Collins; (970) 484–2836.

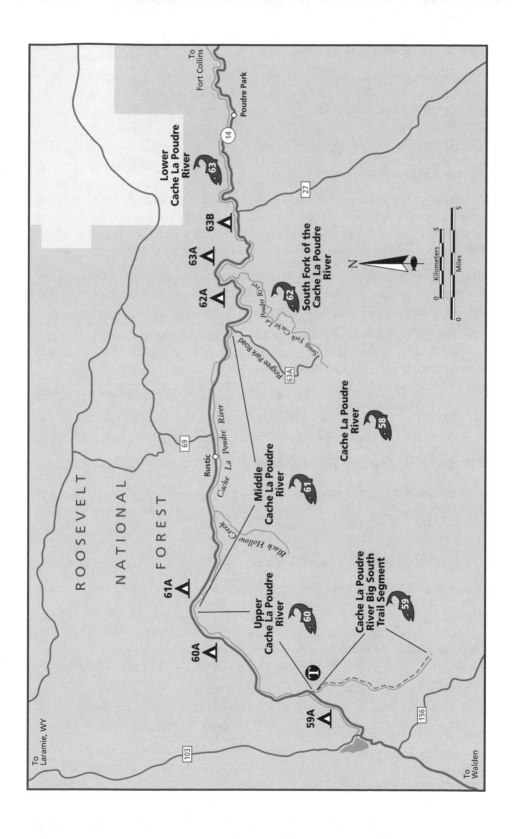

59A Camping: Aspen Glen Area

This small, sunny campground has tables, fire grates, rest rooms, and drinking water. From Fort Collins, drive 10 miles north on U.S. 287 to Ted's Place, then turn west on CO 14 and go 50 miles to the campground.

60 Upper Cache La Poudre River

Key species: Brown trout, rainbow trout.

Description: Beginning at Big Bend Campground, this section extends 7 miles upstream to the Big South trailhead. In this segment the river begins its climb out of the valley and into the alpine region and presents a wide variety of water that holds some of the interesting pools and riffles typical of high-altitude streams.

Tips: Angling pressure is low on this segment of the river; 35,000 rainbow trout fingerlings were stocked in 2002, which should provide catchable-size fish beginning in 2003.

The fishing: With a few exceptions, a 12-inch fish is a big one in this segment. Worms, PowerBait, and salmon eggs are effective, as are small, brightly colored spinners. Small attractor dry flies and nymphs should work well.

Directions: From Fort Collins, drive 10 miles north on U.S. Highway 287 to Ted's Place, then turn west onto Colorado Highway 14 and go 40 miles.

Contact: Colorado Division of Wildlife, Fort Collins; (970) 484–2836.

60A Camping: Sleeping Elephant Area

This campground offers a vault toilet, tables, fire grates, and drinking water. From Fort Collins, drive 10 miles north on U.S. 287 to Ted's Place, then turn west onto CO 14 and go 44 miles to the campground.

61 Middle Cache La Poudre River

Key species: Brown trout, cutbows, rainbow trout.

Description: This section begins at the Pingree Park turnoff and continues 13 miles upstream to the Big Bend Campground. Beginning at Indian Meadows to well above Big Bend, the valley widens and allows slower water conditions as the river meanders through wide, flat meadows and soaks up sunlight, stimulating aquatic vegetation and insect production.

Tips: This is the most productive stretch of the river; 35,000 rainbow trout fingerlings were stocked in 2002, which should provide catchable-size fish beginning in 2003.

The fishing: Browns between 12 and 16 inches predominate in this segment; however, cutbows have been stocked in this section for several years, and some rainbows can be found. The cutbows, some to 16 inches, seem to pod in riffle areas. Midges

The Cache La Poudre River
at Indian Meadows

hatch periodically from April to November, blue-winged olives in April and May and again from September to November, green drakes and red quills from late June to mid-August, caddis flies from June to October, and stoneflies from May to August. Ants, grasshoppers, and beetles become trout fare from July to October. Gold Mepps and Panther Martin spinners are effective pre-runoff and again in fall. The most effective fly patterns will imitate the nymph or emerger stages of these insects, with the exception of dry-fly patterns for ants, grasshoppers, beetles, and blue-winged olives in late summer and early fall.

Whirling disease: Positive.

Directions: From Fort Collins, drive 10 miles north on U.S. Highway 287 to Ted's Place, then turn west onto Colorado Highway 14 and go 26 miles.

Additional information: This section is interspersed with Wild Trout water, with flies-and-lures-only and open-bait regulations in effect.

61A Camping: Big Bend Area

This riverside campground, with three walk-in tent sites and several closely spaced RV sites, offers drinking water, tables, fire grates, and vault toilets. From Fort Collins, drive 10 miles north on U.S. 287 to Ted's Place, then turn west onto CO 14 and go 40 miles to the campground.

Contact: Colorado Division of Wildlife, Fort Collins; (970) 484–2836.

62 South Fork of the Cache La Poudre River

Key species: Brown, rainbow, brook trout, cutbows.

Description: Flowing north out of Rocky Mountain National Park through the Cache La Poudre Wilderness Area, the South Fork joins the main stem of the river just west of Dutch George Flats Campground.

Tips: During low water, hike upstream into a steep canyon just above the confluence with the Poudre River to work the deeper pools. During high water, use the trail beginning at Mountain Park Campground.

The fishing: Browns, brookies, and rainbows up to 12 inches can be caught in the canyon. Cutbows and brookies are in the higher, flat stretches. There are no restrictions on bait. Dry-fly attractor patterns work well.

Whirling disease: Negative.

Directions: From Fort Collins, drive 10 miles north on U.S. Highway 287 to Ted's Place, then turn west onto Colorado Highway 14 and go 22 miles to the Mountain Park Campground. A loop trail runs around the mountain south of the campground. Take the left fork of the trail and hike about 2 miles to the top. The South Fork drainage lies to the east, and the angler must bushwack a mile down into the valley to get there, as there are no formal trails in the wilderness area. Watch out for rattlesnakes.

Contact: Colorado Division of Wildlife, Fort Collins; (970) 484–2836.

62A Camping: Mountain Park Area

This large, popular campground offers modern facilities, including electrical hookups, hot showers, drinking water, and recreational sports areas. From Fort Collins, drive 10 miles north on U.S. 287 to Ted's Place, then turn west onto CO 14 and go 22 miles.

63 Lower Cache La Poudre River

Key species: Rainbow trout, brown trout.

Description: This section begins at the mouth of Poudre Canyon, and ends at Pingree Park Road, 20 miles upriver. This stretch of river has moderate to steep valley walls on its lower and upper ends and a truly ferocious section of fast water known as "The Narrows" just about in the middle. High recreational use—car camping, hiking, rock climbing, rafting, resorts, and, of course, fishing—characterize this segment.

Tips: This section was heavily stocked with 10-inch rainbow trout in 2002, the first time in many years. Since many anglers practice catch-and-release fishing, there should be good population holdovers.

The fishing: Recent stocking has drastically improved the quality of fishing in the lower canyon; the fish rise to attractor flies and flies that imitate any hatches taking place. Beginning in midsummer, terrestrial patterns such as grasshoppers, ants, and beetles work well. Brown trout will come up during hatches but have been heavily fished and are extremely wary and difficult to catch. Worms and PowerBait are the main baits used, usually weighted and fished deep into holes or on slow edges when the water recedes enough to find them. Brightly colored Mepps or Panther Martins retrieved quickly through slower water will make short work of newly stocked rainbows as well as the more elusive brown trout. At low water, pools in The Narrows can produce some browns up to 16 inches.

Whirling disease: Positive.

Directions: From Fort Collins, drive 10 miles north on U.S. Highway 287 to Ted's Place, then turn left onto Colorado Highway 14 for 2 miles to Poudre Canyon.

63A Camping: Dutch George Area

This campground offers great views, vault toilets, tables, fire grates, and drinking water. From Fort Collins, drive 10 miles north on U.S. Highway 287 to Ted's Place, then turn west onto CO 14 and go 21 miles to the campground.

63B Camping: Stove Prairie Area

This campground offers walk-in, shaded tent sites and sites for medium-size RVs and has vault toilets, tables, drinking water, and fire grates. From Fort Collins, drive 10 miles north on U.S. 287 to Ted's Place, then turn west onto CO 14 and go 16 miles to the campground.

64 Rocky Mountain National Park

Key species: Greenback cutthroat trout, cutthroat trout hybrid, brown trout, brook trout, rainbow trout.

Description: Rocky Mountain National Park covers approximately 260,000 acres along both sides of the Continental Divide about 70 miles northwest of Denver. High mountain lakes, streams, and rivers are found throughout the park and most require some hiking, with various degrees of difficulty to access. The park is the stronghold of the greenback cutthroat trout recovery area.

Directions: From Denver, take I–25 for 20 miles north, then go west on Colorado Highway 66 for 17 miles to Lyons. From Lyons, take U.S. Highway 36 for 19 miles to Estes Park.

Additional information: A daily entrance fee or a National Parks season pass is required. All anglers must possess a valid Colorado fishing license. Backcountry users must have a permit. Only artificial flies and lures may be used, and lures must have only one single, double, or treble hook with a common shank. All hooks must be barbless. Possession limits vary, but all cutthroat trout must be returned immediately to the water. The entry stations have current information on possession limits, as well as pictures to aid in identification of each species. No stocking occurs within the park.

Contact: Rocky Mountain National Park; (970) 586–1206.

65 Colorado River

Key species: Rainbow trout, brook trout, brown trout, cutthroat trout hybrid.

Description: The headwaters of the Colorado River are in the alpine basins on the west side of Rocky Mountain National Park and the Neversummer Range to the west. The tributaries come together in the beautiful Kawuneeche Valley, where the river meanders several miles down the long valley.

Tips: Try salmon egg patterns in the fall to bring up the few big browns that are in the river.

The fishing: This is a small- to medium-size stream and holds, for the most part, 8- to 10-inch fish. Cast dry flies like an Elk Hair Caddis or parachute Adams in pocket water when the river is high, and cast small spinners, streamers, or bead-head

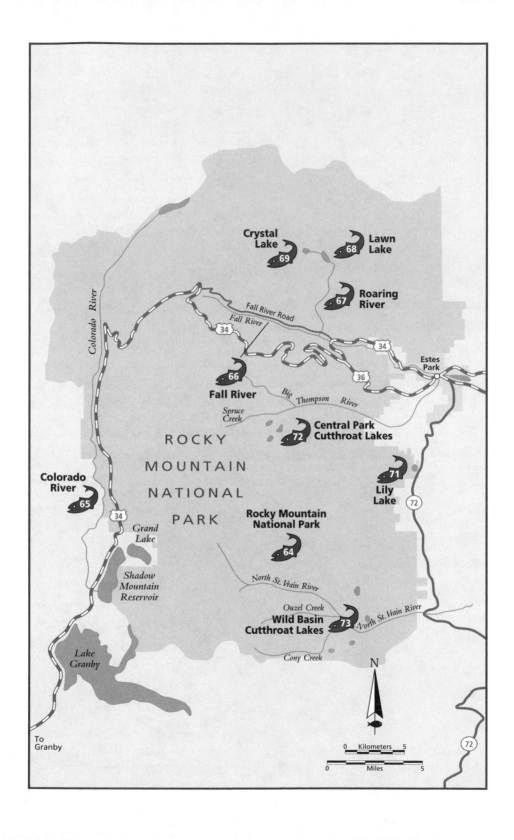

Crystal
Lake **69**

Lawn
Lake **68**

Roaring
River **67**

Colorado River

Fall River Road

Fall River

34

34

36

Estes
Park

66
Fall River

Big Thompson River

Spruce Creek

Central Park
Cutthroat Lakes **72**

R O C K Y

M O U N T A I N

N A T I O N A L

P A R K

Colorado
River **65**

34

Grand Lake

Shadow Mountain Reservoir

Rocky Mountain National Park

64

Lily
Lake **71**

72

North St. Vrain River

Ouzel Creek

Wild Basin
Cutthroat Lakes **73**

North St. Vrain River

72

Lake Granby

Cony Creek

To
Granby

N

0   Kilometers   5

0   Miles   5

72

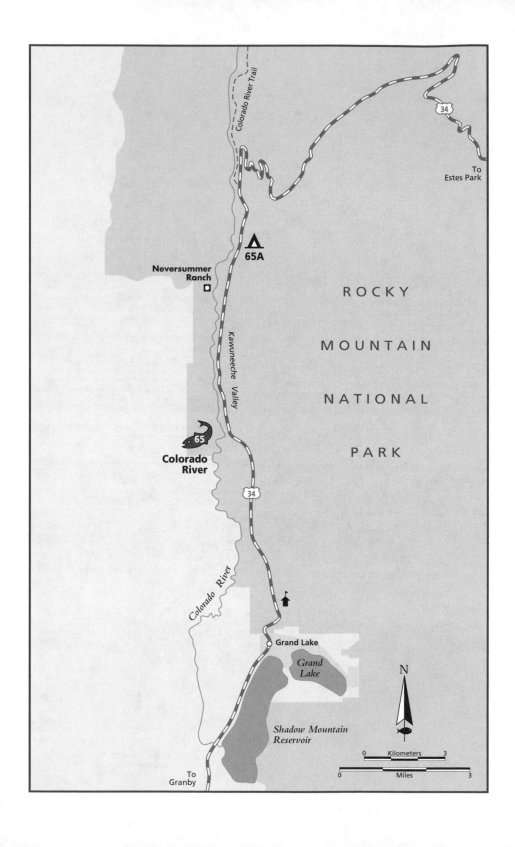

Colorado River Trail

34

To
Estes Park

△
65A

Neversummer
Ranch

Kawuneeche Valley

ROCKY

MOUNTAIN

NATIONAL

PARK

65
Colorado
River

34

Colorado River

Grand Lake

Grand
Lake

N

Shadow Mountain
Reservoir

0   Kilometers   3

0   Miles   3

To
Granby

Pheasant Tail or Prince nymphs into undercut banks when the water slows down. Ant and grasshopper patterns work well in the late summer. If you find a nice undercut bank over a deep hole, fish it in the early morning or late in the day with a minnow, leech, or caddis pattern to nail the big browns that might live there.

Whirling disease: Negative.

Directions: From Estes Park, take U.S. Highway 34 (Trail Ridge Road) across the park about 36 miles to the upper Kawuneeche Valley. From Granby, drive 16 miles north on U.S. 34 to the park entrance. The river parallels the highway almost to the town of Grand Lake. Access begins where the river parallels the road, but a good stretch of water is between the Neversummer Ranch picnic site 9 miles north of the Kawuneeche Visitor Center north of Grand Lake and the Timber Creek Campground 0.5 mile upstream. Lots of good pocket water can be reached by taking the Colorado River Trail 2 miles north of the Timber Creek Campground.

Contact: Rocky Mountain National Park; (970) 586–1206.

65A Camping: Timber Creek Area

This medium-size, riverside campground is in an aspen grove and offers drinking water, toilets, fire grates, and tables. From Granby, drive 16 miles north on U.S. 34 to the park entrance, then go another 9.5 miles north.

66 Fall River

Key species: Brook trout, cutthroat trout hybrid, brown trout, rainbow trout.

Description: From the eastern edge of the Continental Divide, the Fall River tumbles beside Fall River Road, the old highway across the park, through Horseshoe Park, then into the town of Estes Park.

Tips: A stealthy approach, delicate casts, and fine tippits are necessary to catch these spooky fish.

The fishing: The pocket water above the confluence of the Roaring River holds some fish up to 12 inches, which can be caught by using standard weighted nymphs. In slower water try lightly dropping a Royal Wulff or tiny Adams dry fly and be ready for a quick strike. The short feeding season at this altitude can make the fish incautious but not necessarily stupid. If you miss a couple of strikes, move to another spot. Back toward Estes Park the river meanders slowly through Horseshoe Park, where even more finesse is required.

Whirling disease: Negative.

Directions: From Estes Park, go 5 miles on U.S. Highway 34 to the Fall River park entrance. The river runs along the south side of U.S. 34 then parallels Fall River Road well up into the park.

66A Camping: Aspenglen Area

This popular campground for tents and RVs has paved RV pads, drinking water, tables, fire grates, and flush toilets with electrical outlets, but no dump stations or showers. From Estes Park, go 5 miles west on U.S. 34 to the Fall River park entrance and turn south just beyond the entrance.

67 Roaring River

Key species: Greenback cutthroat trout.

Description: This river literally tumbles off the north side of Fall River Canyon amid a path of great destruction caused by a dam breach in 1982 at Lawn Lake, 6 miles up the mountain. Fast water predominates, but pools and pocket water abound in the litter caused by the flood.

Tips: The best section of water is a climb to an altitude of about 900 feet and 2 miles up the trail.

The fishing: Colorful attractor dry flies work well in the slow-water spots.

Whirling disease: Negative.

Directions: From the Fall River park entrance west of Estes Park, take U.S. Highway 34 for about 2 miles to the Lawn Lake trailhead on the north side of the highway. The path runs parallel to the river about 1 mile up the trail.

Additional information: Fishing is restricted to flies and lures only, and all cutthroat trout must be returned immediately to the water.

Contact: Rocky Mountain National Park; (970) 586–1206.

68 Lawn Lake

Key species: Greenback cutthroat trout.

Description: Lawn Lake was once a reservoir, but the dam broke in 1982, causing a flood that roared down the slopes of Fall River Canyon and into Estes Park. Long and narrow, the lake looks a little like a bathtub half full of water.

Tips: The short season makes these fish hit anything that lands on the water.

The fishing: Standard attractor dry-fly patterns like a Royal Wulff, Adams, Elk Hair Caddis, or red Humpy work well on a fly rod or behind a bubble on a spinning outfit. Cast to fish cruising the lake's perimeter, let the fly sit for a few seconds, then retrieve it slowly.

Directions: From the Fall River park entrance west of Estes Park, take U.S. Highway 34 for about 2 miles to the Lawn Lake trailhead on the north side of the highway. The hike to the lake is about 6 miles on a moderate to difficult trail.

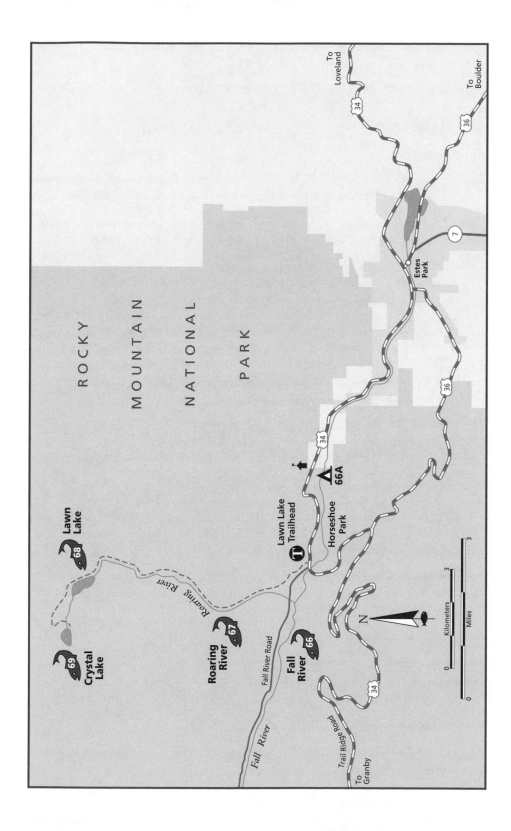

Additional information: Fishing is restricted to flies and lures only, and all cutthroat trout must be returned immediately to the water.

Contact: Rocky Mountain National Park; (970) 586–1206.

69 Crystal Lake

Key species: Greenback cutthroat trout.

Description: Crystal Lake is a high-altitude, remote 25-acre lake at the top of the Roaring River drainage near the north rim of Rocky Mountain National Park.

Tips: This lake requires a long hike through beautiful subalpine forests and alpine meadows but could reward anglers with the largest greenback cutthroat to be found in the wild.

The fishing: The long hike in and the coldness of the water at 9,500 feet makes Crystal Lake a natural for spin-fishing gear, particularly a fly-and-bubble rig, though the banks are open and the east side of the lake is wadeable for standard fly-fishing. With spinning gear, cast a colorful dry fly as far out as possible, then slowly retrieve it back to the bank. With a fly rod, cast a weighted natural nymph, let it sink a little, then reel it in with short, slow retrievals to attract one of the big cutthroat that cruise the perimeter of the lake. A rainbow-hued spinner can be effective on occasion by dragging it into a cruising fish's path.

Directions: From the Fall River park entrance west of Estes Park, take U.S. Highway 34 for about 2 miles to the Lawn Lake trailhead on the north side of the highway. From the trailhead, Crystal Lake is a 7.5-mile hike on a trail that varies from easy to moderate, with a few steep sections.

Additional information: The stream below Crystal Lake all the way down to the Lawn Lake trailhead is part of the greenback recovery program under the Endangered Species Act. Fishing on the stream is limited to flies and lures only, and all fish must be returned immediately to the water.

Contact: Rocky Mountain National Park; (970) 586–1206.

70 Upper Big Thompson River

Key species: Brown trout, brook trout, cutthroat trout hybrid.

Description: From the Continental Divide, the Big Thompson tumbles east through the steep walls of Forest Canyon before entering Moraine Park, where it meanders through willow-choked banks in the scenic valley.

Tips: When the river is clear, attractor dry flies work best.

The fishing: The fish are small, topping out at about 10 inches. Small colorful spinners and attractor nymphs, like the Zug Bug, Prince, and Hare's Ear, floated into undercut banks and pools work well. Stay back from the bank and cast into likely areas.

Whirling disease: Negative.

Directions: From Estes Park, take U.S. Highway 36 west for about 4 miles to the Beaver Meadow park entrance. Turn south just past the entrance and drive 1 mile to Moraine Park. The river runs through Moraine Park and is paralleled by Moraine Park Road for 2 miles, then the Fern Lake Trail for another 2 miles, where it heads northwest into the upper reaches of Forest Canyon.

Contact: Rocky Mountain National Park; (970) 586–1206.

70A Camping: Moraine Park Area

This large campground, with fantastic scenery and wildlife viewing, has fire grates, tables, drinking water, and flush toilets with electrical outlets. From Estes Park, take U.S. 36 west for about 4 miles to the Beaver Meadow park entrance. Turn south just past the entrance and drive 1.6 miles, then turn right and follow the signs to the campground.

71 Lily Lake

Key species: Greenback cutthroat trout.

Description: Lily Lake, as the name suggests, is a lily-pad-covered, mirrored mountain tarn just outside Rocky Mountain National Park's east boundary.

Tips: This is the best drive-up greenback cutthroat fishing on the planet.

The fishing: Lily Lake is home to a brood population of greenback cutthroat trout that stay fat on the insects growing in the pond's lush vegetation, and they can be picky with all that food to eat. The best fishing is just after ice-out with small lures and spinners or attractor wet flies, then again in late June when the damselflies hatch. Both Renegades and bead-head Hare's Ears work well during the damselfly hatch. During the heat of day in midsummer, the action tapers off, but nymphs, Woolly Buggers, and scuds worked around the edges of the weed beds can be effective. Just after the sun goes down on those hot days, swarms of caddis flies and midges cover the water and bring up the lake's bigger fish, some up to 16 inches.

Directions: From Estes Park, take Colorado Highway 7 for about 3 miles south to the Lily Lake parking lot.

Additional information: In addition to catch-and-release, flies-and-lures-only restrictions, anglers must use only barbless hooks. There is a wheelchair-accessible dock next to the parking area.

Contact: Rocky Mountain National Park; (970) 586–1206.

72 Central Park Cutthroat Lakes

Key species: Greenback cutthroat trout.

Description: All the following cutthroat lakes are very high-altitude waters and tend to be covered with ice until July during normal-snow years. Weather at these altitudes can change very rapidly, and lightning presents a very real danger, especially to someone holding a graphite rod. Many of the lakes can only be reached by strenuous hiking. Take warm clothes, a first-aid kit, and food. Know your level of fitness, and when fishing keep track of the time so you can reach your base camp or car before dark.

The fishing: These waters support reproducing populations of pure greenback cutthroat trout and are the backbone of the government's recovery program, which was mandated by the Endangered Species Act. The lakes are capable of growing cutthroat trout to fairly large sizes, some reported up to 18 inches, but most will be in the 7- to 12-inch range. Standard attractor dry-fly patterns like a Royal Wulff, Adams, Elk Hair Caddis, or red Humpy work well on a fly rod or behind a bubble on a spinning outfit. Cast to fish cruising the lake's perimeter, let the fly sit for a few seconds, then retrieve it slowly. If there's no surface activity, cast a weighted natural nymph like a bead-head Hare's Ear, let it sink a little, then reel in short, slow retrievals. In the streams, cast medium to small attractor patterns or lightly weighted nymphs. Heavy spinners hitting the water will often scare the fish.

Directions: From Estes Park, take U.S. Highway 36 west for about 4 miles to the Beaver Meadow park entrance.

Contact: Rocky Mountain National Park; (970) 586–1206.

72A Fern Lake

Directions: Turn south just past the Beaver Meadow park entrance and drive 1 mile to Moraine Park, then take Moraine Park Road west for 2 miles to the Fern Lake trailhead and hike 2.8 miles to the lake.

72B Odessa Lake

Directions: From Fern Lake, take the Odessa Lake trail south around Fern Lake for 1 mile.

72C Spruce Lake

Directions: From Fern Lake, take the Spruce Lake Trail west for 0.8 mile.

73 Wild Basin Cutthroat Lakes

Key species: Greenback cutthroat trout.

Description: All the following cutthroat lakes are very high-altitude waters and tend to be covered with ice until July during normal-snow years. Weather at these altitudes can change very rapidly, and lightning presents a very real danger, especially

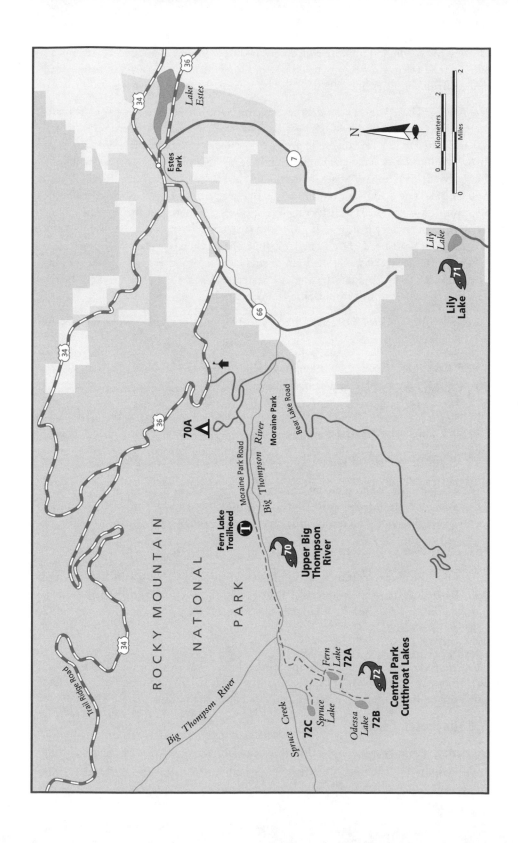

to someone holding a graphite rod. Many lakes can only be reached by strenuous hiking. Take warm clothes, a first-aid kit, and food. Know your level of fitness, and time your fishing so you can reach your base camp or car before dark.

The fishing: These waters support reproducing populations of pure greenback cutthroat trout and are the backbone of the government's recovery program, which was mandated by the Endangered Species Act. The lakes are capable of growing cutthroat trout to fairly large sizes, some reported up to 18 inches, but most will be in the 7- to 12-inch range. Standard attractor dry-fly patterns like a Royal Wulff, Adams, Elk Hair Caddis, or red Humpy work well on a fly rod or behind a bubble on a spinning outfit. Cast to fish cruising the lake's perimeter, let the fly sit for a few seconds, then retrieve it slowly. If there's no surface activity, cast a weighted natural nymph like a bead-head Hare's Ear, let it sink a little, then reel it in with short, slow retrievals. In the streams, cast medium to small attractor patterns or lightly weighted nymphs. Heavy spinners hitting the water will scare the fish, as most in the streams are too small to be predacious on other fish.

Directions: From Estes Park, take Colorado Highway 7 south for 9 miles to the Wild Basin park entrance.

Contact: Rocky Mountain National Park; (970) 586–1206.

73A Sandbeach Lake

Directions: Just past the entrance station, park in the Sandbeach Lake trailhead parking lot and take the trail 4.2 miles west to the lake.

73B Ouzel Creek, Ouzel Lake

Directions: From the entrance station, drive 2 miles on Wild Basin Road to the Wild Basin Ranger Station parking lot and follow the Ouzel Lake Trail signs 3.1 miles west to Ouzel Creek. The trail parallels the creek another 1.8 miles to the lake.

73C Pear Lake

Directions: From the entrance station, drive 2 miles on Wild Basin Road to the Wild Basin Ranger Station and hike back along the road 0.25 mile to the Finch Lake trailhead. Take the Finch Lake Trail 4.5 miles to Finch Lake, then another 2 miles to Pear Lake.

73D Cony Creek

Directions: From just west of Finch Lake, the Finch Lake Trail runs west parallel to Cony Creek for 1.5 miles, about 0.25 mile north of the stream.

73E Hutcheson Lakes

Directions: From Pear Lake, the three Hutcheson Lakes are south up the side of the mountain and require bushwacking from 0.3 mile to the bottom lake to nearly 1 mile to the upper lake.

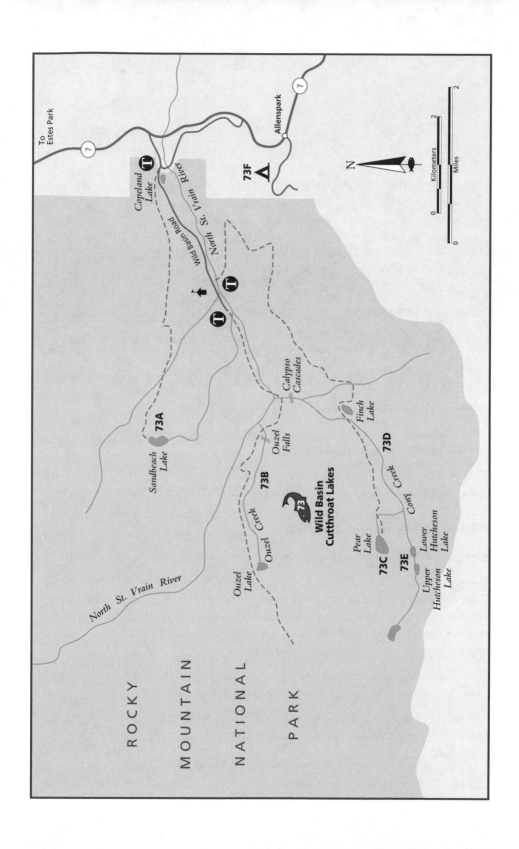

Ouzel Creek in Rocky Mountain National Park's Wild Basin

73F Camping: Olive Ridge Area

This popular campground for tents and RVs offers drinking water, fire grates, tables, and rest rooms. From Estes Park, take CO 7 south for 10 miles.

74 Lower Big Thompson River

Key species: Rainbow trout, brown trout, brook trout.

Description: This section of the Big Thompson River begins below Lake Estes in Estes Park and winds east for about 20 miles through the Big Thompson Canyon into the city of Loveland. A major flood in 1976 blew out much of the canyon but resulted in a significant stream-restoration effort, which has created one of the most popular trout fisheries on the Front Range.

Tips: The lower gradient sections at the upper and lower ends are favored by brown trout. In between, the faster water is favored by rainbow trout.

The fishing: The tailwater below Lake Estes is the most heavily fished stretch and holds the biggest fish, mostly brown trout. The fish are heavily hatch-oriented but not particularly spooky thanks to the constant presence of anglers. Like most Colorado tailwater fisheries, tiny mayfly and caddis fly imitations are the ticket to success. When trout seem scarce try small spinners ripped across likely holding

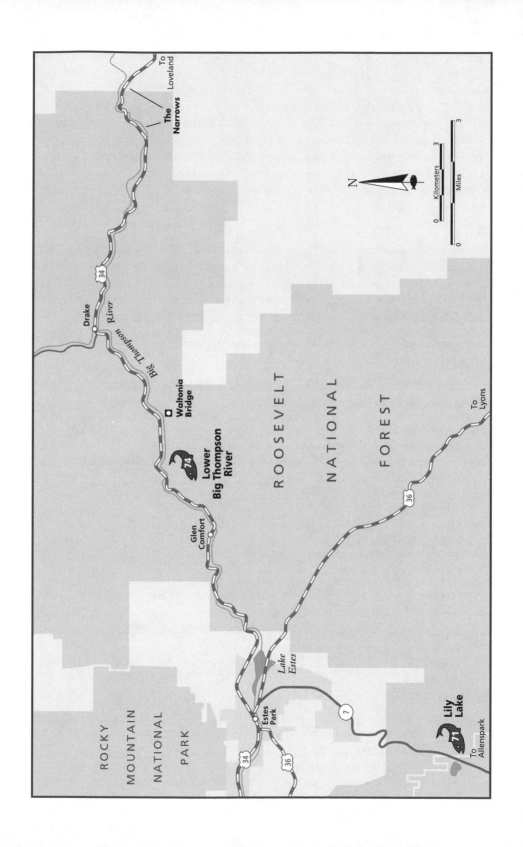

spots or weighted streamers fished jerkily like wounded minnows. In the rainbow trout water downstream, the fish are spookier and a stealthy approach is needed, but fortunately they seem willing to strike at attractor patterns like Elk Hair Caddis, bead-head and flashback Pheasant Tail nymphs, and parachute Adams. The lower canyon, which can be treacherous wading, is marked by steep walls with limited access points, but during low water there are many nice holes where both browns and rainbows up to 16 inches lurk, along with a few smaller fish. These fish are susceptible to the same hatches as in the above stretches, but larger insects, like the green drake and golden stonefly, seem to draw them from their safety holes. Spinners or weighted streamers like the Woolly Bugger fished deep can be effective, as well as salmon eggs and PowerBait fished in deeper holes just off the bottom.

Stream census data: At the habitat-improvement area just below Lake Estes, 1997 surveys estimated 300 fish per acre of surface water. About 60 percent were brown trout, and about 10 percent of them were larger than 14 inches. At a site just below the restricted area at Waltonia Bridge, there were an estimated 1,700 fish per acre of surface water, mostly rainbow trout, but none were larger than 14 inches.

Whirling disease: The Big Thompson River is considered whirling-disease positive, but no population-level effects have been seen yet.

Directions: From Loveland, take U.S. Highway 34 west toward Estes Park. The public water begins at the mouth of The Narrows section, 3 miles west of Loveland.

Additional information: From Lake Estes to the Waltonia Bridge west of the town of Drake, the Big Thompson River is catch-and-release, flies-and-lures-only fishing. The restricted section is well marked. Much of the river is public access, and the places that are private are also well marked.

Contact: Colorado Division of Wildlife, Fort Collins; (970) 484–2836.

75 Douglas Reservoir

Key species: Rainbow trout.

Description: This is a 565-acre reservoir located in the sagebrush and juniper foothills north of Fort Collins.

Tips: Fifty-three thousand rainbow trout were stocked here in 2000.

The fishing: Basic bait-and-bobber and lure fishing will take these easy-to-catch fish. In warmer weather trolling deep with black lead-head jigs will take some holdover rainbows up to 3 pounds.

Directions: From Fort Collins, take U.S. Highway 287 to the north side of town, then take Colorado Highway 1(the Wellington exit) north for 3 miles to Larimer County Road 15. Turn left and drive north for another 1.5 miles to Larimer County Road 60, then west for 0.5 mile to LaVina Drive, which is the entrance to the lake.

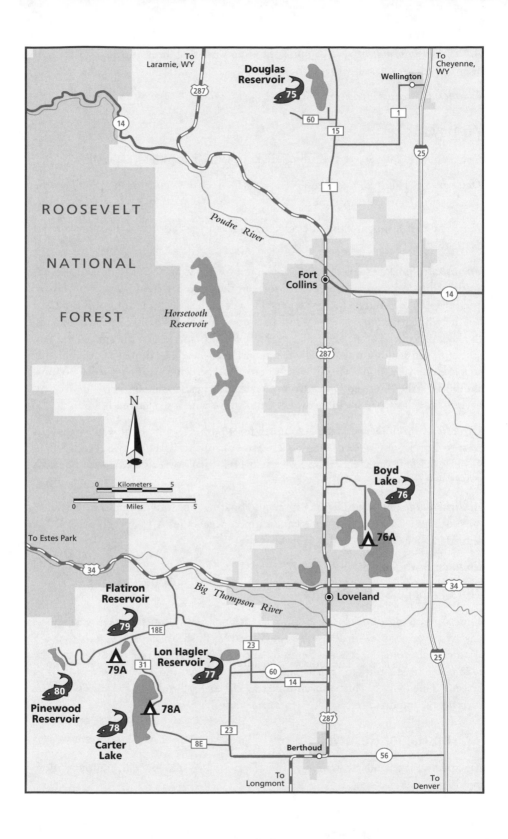

Additional information: No camping, hunting, shooting, fires, or off-road vehicles are allowed. Wakeless boating only.

Contact: Colorado Division of Wildlife, Fort Collins; (970) 484–2836.

76 Boyd Lake

Key species: Rainbow trout, smallmouth bass, white bass, walleye, perch.

Description: This 1,800-acre reservoir is located in the gently rolling hills on the northeast outskirts of Loveland.

Tips: The best fishing is along the ridges at the southeast corner of the reservoir and at the inlet.

The fishing: Stocked with 24,000 10-inch rainbow trout in 2000, Boyd Lake also has a decent holdover population of rainbows in the 3- to 5-pound range. Lures, bait, and flies all work well on these stockers. However, the real attractions of Boyd Lake are the white bass and walleye. White bass up to 2 pounds are not unusual, making the lake one of the best fisheries in the state for this species. In the spring and fall, white bass in shallow water can be taken with lead-head jigs tipped with rabbit-fur strips, either on a spinning rod or a fly rod. Walleye, which grow up to 10 pounds, should be fished in deep water from a boat with jigs, crankbait, or trolled worm harnesses. Yellow perch can be caught from shore with a worm and bobber.

Directions: From Denver, take I–25 north for 40 miles to U.S. Highway 34 and exit west to Loveland. Go north on Madison Street 1 mile to East Thirty-seventh Street. Go east 0.5 mile on Larimer County Road 11C, turn north and drive to the lake's entrance station.

Additional information: The lake is open to boating, but waterskiing is restricted to its south end. Most facilities are handicapped accessible. A Colorado State Parks season pass or daily use fee is required.

Contact: Boyd Lake State Park; (970) 669–1739.

76A Camping: Boyd Lake Area

This large campground, located near the entrance station on the lake's east shore, has six paved loops with RV pull-though spaces, flush toilets, showers, a first-aid station, and a food concession. Tents are allowed in grassy sites. From Denver, take I–25 north for 40 miles to U.S. 34 and exit west to Loveland. Go north on Madison Street 1 mile to East Thirty-seventh Street. Go east 0.5 mile on Larimer CR 11C, turn north, and drive to the lake's entrance station.

77 Lon Hagler Reservoir

Key species: Tiger muskie, rainbow trout, largemouth bass, bluegill, crappie, yellow perch.

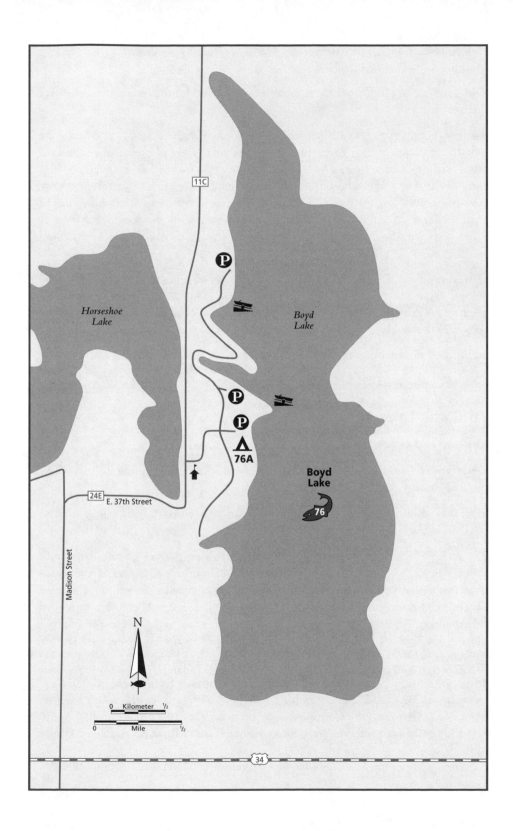

Horseshoe
Lake

11C

Boyd
Lake

76A

Boyd
Lake

76

24E
E. 37th Street

Madison Street

N

0   Kilometer   ½
0   Mile   ½

34

Description: Lon Hagler Reservoir is a 100-acre impoundment in the rolling foothills southwest of Loveland.

Tips: High numbers of stocked rainbows are scheduled for the reservoir for the next few years.

The fishing: With 55,000 10-inch rainbows stocked in 2000 and similar numbers tentatively planned for 3 to 5 years thereafter, this is the place for old-fashioned family fishing. Use a worm and bobber, salmon eggs, PowerBait, spinners, or flies early in the year and catch your limit. The same goes for the lake's numerous varieties of panfish. For the predatory tiger muskie, throw big top-water plugs baited with sucker meat and reel it in. For largemouth bass, cast near subsurface trees or weed beds with buzz bait, popper bugs, Hula Frogs, and rubber worms behind spinners.

Directions: From Denver, take I–25 north for about 35 miles to Colorado Highway 56 and drive into Berthoud to U.S. Highway 287. Go north 3 miles to Colorado Highway 60, then go west 4 miles to Larimer County Road 23; turn north and drive 0.75 mile to the lake.

Additional information: A daily use fee is required. Wakeless boating only.

Contact: Colorado Division of Wildlife, Fort Collins; (970) 484–2836.

78 Carter Lake

Key species: Rainbow trout, kokanee, largemouth bass, perch.

Description: Carter Lake is a 1,100-acre reservoir located behind the Dakota Ridge hogback northwest of Longmont.

Tips: This lake is one of the most heavily stocked with 10-inch rainbow trout (70,000) in the state.

The fishing: The best trout fishing is along the riprap areas of the dam, with PowerBait or salmon eggs, and from the south shore camping area. Trolling for trout is successful with a flashing lure trailing a night crawler. Kokanee salmon are caught by deep-trolling with a Dick Nite or Needlefish lure. Perch are caught in spring and fall by using minnows and small jigs along the west shoreline and in various coves. Bass can be taken on crankbait and jigs in the coves near subsurface structures.

Directions: From Denver, take I–25 north about 35 miles to the Berthoud exit and go west on Colorado Highway 56 for 1 mile past Berthoud to where CO 56 splits from U.S. Highway 287. Continue west, then turn north onto Larimer County Road 23 for 0.5 mile and then west onto Larimer County Road 8E and drive 3 miles to the lake.

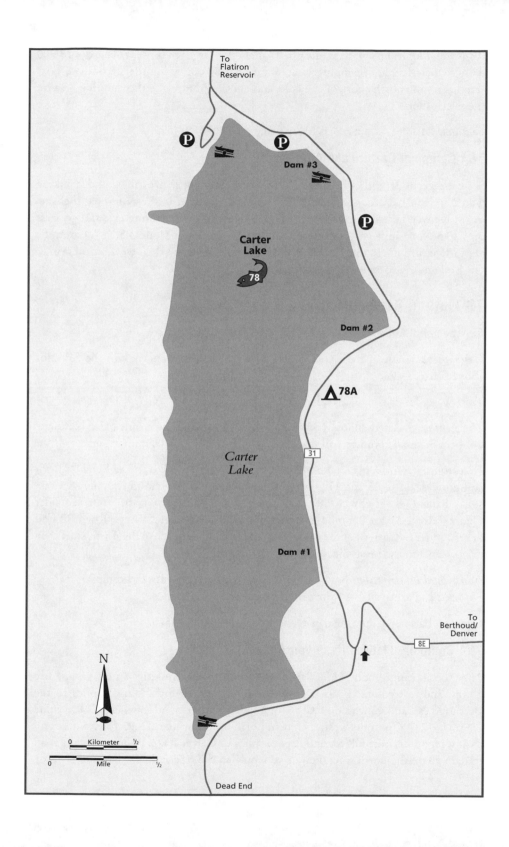

To
Flatiron
Reservoir

Dam #3

Carter
Lake
78

Dam #2

78A

Carter
Lake

31

Dam #1

To
Berthoud/
Denver

8E

N

0 Kilometer ½
0 Mile ½

Dead End

Additional information: Bass must be 15 inches or larger to be kept. There is a $6.00 daily vehicle fee, and camping is an additional $7.00. A multilane concrete boat ramp is on the north shore of the lake, and another ramp is at the camping area on the south shore.

Contact: Larimer County Parks Department; (970) 679–4570.

78A Camping: Carter Lake Area

Six campgrounds with 190 spaces, featuring rest rooms, fire rings, and drinking water, are situated around the lake. There is also a marina and restaurant at the lake. From Denver, take I–25 north for about 35 miles to the Berthoud exit and go west on CO 56 for 1 mile past Berthoud to where CO 56 splits from U.S. 287. Continue west, then turn north onto Larimer CR 23 for 0.5 mile and then west onto Larimer CR 8E and drive 3 miles to the campground.

79 Flatiron Reservoir

Key species: Rainbow trout.

Description: Flatiron Reservoir is a 47-acre power plant afterbay in the foothills above Carter Lake.

Tips: Water levels fluctuate daily.

The fishing: Stocked annually with 28,500 10-inch rainbow trout, basic bait-and-bobbers or small spinners will take these fish from shore all summerlong.

Directions: From Denver, take I–25 north for about 35 miles to the Berthoud exit and go west on Colorado Highway 56 for 1 mile past Berthoud to where CO 56 splits from U.S. Highway 287. Continue west, then turn north onto Larimer County Road 23 for 0.5 mile and then west onto Larimer County Road 8E and drive 3 miles to Carter Lake. Follow the lake road to dam #3 on the north side, then drive 1 mile to the reservoir.

Additional information: No boating is allowed. Park permits and camping fees are required and are available from rangers or at self-service sites.

Contact: Larimer County Parks Department; (970) 679–4570.

79A Camping: Flatiron Reservoir Area

This scenic campground offers tent sites only, with drinking water, tables, fire grates, and rest rooms. From Denver, take I–25 north for about 35 miles to the Berthoud exit and go west on CO 56 for 1 mile past Berthoud to where CO 56 splits from U.S. 287. Continue west, then turn north onto Larimer CR 23 for 0.5 mile and then west on Larimer CR 8E and drive 3 miles to Carter Lake. Follow the lake road to dam #3 on the north side, then drive 1 mile to the reservoir.

80 Pinewood Reservoir

Key species: Rainbow trout.

Description: Pinewood Reservoir is a 97-acre impoundment in a low saddle above Carter Lake.

Tips: The reservoir is likely to be heavily stocked with rainbows for the next few years.

The fishing: Stocked in 2000 with 44,000 10-inch rainbow trout, basic bait-and-bobbers or small spinners will take these fish from shore all summerlong. Fishing from float tubes in the evening is most productive during the warm summer months.

Directions: From Denver, take I–25 north for about 35 miles to the Berthoud exit and go west on Colorado Highway 56 for 1 mile past Berthoud to where CO 56 splits from U.S. Highway 287. Continue west, then turn north onto Larimer County Road 23 for 0.5 mile and then west on Larimer County Road 8E and drive 3 miles to Carter Lake. Follow the lake road to dam #3 on the north side, then drive 1 mile to Flatiron Reservoir. Just past Flatiron Reservoir, turn west on Larimer County Road 18E and drive 3 miles to Pinewood Reservoir.

Additional information: Wakeless boating only. Picnic areas and rest rooms are available.

Contact: Larimer County Parks Department; (970) 679–4570.

81 Union Reservoir

Key species: Wiper, rainbow trout, crappie, catfish, largemouth bass, walleye.

Description: Union Reservoir is a 730-acre impoundment in the rolling farm and pasture lands east of Longmont.

Tips: This reservoir offers the best chance to catch wipers in the state.

The fishing: Wipers move into shallow water near the shore looking for bait-fish schools whenever the water is cool, which means spring and fall, and in the morning and evening during warm summer temperatures. They typically range from 1 to 5 pounds and put up a tremendous fight. Look for boils of shad and cast a top-water minnow imitation, white popping bug, or white or bait-fish-colored streamer into the swirling water and hold on. The reservoir's walleye, ranging up to 7 pounds, stay in deep water, and can be enticed by deep, slow trolling of lures or weighted jigs hopped along the bottom. Nearly 50,000 10-inch rainbow trout are stocked annually, and these fish are caught on bait, small spinners, spoons, and standard flies. Some holdovers reach 2 to 3 pounds. Catfish are caught on dough bait or chicken liver fished on the bottom.

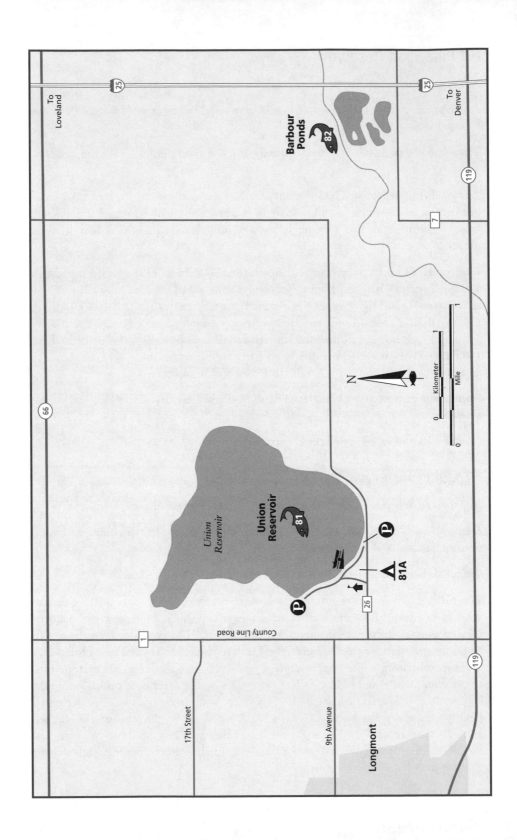

Directions: From Denver, take I–25 north for 24 miles to Colorado Highway 119 and then drive west for 3.5 miles to Weld County Road 1, then go north for 0.5 mile to Weld County Road 26 and take a right to the reservoir's entrance.

Additional information: Wakeless boating only. A $4.00 daily entrance fee is charged, as well as a boat-launching fee. The bank around the north half of the lake is closed to the public.

Contact: City of Longmont; (303) 772–1265.

81A Camping: Union Reservoir Area

There are forty-one primitive sites at Union Reservoir for trailers and tents, with fire grates, drinking water, rest rooms, and tables, but no hookups or dump stations. From Denver, take I–25 north for 24 miles to CO 119 and drive west for 3.5 miles to Weld CR 1, then go north 0.5 mile to Weld CR 26 and take a right. The campsites are on the southwest corner of the lakeshore.

82 Barbour Ponds

Key species: Rainbow trout, largemouth bass, bluegill, crappie.

Description: These four ponds are located along the St. Vrain River just before it crosses under I–25 east of Longmont. The ponds offer wildlife habitat and recreational opportunities, as well as fishing.

Tips: The best fishing is in the spring and again in the fall, when rainbow trout are stocked.

The fishing: With nearly 60,000 10-inch rainbow trout stocked in 2000, Barbour Ponds is the most accessible catch-and-keep rainbow fishery along the northern Front Range. Shore-fishing with spinners and worms works best for trout and panfish. Use a belly boat to work the shoreline, where submerged structures and vegetation hold bass up to 2 pounds, with top-water plugs and weighted jigs.

Directions: From Denver, take I–25 north for 24 miles to Colorado Highway 119 and go west for 1 mile, then turn north onto Adams County Road 7 and proceed 0.25 mile to the ponds' entrance.

Additional information: Only small sailing and hand-propelled craft are allowed. Many of the recreation area's facilities are handicapped accessible. A Colorado State Parks season pass or daily entry fee is required.

Contact: Barbour Ponds State Park; (303) 678–9402.

82A Camping: Barbour Ponds Area

The park offers sixty dispersed campsites with picnic tables, fire grates, rest rooms, drinking water, and two boat ramps. From Denver, take I–25 north for 24 miles to

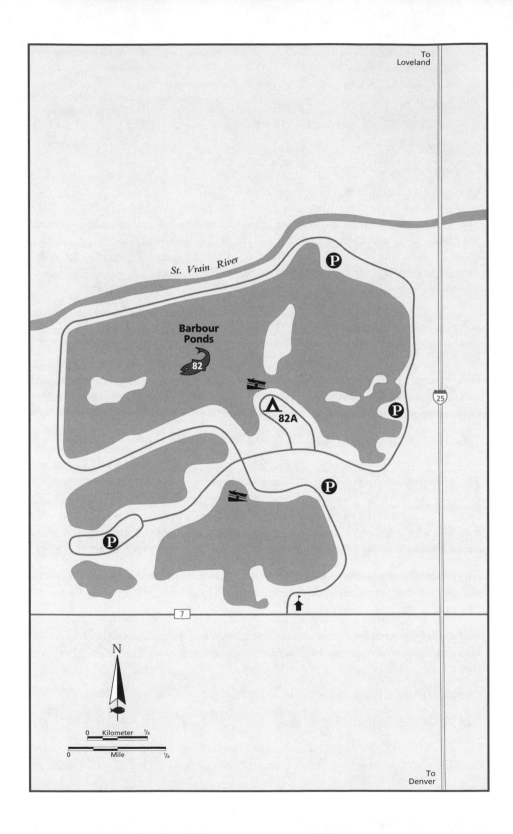

CO 119 and go west for 1 mile, then turn north onto Adams CR 7 and proceed to the ponds' entrance.

83 South Platte River between Spinney Mountain and Elevenmile Reservoirs

Key species: Brown trout, rainbow trout, Snake River cutthroat, cutbows.

Description: This 6-mile stretch of the South Platte River meanders through a wide valley in the ranchland of South Park. An extensive project to restore trout habitat on the 3-mile stretch between Spinney Mountain Reservoir and Park County Road 59 was completed in 2002. The habitat work has returned this section of river to the glory days of its past, which earned it the moniker "Dream Stream."

Tips: Get on the river as early as possible; it gets very crowded nearly every day.

The fishing: While big brown trout are still the main species in this stretch, there has been an increase in big rainbows, cutbows, and Snake River cutthroats in the last couple of years. The browns, rainbows, and cutthroats range from 16 to 24 inches, with an average size of 18 inches. Hatches are prolific here, especially when it is cloudy, so matching the hatch—everything from caddis flies to mayflies and midges—will produce exciting dry-fly action. When trout are feeding below the surface, try bead-head Pheasant tail nymphs, RS-2s, and caddis emergers. Remember, a lot of food comes down from the reservoir, so don't hesitate to use shrimp patterns, Woolly Buggers, spinners, and streamers or even terrestrial patterns in late summer and fall. For the most part, when insects are hatching, the smaller the flies, the better.

Stream census data: There are an estimated 2,000 brown trout per mile in this section of river.

Whirling disease: Positive. The rainbows, Snake River cutthroats, and cutbows come up from Elevenmile Reservoir.

Directions: From Hartsel, go southeast 11 miles on Park CR 59 to Spinney Mountain Park; drive across the dam and park.

Additional information: The entire section below Spinney Reservoir is catch-and-release, flies-and-lures-only fishing. A Colorado State Parks season pass or daily use fee is required to park at Spinney Mountain for access to the river.

Contact: Colorado Division of Wildlife, Fort Collins; (970) 484–2836.

84 South Platte River below Cheesman Reservoir

Key species: Rainbow trout, brown trout.

Description: This 5-mile stretch of the South Platte River, between Cheesman Reservoir and the town of Deckers, is a series of crystalline riffles, runs, and pools

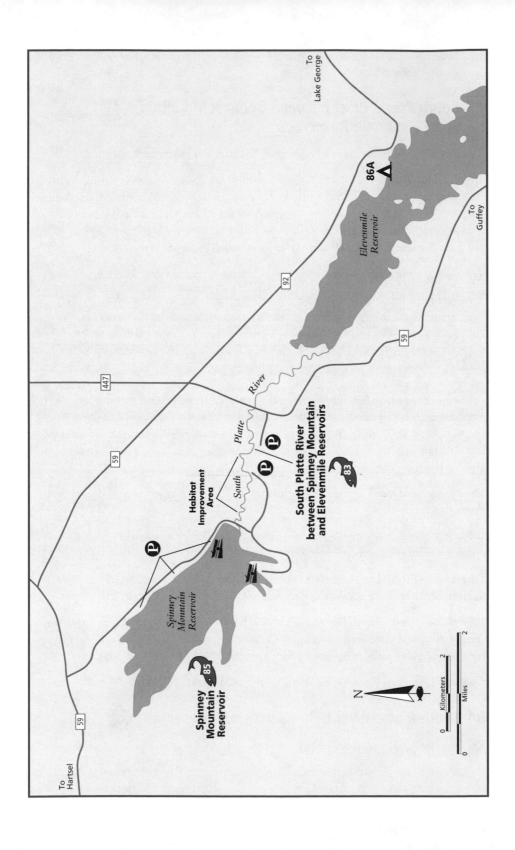

winding its way through a deep granite canyon before opening up into a valley below Deckers.

Tips: Tiny flies are critical to success.

The fishing: Big browns up to 24 inches numerically dominate this section of river, but anglers catch mostly rainbows, from 14 to 28 inches. The key to success is to make the 20- to 30-minute hike into the canyon early enough to get one of the good holes. By the time the sun hits the water and swarms of anglers show up, the best fishing is usually over. Mayflies and midges, with a healthy smattering of mysis shrimp and small fish, make up the prey base for these fish. When a hatch is on, the fish gorge themselves. When it's over, often so is the fishing opportunity. Check with the local flyshop in Deckers to learn what hatches are under way or upcoming. Don't overestimate the fly size; the Cheesman Canyon fish, like those in most of the other famous Colorado tailwaters, prefer size 20 to 24 flies. If they are hitting on top, try a standard Adams or a parachute Adams. However, for the best chance at success, stick with nymphs like the RS-2 weighted for the bottom and fish dead drift, keeping only the leader and tippet in the water by holding your rod tip high. Some lure anglers have reportedly done well in Cheesman Canyon, but they are few

An angler on the South Platte River in Cheesman Canyon

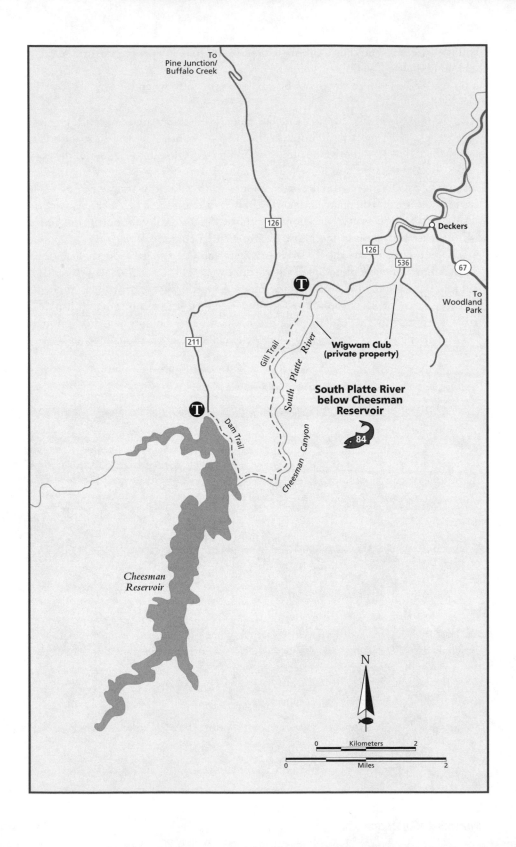

To
Pine Junction/
Buffalo Creek

126

Deckers

126

536

67

To
Woodland
Park

211

T

Gill Trail

South Platte River

**Wigwam Club
(private property)**

**South Platte River
below Cheesman
Reservoir**

84

T

Dam Trail

Cheesman Canyon

*Cheesman
Reservoir*

N

0   Kilometers   2

0   Miles   2

and far between—and they don't share their techniques. However, trailing a weighted nymph below a bubble on spinning gear can be more effective than fishing with a fly rod because more water can be covered, especially when the river is flowing 1,200 cfs.

Whirling disease: The South Platte River is whirling-disease positive throughout its length. However, in 1998 survival of rainbow trout to the age of one year did not decrease for the first time in nearly a decade. The rainbow population is maintained by stocking and fugitives from the Wigwam Club fishing operation.

Directions: From west Denver, take U.S. Highway 285 west for 20 miles to Pine Junction, then turn south on Colorado Highway 126 and drive for 23 miles. There will be several pull-offs at this point. From there, take the Gill Trail west for 3 miles to the canyon. Or stay on CO 126 and access the river past the well-marked Wigwam property and Deckers.

Additional information: From Cheesman Dam downstream 3 miles to the private Wigwam Club, flies-and-lures-only catch-and-release regulations are in place. From the Wigwam Club downstream to Deckers, fishing is flies and lures only, and the bag limit is two fish larger than 16 inches.

Contact: Colorado Division of Wildlife, Fort Collins; (970) 484–2836.

85 Spinney Mountain Reservoir

Key species: Rainbow trout, brown trout, Snake River cutthroats, northern pike.

Description: Spinney Mountain Reservoir is a shallow 3,000-acre impoundment in the southeast corner of South Park.

Tips: The reservoir could be affected by water drawdowns if the current drought persists.

The fishing: An estimated 70,000 10- to 13-inch rainbows were stocked in Spinney Reservoir in 2002, along with 10,000 larger fish from Antero Reservoir. As the reservoir has been known to grow fish as much as 5 inches a year, this could result in an incredible number of huge fish by 2003—and an equally large number of anglers. A float tube or a boat is advised. There are so many food sources in this fertile lake that success will be based upon matching the hatch. Leeches, scuds, and crawfish patterns can be used when there are few bugs coming off the water. The best pike fishing is in spring and early summer, when the big predators move into the shallows to feed on bait fish. Spot a fish, cast a big streamer, and retrieve it across the fish's line of vision; or cast a spoon into deep water.

Directions: From Hartsel, go southeast for 11 miles on Park County Road 59 to the reservoir's entrance.

Additional information: A Colorado State Parks season pass or daily use fee is required. Fishing is restricted to flies and lures, with a bag limit for trout of one fish larger than 20 inches. There is no limit on pike. No camping is allowed.

Contact: Colorado State Parks; (719) 748–3401.

86 South Platte River in Elevenmile Canyon

Key species: Rainbow trout, brown trout.

Description: This section of river runs through a scenic, granite-walled canyon from Elevenmile Reservoir dam nearly all the way to Lake George and features long meanders, riffle-pool-run complexes, deep, slow pools, and cascades.

Tips: If all else fails, tie on a peach-egg pattern.

The fishing: Rainbows, and there are a lot of them, average about 12 inches, but there are many 14 to 16 inches long and a few fish quite a bit larger. Browns tend to be less populous, but many of those are 16 inches or larger. Like in most other tailwaters, midges hatch almost continually, and the fish seem to choose those when a hatch is on. Gray, black, or green midge larvae patterns are consistently effective, but fish will take small mayfly nymphs or emergers when a midge hatch is on, as well as when mayflies are coming off the water. Caddis flies hatch often in midsummer to early fall, and fish seem to like the ice caddis patterns as larvae or emergers. While there are large numbers of browns in the canyon, they seem to wait until fall to bite. Matching the hatch, or fishing through pools and deeper meanders with peach eggs or Woolly Buggers or streamers, can be effective. Spin fishers should throw blue Kastmaster lures across deep holes and quickly retrieve them. In the unrestricted section of the river, try worms or PowerBait, blue Kastmasters, or attractor dry flies.

Stream census data: A 2002 stream census indicates that the 3-mile stretch below the dam exceeds Gold Medal standards, but specific data were not available.

Whirling disease: This section of river is considered whirling-disease positive, but the disease has not affected the rainbow trout population.

Directions: From Colorado Springs, drive 38 miles west on U.S. Highway 24 to Lake George, then turn south onto Elevenmile Canyon Road and drive 1 mile to the canyon entrance.

Additional information: Fishing in the 3-mile stretch from Forest Road 244 upstream to the dam is restricted to flies and lures, catch and release. Below that section anglers can keep four fish a day. The unrestricted section has been regularly stocked with rainbows. A daily use fee is required.

Contact: Colorado Division of Wildlife, Fort Collins; (970) 484–2836.

86A Camping: Elevenmile Reservoir Area

There are eight campgrounds with 370 campsites available at Elevenmile Reservoir,

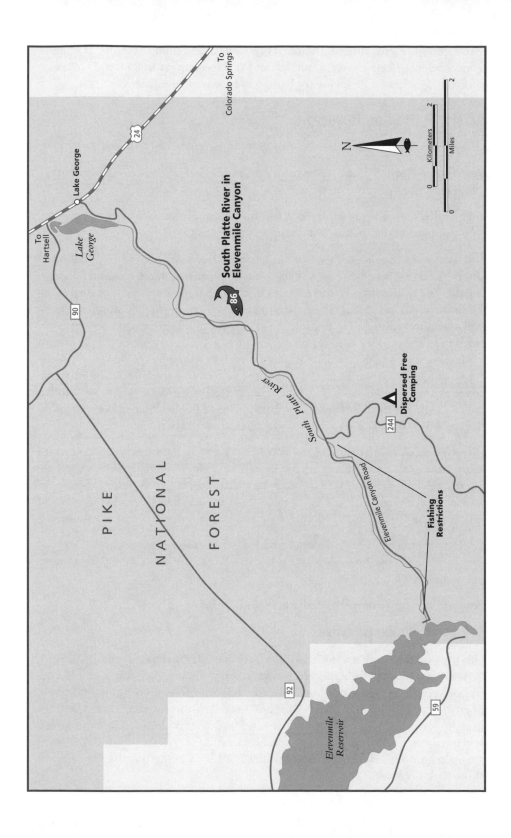

South Platte River in
Elevenmile Canyon

86

Dispersed Free
Camping

Fishing
Restrictions

Elevenmile Canyon Road

South Platte River

PIKE

NATIONAL

FOREST

Lake
George

Lake George

To
Hartsell

To
Colorado Springs

Elevenmile
Reservoir

90

92

59

24

244

N

Kilometers

Miles

with tables, fire pits, drinking water, vault toilets, and dump stations. A camper services building has showers, a laundry, and an RV dump station. From Hartsel, go southeast 17 miles on Park County Road 59 to the park entrance.

87 North Sterling Reservoir

Key species: Wiper, walleye, rainbow trout, bass, perch, bluegill, catfish.

Description: North Sterling Reservoir is a 3,000-acre irrigation impoundment in the rolling hills of northeast Colorado.

Tips: This is one of the best places to fish for wipers in the state. If you catch one, keep fishing the same area, as wipers are schooling fish.

The fishing: As wipers go, these are not large, with some fish up to 10 pounds and lots in the 3- to 5-pound range. Throw shallow-running lures like Rat-L-Traps, Rapalas, and Kastmasters or surface lures like Zara Spooks into swells of shad along the shore in the spring and fall or morning and evening during the summer. Deep-troll a shad imitation during summer days. Catches of fifty to seventy-five wipers a day during the peak of the season are not unusual. The best trout action is with worms, salmon eggs, and pink or yellow PowerBait fished on the bottom. Walleye can be caught by jigging along the face of the dam or by bottom-bouncing flashers tipped with night crawlers along cove arms or near subsurface structures. Panfish can be caught on small jigs or worms fished below a bobber. Catfish are caught on chicken livers, stink bait, or night crawlers fished on the bottom.

Directions: Exit I–76 at Sterling and take U.S. Highway 6 northwest 0.25 mile into town, where it becomes Chestnut Street. Go 4 blocks to Division Avenue, where Chestnut Street turns west and becomes Platte Street. Head west 5 blocks to Seventh Street; turn north and go 12 miles (Seventh becomes Logan Country Road 39). At Logan County Road 46, turn west and go 2.5 miles to the park entrance.

Additional information: A Colorado State Parks season pass or daily use fee is required. Three boat ramps are available and designed to allow launching at low- and high-water levels.

Contact: Sterling Reservoir State Park; (970) 522–3657.

87A Camping: The Elks Area

This area on the northeast corner of the park has fifty campsites, with a laundry, showers, rest rooms, shade shelters, picnic tables, grills, drinking water, and electrical hookups. Exit I–76 at Sterling and take U.S. 6 northwest 0.25 mile into town, where it becomes Chestnut Street. Go 4 blocks to Division Avenue, where Chestnut Street turns west and becomes Platte Street. Head west 5 blocks to Seventh Street; turn north and go 12 miles (Seventh becomes Logan CR 39). At Logan CR 46, turn west and go 2.5 miles to the park entrance. The Elks Campground is 1 mile north of the park's entrance.

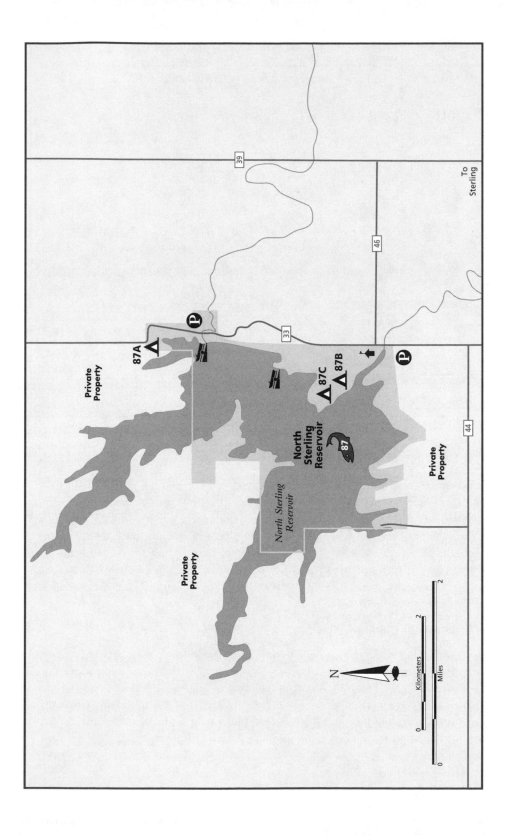

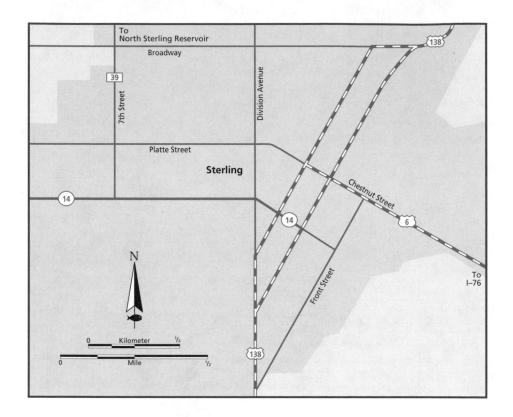

87B Camping: Inlet Grove Area

This campground on the south side of the park has forty-seven pull-through sites near the water's edge, with electrical hookups, drinking water, rest rooms, shade shelters, and grills. Exit I–76 at Sterling and take U.S. 6 northwest 0.25 mile into town, where it becomes Chestnut Street. Go 4 blocks to Division Avenue, where Chestnut Street turns west and becomes Platte Street. Head west 5 blocks to Seventh Street; turn north and go 12 miles (Seventh becomes Logan CR 39). At Logan CR 46, turn west and go 2.5 miles to the park entrance. The campground is just behind the park entrance.

87C Camping: Chimney View Area

Set a little higher than the reservoir on the south side of the park, this area has forty-seven campsites offering drinking water, shade shelters, rest rooms, and grills, but no electricity. Exit I–76 at Sterling and take U.S. 6 northwest 0.25 mile into town, where it becomes Chestnut Street. Go 4 blocks to Division Avenue, where Chestnut Street turns west and becomes Platte Street. Head west 5 blocks to Seventh Street; turn north and go 12 miles (Seventh becomes Logan CR 39). At Logan CR 46, turn west and go 2.5 miles to the park entrance. This campground is just north of Inlet Grove Campground.

Southeast Colorado

88 John Martin Reservoir

Key species: Saugeye, walleye, wiper, white bass, channel catfish, largemouth bass, rainbow trout.

Description: An impound of the Arkansas River, John Martin Reservoir covers about 13,000 acres on the eastern Colorado sagebrush plains.

Tips: Low water in 2002 made boat ramps unusable.

The fishing: Early spring and late fall are the best times to fish this reservoir. The primary forage fish is gizzard shad. Saugeye up to 20 inches have become increasingly common. The best action is in May and early June along the dam or near any shoreline obstruction. Fish with minnows, Mister Twister grubs, or lead-head jigs tipped with a night crawler. Use a slow retrieval, the slower the better. Wipers run in the 15- to 22-inch range, with some larger ones caught every year. Without heavy gear, these fish will get away from you. In May and June for wipers use a silver Rat-L-Trap, Rapala, or Kastmaster lure or a chartreuse Mister Twister tail grub cast from the shore or a boat into boils of shad feeding in the shallows. Fly anglers can cast from the shoreline or use a belly boat to drop 3- to 4-inch floating streamers to imitate the shad. Use plenty of action. Smallmouth and largemouth bass can be caught in weed beds and near submerged structures using the wiper lures listed above. When the water warms up in summer, anglers find success by deep-trolling in cooler water or going after channel catfish, which average 4 to 8 pounds but range up to 20 pounds, on shrimp, liver, night crawlers, and cut bait. More than 77,000 rainbow trout are stocked annually, but in such a large reservoir they aren't an important part of the fishery.

Directions: From Las Animas, take U.S. Highway 50 east for about 5 miles to where access begins with several roads leading to the reservoir. The main access is Colorado Highway 260 at the east end of the reservoir.

Additional information: A Colorado State Parks season pass or daily use fee is required. The entire reservoir is open to primitive camping, but the shores are treeless and rest rooms are scarce. There are three boat ramps, one of which is long enough to be functional at low-water levels in most seasons. The reservoir is open all year, with no fees. Water drawdowns during dry years can affect fishing—check locally.

Contact: John Martin Reservoir State Park; (719) 829–1801.

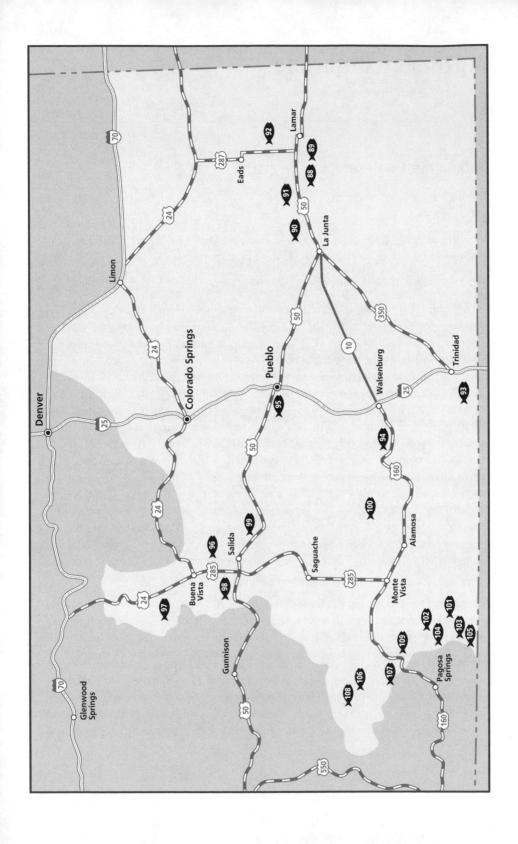

89 Lake Hasty

Key species: Catfish, saugeye, walleye, wiper.

Description: This 75-acre lake lies literally at the foot of John Martin Dam. It was created when a barrow pit, used to provide material for the dam, filled up with water.

Tips: Lake Hasty is excellent for shore-fishing, wading, float tubes, and nonmotorized craft.

The fishing: There are plenty of fish, but not as many large fish as John Martin Reservoir. Use the same tactics and lures as at John Martin.

Directions: From Las Animas, take U.S. Highway 50 east for 20 miles to Colorado Highway 260, then turn south and drive 1.5 miles to the lake.

Contact: John Martin Reservoir State Park; (719) 829–1801.

89A Camping: Lake Hasty Area

This shady campground, nestled on the north side of Lake Hasty, is one of the nicer all-around facilities on the plains and offers sites for tents and RVs of all sizes, with modern bathrooms, hot showers, and electrical hookups, as well as tables, fire grates, a waste disposal station, phones, and a boat ramp. From Las Animas, take U.S. 50 east for 20 miles to CO 260, then turn south and drive 1.5 miles to the campground.

90 Meredith Reservoir

Key species: Wiper.

Description: Meredith Reservoir is a shallow, windswept 3,000-acre impoundment on the plains of southeast Colorado.

Tips: Wipers are schooling fish. If you catch one, keep fishing in the same spot.

The fishing: From a boat, cast shallow-running crankbait, silvery surface lures, streamers in white or bait-fish colors, or popping bugs into boils of bait fish in shallow water, or deep-troll jigs or shad imitations in the warm summer months. A group of five anglers reported catching and releasing 200 pounds of wipers in six hours on this remote lake, fished mostly by locals.

Directions: From Pueblo, take Colorado Highway 96 east for 38 miles to Ordway then for another 3 miles east to Crowley County Road 21 and turn south into the parking area.

Additional information: Water drawdowns during dry years can affect the fishing—check locally.

Contact: Colorado Division of Wildlife, Colorado Springs; (719) 473–2945.

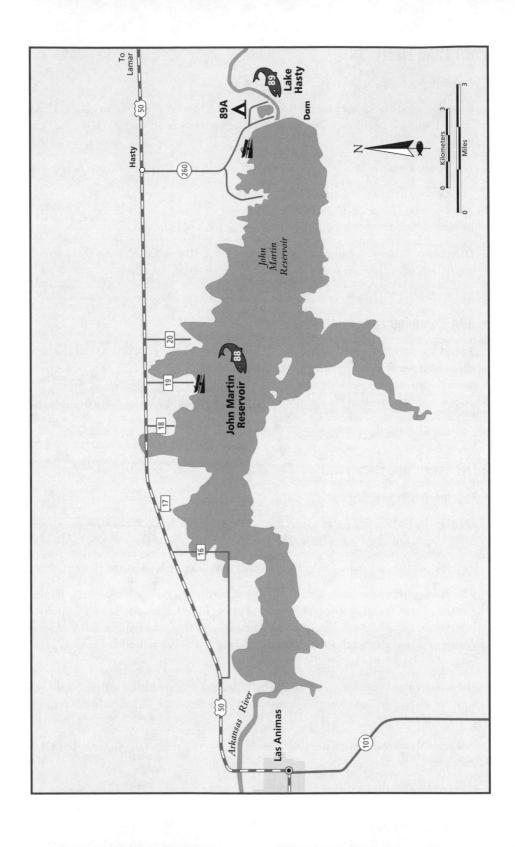

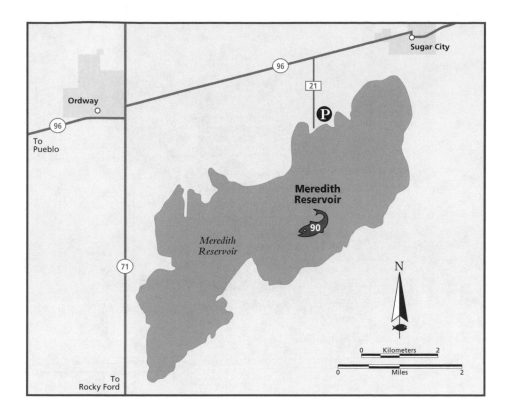

91 Adobe Creek Reservoir

Key species: Crappie, channel catfish, blue catfish.

Description: Adobe Creek Reservoir is a 5,000-acre shallow impoundment on the windswept eastern plains.

Tips: Some of the best crappie fishing in Colorado can be found here. A few anglers have reported catching one hundred fish a day.

The fishing: Crappies averaging 13 inches are plentiful. Troll white or yellowish green lead-head jigs near weed lines. The reservoir also has blue catfish up to 10 pounds and 8- to 20-pound channel cats. Use stink bait, cut bait, or gobs of night crawlers at night to catch these fish.

Directions: From Pueblo, take U.S. Highway 50 east for 65 miles to Las Animas, then go north for 11 miles on Bent County Road 10 to the reservoir.

Additional information: Two boat ramps are available but often don't reach the water when the lake is drawn down. Open camping is available on the south side of the reservoir, but there are no trees and therefore no shade. Water drawdowns during dry years can affect the fishing—check locally.

Contact: Colorado Division of Wildlife, Colorado Springs; (719) 473–2945.

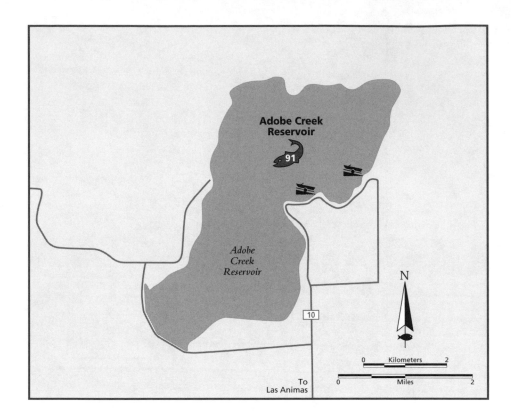

92 Nee Noshe and Nee Gronda Reservoirs

Key species: Wiper, white bass, saugeye, walleye, crappie, catfish.

Description: These lakes are low-elevation plains impoundments of about 3,500 acres (Nee Gronda) and 9,700 acres (Nee Noshe) during normal-water-level years.

Tips: Nee Noshe has slightly, but not significantly, better fishing.

The fishing: Both lakes have good crappie fishing. Nee Gronda reportedly is better for white bass, averaging 12 to 17 inches. Nee Noshe produced a state record wiper in 1996, a 23.9-pound, 34-inch monster, and also had the highest catch of saugeye, ranging from 15 to 26 inches, in lakes sampled in 1999. Crappies can be caught by using white jigs and minnows around submerged brush and trees, and worms and bobbers work in the evening during the summer. Walleye and saugeye can be taken by slow-trolling flashers tipped with night crawlers or other worms and by casting Twister tail jigs into submerged cover. Wipers and white bass can be caught with shallow-running crankbait or surface lures cast into feeding areas and by trolling jigs or shad imitations in the summer. Catfish fall to stink bait, shrimp, and night crawlers fished on the bottom.

Directions: From Las Animas, take U.S. Highway 50 east for 32 miles to U.S. Highway 287. To reach Nee Gronda, go north 12 miles to the reservoir's entrance

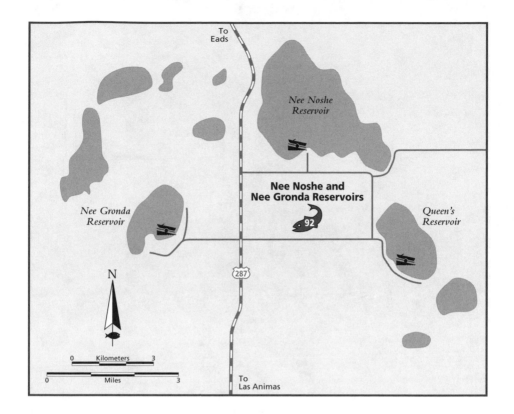

and turn west. To reach Nee Noshe, go another 1.5 miles north on U.S. 287 to the reservoir's entrance and turn east.

Additional information: There is open free camping at both reservoirs, but the only facilities are pit toilets. Nee Noshe has a concrete boat ramp. Nee Gronda has a gravel boat ramp that is difficult for larger boats. Water drawdowns during dry years can affect the fishing—check locally.

Contact: Colorado Division of Wildlife, Colorado Springs; (719) 473–2945.

93 Trinidad Reservoir

Key species: Rainbow trout, Snake River cutthroat trout, saugeye.

Description: Trinidad Reservoir is an 800-acre reservoir in the Purgatoire River Valley on the east side of the Sangre de Cristo Range near the New Mexico border.

Tips: Due to its remote location, this reservoir is underutilized by anglers.

The fishing: Saugeye up to 16 inches can be caught by slowly retrieving a Rat-L-Trap or Mister Twister grub along dams and shoreline structures. Trinidad also offers a strong component of rainbow trout, including 115,000 stockers in 2000, with some monsters up to 27 inches and consistent catches of 16- to 18-inch fish, as

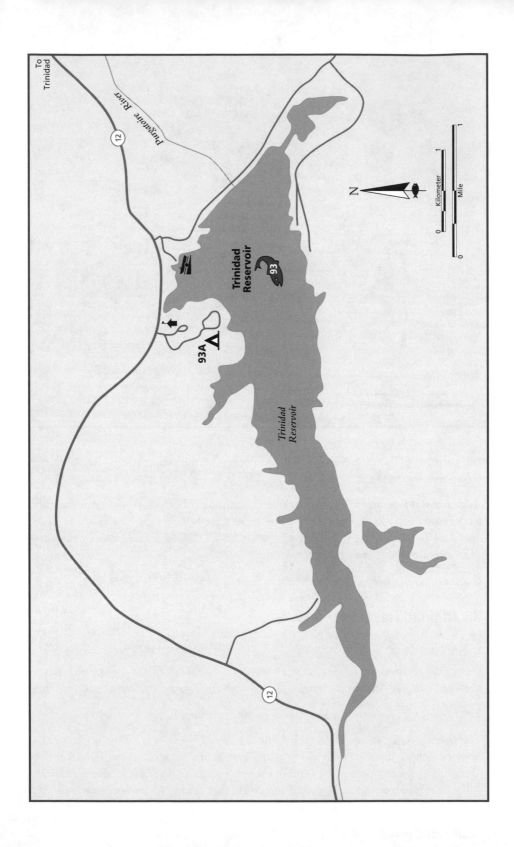

well as big browns and Snake River cutthroat. With such a variety of trout, almost any method of fishing will catch something, but go after the big trout in deep water, using lures and streamers that imitate bait fish. Or catch the damselfly hatch and fish nymphs near the bank by dropping them deep and retrieving towards the shore. In the spring and fall, use salmon eggs or their imitations, retrieving them slowly on the bottom.

Directions: From Trinidad, go 2.5 miles west on Colorado Highway 12 to the lake.

Additional information: A Colorado State Parks season pass or daily use fee is required. Water levels can drop during drought years.

Contact: Trinidad State Park; (719) 846–6951.

93A Camping: Carpios Ridge Area

This campground sits on the north shore of the lake and features electrical hookups, flush toilets, showers, drinking water, tables, fire grates, a laundry, and a dump station. From Trinidad, go 2.5 miles west on CO 12 to the lake. The campsite is south of the park entrance.

94 Horseshoe and Martin Reservoirs

Key species: Rainbow trout, Snake River cutthroat trout, tiger muskie, largemouth bass, walleye, saugeye, wiper, channel catfish.

Description: These reservoirs are situated in the piñon and juniper foothills east of the spectacular Spanish Peaks in southern Colorado. Horseshoe Reservoir covers 170 acres and is 25 feet deep. Martin Reservoir covers 200 acres and is 27 feet deep.

Tips: Lathrop State Park has a nine-hole golf course, so bring your clubs.

The fishing: Horseshoe Reservoir holds the Colorado freshwater barracuda, otherwise known as the tiger muskie, some confirmed as large as 44 inches, as well as rainbows and Snake River cutthroat up to 22 inches. Big channel cats up to 20 pounds and largemouth bass up to 8 pounds will be lurking in the water. Big topwater plugs baited with sucker meat are effective on the tiger muskies. Let the lure plop loudly and sit still for about thirty seconds, then reel it in slowly 5 to 10 feet at a time. The big trout can be caught by trolling pop gear baited with worms or from shore using bait and bobbers or standard dry flies and nymphs trailed behind a bubble, especially in the morning and evening. Look for the lunker bass almost anywhere in this shallow reservoir, and drop a bunny fly or rabbit-strip minnow into deeper water or use foam or wood popper bugs near subsurface structures or weeds to draw the fish to the top. Channel catfish can be caught from the shore after dark using stink bait, chicken livers, or night crawlers. At Martin Reservoir walleye in the 10- to 12-pound range can be caught by trolling worm harnesses, casting deep-diving lures, and vertical jigging in deep water. A good wiper population, with fish up to 10 pounds, exists in this lake and can be caught on surface lures

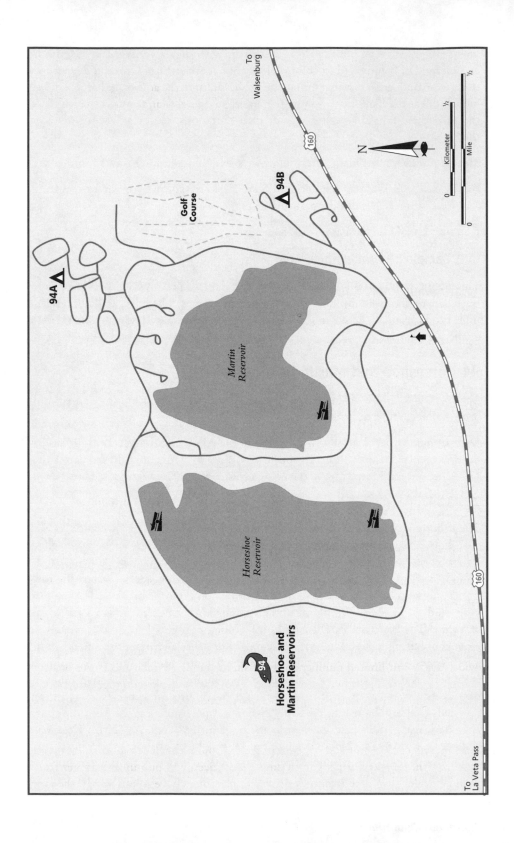

or streamers dropped onto swells of gizzard shad in shallow water. The saugeye are a little small, but the population is high enough that some anglers report catching a 12-incher on nearly every cast during peak conditions. Lead-head jigs tipped with night crawlers or minnows should be retrieved along subsurface structures to catch these fish.

Directions: From Walsenburg, take U.S. Highway 160 west for 3 miles to the Lathrop State Park entrance.

Additional information: A Colorado State Parks season pass or daily use fee and camping fees are required. Tiger muskies must be at least 30 inches to be kept, and there is a one-fish limit. Smallmouth and largemouth bass must be 15 inches or larger, with a five-fish bag limit.

Contact: Lathrop State Park; (719) 738–2376.

94A Camping: Piñon Area

This modern campground serves RVs, trailers, and tents and offers showers, flush toilets, electrical outlets, a dump station, a laundry, and a playground. From Walsenburg, take U.S. 160 west for 3 miles to the Lathrop State Park entrance. The campground is on the northeast corner of Martin Reservoir.

94B Camping: Yucca Flats Area

This primitive campsite has drinking water, tables, and fire grates. From Walsenburg, take U.S. 160 west for 3 miles to the Lathrop State Park entrance. The campground is on the east side of Martin Reservoir.

95 Pueblo Reservoir

Key species: Rainbow trout, walleye, wiper, largemouth bass, smallmouth bass, channel catfish.

Description: Pueblo Reservoir is a 5,000-acre impoundment situated in the limestone cliffs and buttes in the foothills west of the city of Pueblo.

Tips: Due to the high level of recreational boating at the reservoir, on weekends the fishing is best during the off-hours.

The fishing: This is the granddaddy of warm-water sportfishing and serves up a wide variety but limited numbers of big fish, including 18-inch and larger walleye, wipers up to 20 pounds but with lots of fish in the 4- to 8-pound range, largemouth and smallmouth bass, catfish up to 30 pounds, and rainbow trout up to 24 inches. An estimated 260,000 fingerling and 130,000 10-inch rainbow trout were stocked in 2000, but annual stockings vary. Trout-fishing continues to be the main attraction at Pueblo, and casting bait and bobbers or small spinners from the shore will take the smaller fish. Rapala and Daredevle lures fished deep will pull up the bigger trout. Winter anglers can take rainbows on gravel bars or in coves, particularly the large cove east of the North Shore Marina, with minnows and lures. In March 3- to 9-pound walleye school in the estuary where the river meets the lake. Clouser Minnows, Zonkers, or small spinners cast from a boat or float tube into the deep water at the base of bluffs can bring up smallmouths, crappies, and rainbows in warmer weather. Also work the coves and submerged brush for these species.

Directions: From Pueblo, take U.S. Highway 50 west for 4 miles, then turn south on Pueblo Boulevard and go 4 miles to Thatcher Avenue, turn west and go 6 miles to the park entrance.

Additional information: A Colorado State Parks season pass or daily use fee, as well as camping fees, are required. Reservations are suggested from April to September.

Contact: Pueblo Reservoir State Park; (719) 561–9320.

95A Camping: Northern Plains Area

This campground offers both primitive camping for tents, with drinking water, vault toilets, tables, and fire grates, and RV and trailer camping with electrical outlets, flush toilets, showers, a dump station, and telephones. From Pueblo, take U.S. 50 west for 4 miles, then turn south on Pueblo Boulevard and go 4 miles to Thatcher Avenue, turn west and go 6 miles to the park entrance, then turn north and drive across the dam. The campground is 5 miles from the dam, on the northeast corner of the reservoir.

95B Camping: Juniper Breaks Area

This primitive campground is on the north shore of the reservoir and offers vault toilets, tables, and fire grates. From Pueblo, take U.S. 50 west for 4 miles, then turn south on Pueblo Boulevard and go 4 miles to Thatcher Avenue, turn west and go 6 miles to the park entrance, then turn north and drive across the dam. The campground is 3.5 miles from the dam.

95C Camping: Southshore Marina Area

This campground is primarily for trailers and RVs and features electrical outlets, showers, drinking water, flush toilets, tables, a dump station, and a boat ramp. From Pueblo, take U.S. 50 west for 4 miles, then turn south on Pueblo Boulevard and go 4 miles to Thatcher Avenue, turn west and go 6 miles to the park entrance. Once inside the park, turn west and drive 0.5 mile.

96 Arkansas River

Key species: Brown trout, rainbow trout, wiper.

Description: The Arkansas River begins in the high mountains above Leadville and runs 300 miles to the Kansas border. Due to drainage from the Sawatch Mountains, the highest mountain range in the lower forty-eight states, runoff creates an unfish-

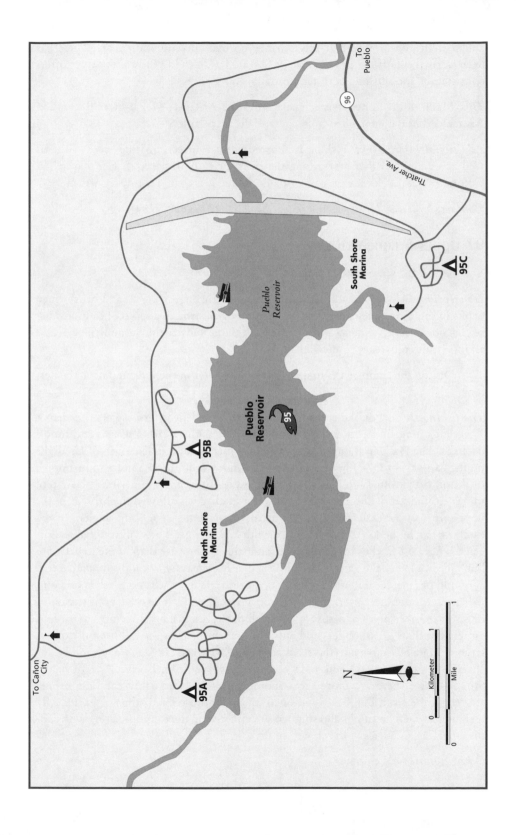

Pueblo Reservoir

Pueblo
Reservoir

95

95A

95B

95C

North Shore
Marina

South Shore
Marina

To Cañon
City

To
Pueblo

96

Thatcher Ave.

N

Kilometer
0   1

Mile
0   1

able torrent mid-May to mid-July during "normal" precipitation years. There has been normal runoff the past two years. At moderate to low flows, the river offers consistently good fishing between Leadville and Cañon City.

Tips: Much of the upper river is managed as the Arkansas Headwaters Recreation Area and is heavily patrolled by rangers. Follow the rules.

Additional information: Fishing is allowed at all fourteen boating access sites, as well as numerous other areas along the river. Private property is well marked. A Colorado State Parks season pass or daily use fee is required for many areas.

Contact: Arkansas Headwaters Recreation Area; (719) 539–7289.

97 Upper Arkansas River

Key species: Brown trout.

Description: Below Leadville the river meanders through willow- and brush-lined banks in the wide valley near Granite, then plunges through a series of canyons that begins below its confluence with Clear Creek and ends at the Stone Bridge access about 5 miles upstream from Salida.

Tips: During the summer the first anglers on the river in the morning have the best luck.

The fishing: A new public-access stretch below Leadville offers anglers the chance to get into some underutilized brown trout water as the weather warms and runoff declines. The Hayden Ranch access, which begins about 8 miles south of Leadville on the east side of U.S. Highway 24 and continues south for 5.5 miles to just north of the outflow from Twin Lakes Reservoir, is benefiting from Superfund cleanup of mines around Leadville. The improved water quality has allowed the browns in the upper river to increase their size and density in recent years. Some anglers report catching fish in the 18- to 20-inch range, with knowledge of brown trout habits crucial to success. Hatches here are lighter and later in the year than in the lower river but still should be taken advantage of. Whether it's a mayfly or caddis fly hatch, trail a nymph or emerger imitation behind an appropriate dry fly. If no hatch is obvious, fish attractor nymph patterns near the bottom early and late in the day or streamers or spinners over holes and stream cover all day. October or November terrestrial patterns such as grasshoppers and ants will pull in fish. In the fall brown trout as large as 24 inches move into this reach to spawn. Between Hayden Ranch and Buena Vista, private property limits river access. However, from Buena Vista to below Stone Bridge, there are more access points to what is arguably the best fishing stretch in the river, but a raft will open up the entire river to the angler. Heavily weighted stonefly nymphs and spinners are effective in the canyons, along with caddis emergers and dries in the slower spots.

Whirling disease: Positive.

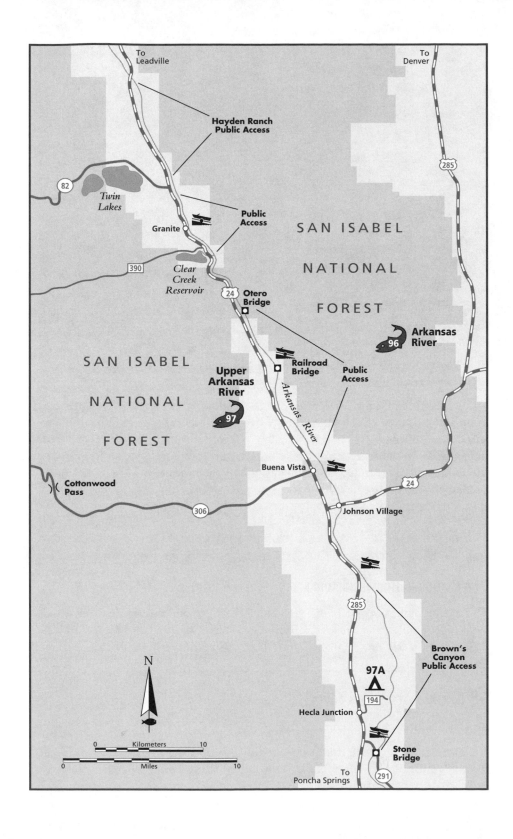

To Leadville

To Denver

**Hayden Ranch
Public Access**

285

*Twin
Lakes*

82

**Public
Access**

Granite

SAN ISABEL

390

*Clear
Creek
Reservoir*

24

**Otero
Bridge**

NATIONAL

FOREST

**Arkansas
River**

96

SAN ISABEL

**Railroad
Bridge**

**Public
Access**

NATIONAL

**Upper
Arkansas
River**

97

Arkansas River

FOREST

Buena Vista

**Cottonwood
Pass**

306

24

Johnson Village

285

**Brown's
Canyon
Public Access**

N

97A

194

Hecla Junction

**Stone
Bridge**

0   Kilometers   10

0   Miles   10

To
Poncha Springs

291

The upper Arkansas River outside of Leadville

Directions: From Denver, drive west on U.S. Highway 285 for 114 miles to U.S. 24 in Buena Vista. From Colorado Springs, drive west on U.S. 24 for 91 miles to Buena Vista. From Buena Vista the river parallels U.S. 24 for 30 miles to the north, with public access on more than half the section. Or go south on U.S. 285 from Buena Vista about 18 miles to Colorado Highway 291, then turn east and go 0.5 mile to reach the Stone Bridge access.

Additional information: The Hayden Ranch access is flies and lures only, with a bag limit of one fish smaller than 12 inches.

Contact: Arkansas Headwaters Recreation Area; (719) 539–7289.

97A Camping: Hecla Junction Area

This campground sits on a bluff overlooking the river and features drinking water, vault toilets, tables, and fire grates. From Buena Vista, drive south 14 miles on U.S. 285, then turn east on Chaffee County Road 194 and drive 0.5 mile to the campground.

98 Middle Arkansas River

Key species: Brown trout, rainbow trout.

Description: Below Stone Bridge the river opens into a wide valley that spreads all the way to Parkdale. From Salida downstream U.S. Highway 50 parallels the river to Parkdale.

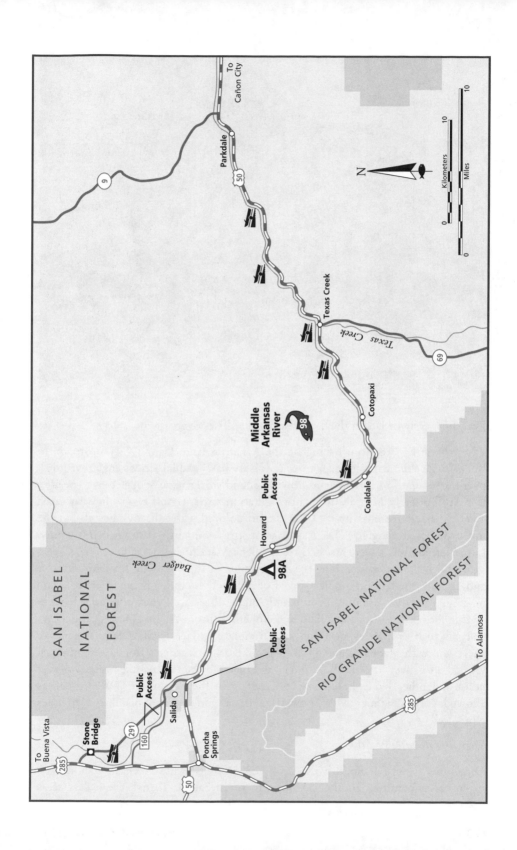

The middle Arkansas River in Brown's Canyon

Tips: Fish early or late in the day or when the sky is overcast.

The fishing: Early-season fishing on the Arkansas from Cañon City upstream to Buena Vista culminates in the famous caddis fly hatch, which draws anglers from all over the region. The hatch begins downriver and works its way upstream to peak in late April or early May. In normal precipitation years, runoff begins in early May, and as the river reaches up to 3,000 cfs, off-colored water discourages all but the most dedicated angler. The Arkansas is predominantly brown trout water. However, rainbows were stocked from Buena Vista to below Salida several years ago, and they are now reaching the upper limits of their growth. Preceding runoff and again in the fall, little blue-winged olive mayflies come off the river from late morning to early afternoon. In July and August there are light but regular hatches of pale morning duns, caddis flies, and stoneflies. From August until October terrestrials such as grasshoppers and ants stimulate surface feeding. Spin fishers are successful with Mepps #2 and #3, Rooster Tails, and Warden's Root Beer spinners. Use gold or silver lures in the summer and black in the fall. A quick retrieval over holes and other likely holding areas is effective for big browns. Where bait is allowed worms, night crawlers, PowerBait, or salmon eggs dropped into deep holes work well.

Whirling disease: Positive.

Directions: From Pueblo, drive west on U.S. 50 for 38 miles to reach Cañon City. From there, continue another 53 miles to reach Salida. To fish the access areas upstream from Salida, go northwest 9 miles on Colorado Highway 291 from its intersection with U.S. 50 in downtown Salida. A large portion of the river between Cañon City and Salida is public access.

Additional information: Only flies and lures are allowed from the Stockyard Bridge in Salida to the river's confluence with Badger Creek, 7.5 miles southeast on U.S. 50. All rainbows must be returned immediately to the water.

Contact: Arkansas Headwaters Recreation Area; (719) 539–7289.

98A Camping: Rincon Area

This campground has drinking water, vault toilets, tables, and fire grates. From Salida, drive 7 miles east on U.S. 50 to the campground entrance.

99 Lower Arkansas River

Key species: Brown trout, rainbow trout, wiper.

Description: This stretch of the Arkansas River begins in Parkdale and ends at the Pueblo Reservoir. Much of it is physically inaccessible or on private property.

Tips: The best access is around Cañon City, Florence, and Pueblo Reservoir.

The fishing: Brown trout populations are lower here but steady, with the possibility of big browns lurking in deep holes. The river is wide and deep in this section

The lower Arkansas River above Cañon City

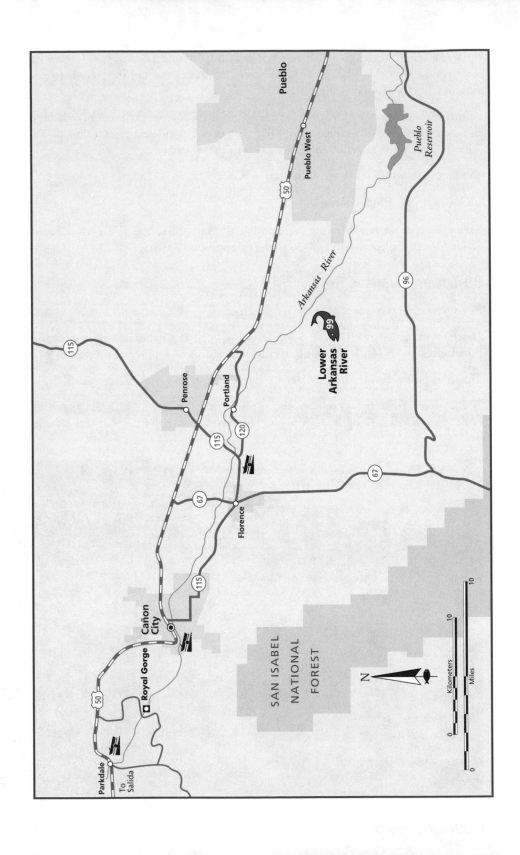

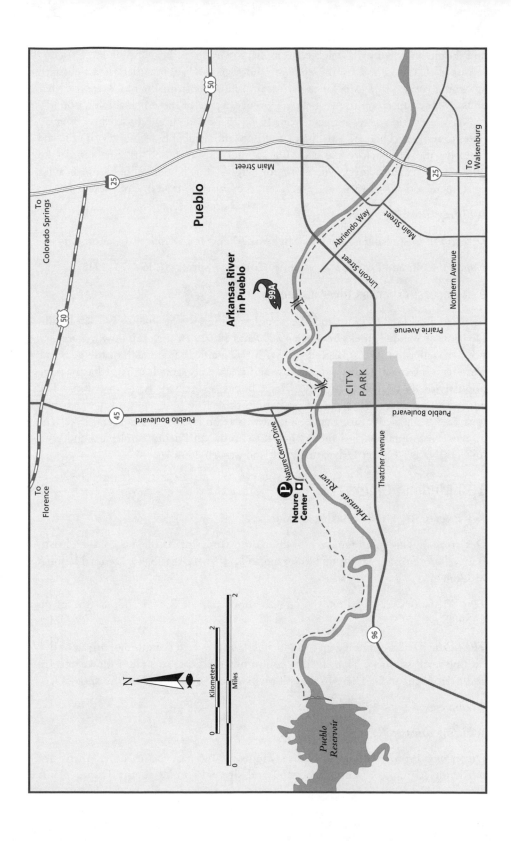

Arkansas River
in Pueblo

99A

and should be fished with weighted nymphs, streamers, or heavy spinners. The consensus is that the good fishing ends around Cañon City, but there is a February spawning run of Lake McConaughy–strain rainbows from Pueblo Reservoir that ends 25 miles upstream to just below Florence. Some of these fish reach 5 pounds. In May reservoir wipers ranging from 10 to 15 pounds travel upstream about 20 miles to the gravel bars near the hamlet of Portland, probably to munch on rainbow trout fry moving back to the lake. Big spinners, spoons, and streamers will take rainbows. The same lures will work for wipers, but anglers should use heavier equipment and 10- to 15-pound test line if they want to land one of these fish.

Whirling disease: Positive.

Directions: From Salida, take U.S. Highway 50 east for 57 miles to Cañon City.

Contact: Colorado Division of Wildlife, Colorado Springs; (719) 473–2945.

99A Access: Arkansas River in Pueblo

Between Pueblo Reservoir and the middle of the city of Pueblo, the Colorado Division of Wildlife stocks between 40,000 and 50,000 10-inch rainbow trout every year, as well as up to 200 larger brood fish twice a year. For much of the year, the water coming from the reservoir is low and clear. This stretch of river has become popular for fly anglers during the winter but is open to all types of fishing. The entire river is accessible by a hiking/biking trail. The best chance for big fish is upstream from the Nature Center, and downstream is best for numbers. Take U.S. 50 west from Pueblo for 4 miles, then turn south on Pueblo Boulevard and go 4 miles to Nature Center Drive, turn west and drive 1.25 miles.

100 Medano Creek

Key species: Rio Grande cutthroat trout.

Description: This mountain stream drains the west side of the Sangre de Christo Range before disappearing into the sand hills of the Great Sand Dunes National Monument.

Tips: Medano Creek harbors the largest population of Rio Grande cutthroat on public land.

The fishing: The trout range up to 12 inches. Use standard imitation or attractor dry flies or small spinners. Tight fishing conditions exist due to streamside vegetation and narrow channels. These fish aren't picky eaters, but they are easily spooked.

Stream census data: 1,000 fish per mile.

Whirling disease: Negative.

Directions: From Alamosa, take U.S. Highway 160 east for 15 miles, then turn north on Alamosa County Road 150 and drive 18 miles to the Dunes picnic

The author holds a nice rainbow caught on the Arkansas River in the city of Pueblo.

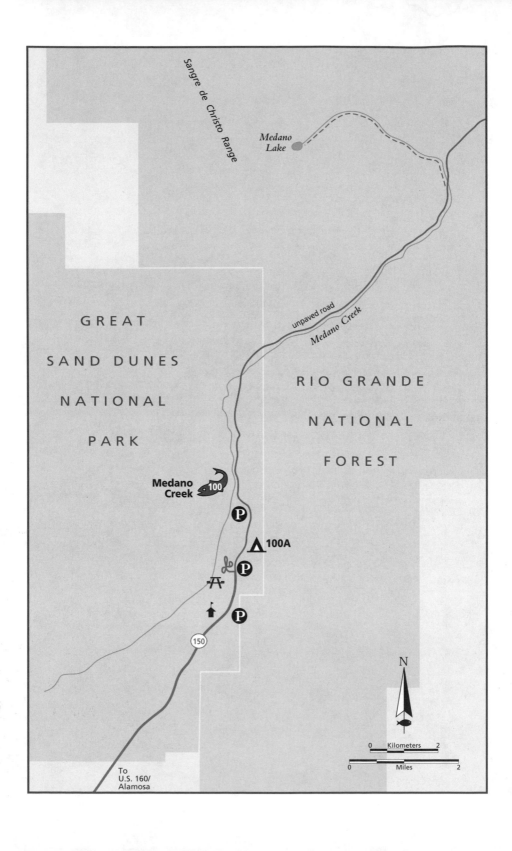

Sangre de Christo Range

Medano
Lake

unpaved road

Medano Creek

GREAT

SAND DUNES

NATIONAL

PARK

RIO GRANDE

NATIONAL

FOREST

**Medano
Creek** 100

P

100A

P

P

150

N

0 — Kilometers — 2

0 — Miles — 2

To
U.S. 160/
Alamosa

grounds. Park and walk west a few yards to the creek. A four-wheel-drive road runs parallel to the creek for several miles.

Additional information: The Rio Grande cutthroat has been proposed for listing as an endangered species. No bait-fishing is allowed, and all fish must be returned immediately to the water. Handle these fish with care. A National Parks entrance fee is required.

Contact: Great Sand Dunes National Park; (719) 378–2312.

100A Camping: Piñon Flats Area

Set in a piñon and juniper forest, these campsites have tables, fire grates, flush toilets, and drinking water. From Alamosa, take U.S. 160 east for 15 miles, then turn north on Alamosa CR 150 and drive 18.5 miles to the campground.

101 Conejos River

Key species: Brown trout, rainbow trout, brook trout, Rio Grande cutthroat trout.

Description: The Conejos River flows 70 miles from its headwaters along the east side of the Continental Divide in the south San Juan Mountains through high lush meadows, steep canyons, and broad valleys to its confluence with the Rio Grande River.

Tips: In July and August water releases from Platoro Reservoir can shoot the water level up to 300 cfs without warning. If you are fishing in an area with steep banks or canyon walls, keep an eye on the water level and get out if it starts to rise.

The fishing: With an altitude drop of nearly 5,000 feet, the diversity of habitat has created incredible fishing conditions in some of the most spectacular scenery you will find in Colorado. Fishing techniques must be adapted to the varied landscapes of the Conejos River. Small streams above Platoro Reservoir offer up browns, rainbows, and brookies up to 12 inches but tending to be smaller. Small- to medium-size attractor patterns like an Adams, Royal Wulff, Humpy, or Stimulator work well, as do worms and small, brightly colored spinners. Below the reservoir the river widens and offers bigger fish, with browns and rainbows averaging 12 inches but occasionally climbing to 16 inches. The size and density of brown trout in the middle section is near Gold Medal standards. Add stonefly imitations to the mix at the end of runoff, with mayfly and caddis fly patterns becoming increasingly effective as the water drops. Below the river's confluence with Lake Fork Creek, a deep and sometimes treacherous canyon near the Pinnacles holds the largest fish in the river, with browns up to 22 inches. Large weighted nymphs or streamers will pull these trout out of their holding lies, as will large spinners fished deep. As the river exits the canyon, it enters a wide glacial valley, with quite a bit of private land limiting access to the water. Two miles downstream from where Colorado Highway 17 crosses the river, a 4-mile stretch of public access begins below Menkhaven Resort. This meandering section offers pools, riffles, deep runs, undercut banks, gravel bars,

The Conejos River below Aspen Glade Campground

and at least one bank flat and clear of brush. It's often a steep hike down from the road. Heavy insect hatches are characteristic of this stretch, with caddis fly and stonefly hatches beginning during runoff. The caddis flies will continue to come off throughout the summer. Pale morning dun, red quill, and blue-winged olive mayflies hatch during normal flows from midsummer to late October. Nymph, emerger, and dry-fly patterns of these insects are effective. Check with local fishing stores for more specific information.

Whirling disease: Positive due to earlier stocking with infected fish. However, lack of stocking in recent years is the likely cause of the rainbow trout population decline.

Directions: From Alamosa, drive south on U.S. Highway 285 for 34 miles to Antonito, then take CO 17 west for 17 miles to Aspen Glade Campground. Public access begins here.

Additional information: Only flies and lures are allowed from the Saddle Creek Bridge below Platoro Reservoir to the river's confluence with the South Fork. Below Menkhaven Resort fishing is restricted to flies only. Both stretches have a bag limit of two fish 16 inches or larger.

Contact: Colorado Division of Wildlife, Colorado Springs; (719) 473–2945.

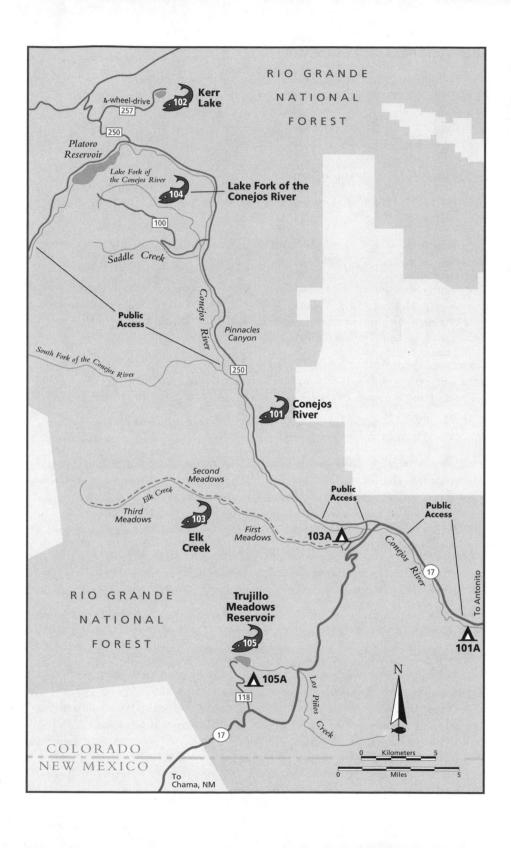

101A Camping: Aspen Glade Area

This campground for RVs and tents is on the north bank of the river and features drinking water, tables, toilets, rest rooms, and fire grates. From Antonito, take CO 17 west for 17 miles.

102 Kerr Lake

Key species: Rio Grande cutthroat trout.

Description: This is a 40-acre natural lake high in the San Juan Mountains north of Platoro Reservoir.

Tips: Kerr Lake is one of two lakes stocked with Rio Grande cutthroat that are accessible by vehicle.

The fishing: Medium- to large-size attractor dry flies should be cast into rise forms, then slowly retrieved towards shore. Weighted nymphs should be allowed to sink, then retrieved with intermittent hesitations and hand twists. Fish average 8 to 10 inches, with some as large as 14 inches.

Directions: From Antonito, take Colorado Highway 17 west for 23 miles, then go northwest on Forest Road 250 for 22 miles to Mix Lake, turn north on Forest Road 257 and drive for 3 miles to the lake.

Additional information: FR 257 is a four-wheel-drive track. Only flies and lures are allowed, with a two-fish bag limit.

Contact: Colorado Division of Wildlife, Colorado Springs; (719) 473–2945.

103 Elk Creek

Key species: Brown trout, rainbow trout.

Description: Elk Creek drains the southeast rim of the South San Juan Wilderness area and runs through steep canyons and wide meadows for 11 miles before its confluence with the Conejos River.

Tips: It's a tough hike to the creek, but it's into one of the most beautiful, remote wildernesses in Colorado and worth the effort.

The fishing: Anglers following the steep trail will be rewarded with narrow canyons full of plunge pools, cascades and riffles holding browns and rainbows from 8 to 14 inches. Golden stonefly imitations and small yellow or gold spinners will work well in the pools and pocket water. The stretch of meadow 3 miles up the trail known as First Meadows holds spooky browns up to 16 inches. In this open section stealth and delicate presentation are musts. Mayfly imitations and nymphs work well in this stretch in July and August. Four miles farther up the trail lies Second Meadows, where the trout are bigger and, having seen fewer people, are not so spooky. Throw weighted streamers or small spinners into pools and undercut banks.

Directions: From Antonito, take Colorado Highway 17 west for 23 miles, cross the Conejos River and take the Elk Creek campground exit, then drive 1 mile past the campground to the trailhead and take Forest Trail 731, which runs on the north side of the stream.

Additional information: There are no restrictions on bait. A four-fish bag limit applies.

Contact: Colorado Division of Wildlife, Colorado Springs; (719) 473–2945.

103A Camping: Elk Creek Area

Nestled at the confluence of Elk Creek and the Conejos River, this campground offers small RV and tent sites, with drinking water, tables, rest rooms, and fire grates. From Antonito, take CO 17 west for 23 miles, then cross the river and turn right into the campground.

104 Lake Fork of the Conejos River

Key species: Rio Grande cutthroat trout, brown trout.

The Conejos River Valley below Platoro Reservoir

Description: The Lake Fork of the Conejos River is a tumbling little stream, criss-crossed by fallen timber, with plenty of pools and pocket water.

Tips: Catch and keep your limit of brook, brown, and rainbow trout to protect the Rio Grande cutthroat trout in this stream.

The fishing: This is classic dry-fly, small-stream water so stick with the standards like medium-size Adams, Stimulators, and Elk Hair Caddis or small, brightly colored spinners.

Whirling disease: Negative.

Directions: From Antonito, take Colorado Highway 17 west for 23 miles, then take Forest Road 250 north for about 15 miles to Forest Road 100 and go west about 0.25 mile then north about 0.5 mile to the Lake Fork Creek trailhead. Hike upstream.

Additional information: Only flies and lures may be used. All cutthroat trout must be returned immediately to the water. A four-fish-per-day bag limit applies to other species.

Contact: Colorado Division of Wildlife, Colorado Springs; (719) 473–2945.

105 Trujillo Meadows Reservoir

Key species: Brown trout, brook trout, rainbow trout.

Description: Trujillo Meadows Reservoir is a 70-acre reservoir with open banks in a high-mountain meadow bordered by thick Douglas fir trees.

Tips: The reservoir was heavily restocked in 1999 after the dam was breached in 1998 for repair work, and many big fish were released downstream into Los Piños Creek.

The fishing: With a full menu of cold-water species, it's hard to go wrong in this reservoir. These fish can be taken on standard flies, lures, and bait from the bank. The upper end of the reservoir is wadeable.

Directions: From Antonito, go 34 miles west on Colorado Highway 17 to Forest Road 118 and drive 3 miles north to the reservoir.

Additional information: Wakeless boating is allowed. There is a concrete boat ramp on the south side of the reservoir.

Contact: Colorado Division of Wildlife, Colorado Springs; (719) 473–2945.

105A Camping: Trujillo Meadows Reservoir Area

Located on a hillside above the reservoir, this campground accommodates tents and medium-size RVs and has rest rooms, drinking water, tables, and fire grates. From Antonito, go 34 miles west on CO 17 to FR 118 and drive 2.5 miles north to the campground.

106 Rio Grande

Key species: Brown trout, rainbow trout.

Description: The Rio Grande, the second longest river in the United States, begins its journey in the Weminuche Wilderness of the San Juan Mountains as a tumbling mountain stream and, for Colorado trout-fishing purposes, ends about 70 miles later, just west of Del Norte. At its upper end is the Rio Grande Reservoir, below which it spreads out through meadows before hurtling through Box Canyon. Below the canyon, the river is a succession of crashing rapids and, upon entering a long wide valley, a series of riffle-pool-run complexes all the way down to its confluence with the South Fork of the Rio Grande. At the town of South Fork, the river heads east into the agricultural lands of the San Luis Valley.

Tips: Floating is the best way to fish the river, but plenty of wading opportunities are available in July after the runoff.

The fishing: Three stretches of the river are particularly appealing to anglers who want to wade. The 2-mile stretch below Rio Grande Reservoir to River Hill Campground is close to the road and is often shallow enough to wade its braided channels by late June or early July. Deep seams hold browns and rainbows in the 12- to 14-inch range. Salmonflies and stoneflies are the main food source here in June and July, and dead-drifting big nymphs into the troughs will tempt the reclusive browns out of their holes. Later in the season mayfly and caddis fly imitations will draw strikes in slow backwaters. Some of the biggest fish in the river are found in Box Canyon, about 5 miles downstream from the reservoir. This canyon is inaccessible and extremely dangerous during high water. It also requires bushwacking about 2 miles downstream, as no trail exists. During August and September the water is lower and allows access. Less angling pressure makes the fish in the canyon less wary. Big weighted stonefly or Prince nymphs dead-drifted into pocket water or high-floating Stimulators or Humpies will draw strikes from rainbows and browns as large as 20 inches. As always, streamers like black and brown Woolly Buggers and Zonkers and small spinners will catch fish when they are not hitting anything else, especially on cloudy days. The next wadeable section is the 6-mile stretch from Palisade Campground downstream to the Coller State Wildlife Area. This area gets quite a bit of pressure, but it's big water and there's plenty of room. The fish are generally smaller in this stretch. Locate holding areas and dead-drift big nymphs into pockets or cast caddis dry flies and Royal Wulffs into slack water along the edges of currents or beneath overhanging vegetation along the banks. A long rod is necessary to fish this water effectively. Fish the Gold Medal stretch east of South Fork at the end of runoff in mid-June with stonefly nymphs and with caddis emergers and dries, then from the end of June to mid-July with green drake nymphs and dries. The recent drought and fires of 2002 have taken a toll on the stretch, and it may no longer rate as a Gold Medal water.

Whirling disease: Positive. Rainbow trout have shown a dramatic decline in numbers but appear to be more prevalent in the upper stretches of the river.

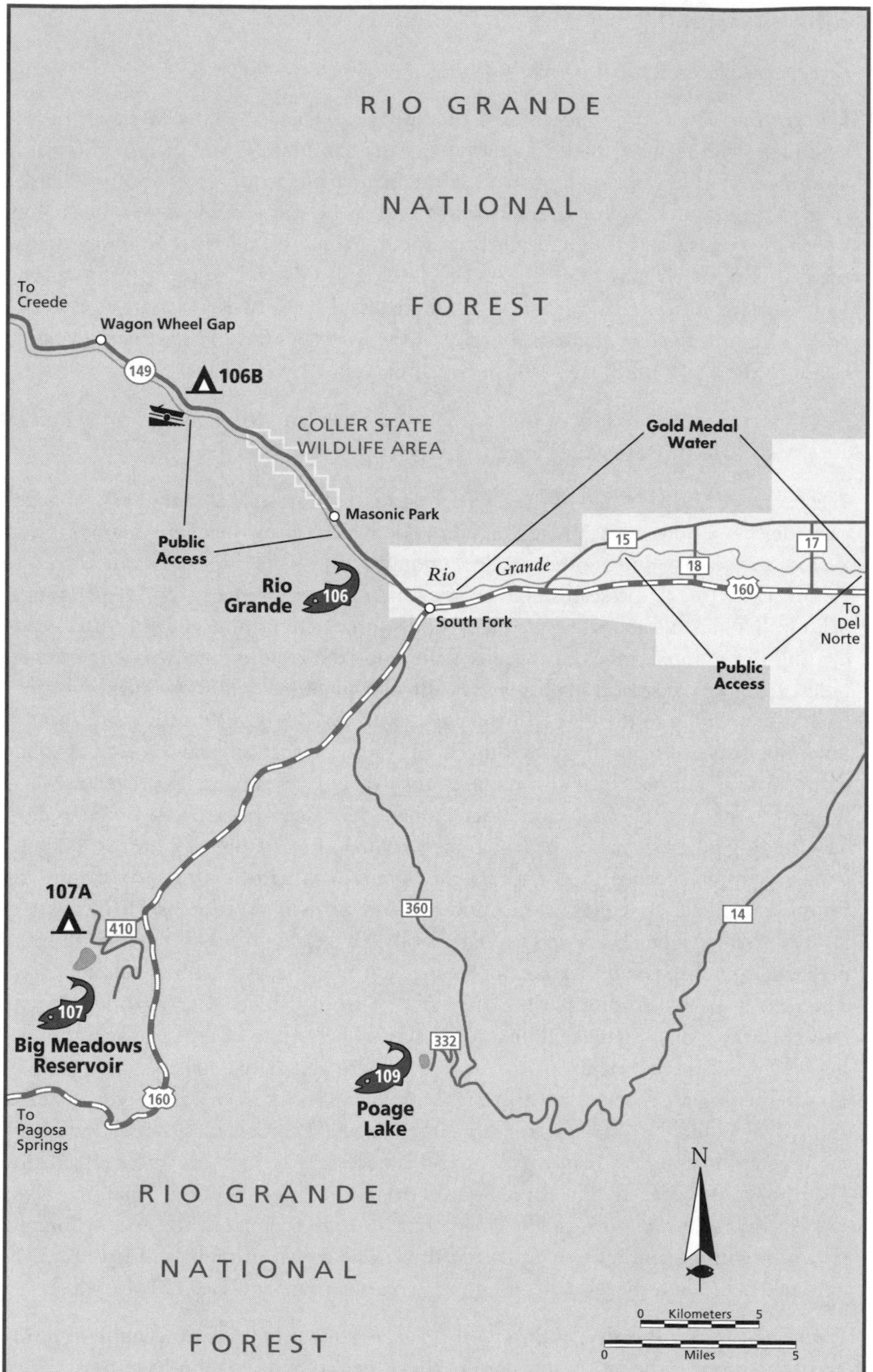

RIO GRANDE

NATIONAL

FOREST

To Creede

Wagon Wheel Gap

149

▲106B

COLLER STATE
WILDLIFE AREA

Gold Medal
Water

Public
Access

Masonic Park

Rio   Grande

15

18

17

Rio
Grande

106

160

South Fork

To
Del
Norte

Public
Access

107A
▲

410

360

14

107

332

Big Meadows
Reservoir

160

109

Poage
Lake

To
Pagosa
Springs

RIO GRANDE

NATIONAL

FOREST

N

0   Kilometers   5

0   Miles   5

Directions: From South Fork, take U.S. Highway 160 east for 7 miles to Rio Grande County Road 18 and drive north 1 mile to reach the Gold Medal stretch of the river. One or both banks for 2 miles upstream and 3 miles downstream are accessible to the public. From South Fork, take Colorado Highway 149 northwest for 3.5 miles to reach the Coller State Wildlife Area. To reach Box Canyon, continue west on CO 149 for 43 miles, then turn west on Forest Road 520 and drive 10 miles to the River Hill Campground below Rio Grande Reservoir. Hike 2 miles downstream.

Additional information: From the River Hill Campground downstream to Masonic Park, only flies and lures are allowed, with a brown trout bag limit of two fish up to 12 inches long. From CO 149 downstream to Rio Grande County Road 17, the fishing is flies and lures only, with a brown trout bag limit of two fish 16 inches or longer. All rainbows must be returned immediately to the water. Anglers floating the river should check locally on water conditions, as there are several stretches of dangerous rapids.

Contact: Colorado Division of Wildlife, Colorado Springs; (719) 473–2945.

106A Camping: River Hill Area

This riverside campground has fire grates, drinking water, tables, vault toilets, and a launch site for rafts. From South Fork, take CO 149 northwest for 43 miles, then turn west on FR 520 and drive 10 miles.

106B Camping: Palisade Area

This riverside campground has fire grates, drinking water, tables, vault toilets, and a launch site for rafts. From South Fork, take CO 149 northwest for 9 miles.

107 Big Meadows Reservoir

Key species: Rainbow trout, brook trout.

Description: Big Meadows Reservoir is a 110-acre reservoir in the headwaters of the South Fork of the Rio Grande.

Tips: Sizable numbers of 10-inch rainbow trout are still being stocked in this reservoir.

The fishing: Brook trout lake-fishing is quite a bit different than stream-fishing. The big brookies will run up into the shallows in the spring and fall and can be taken on small spinners, salmon eggs, and streamers like black leeches. In the summer they'll stay below 20 feet deep, so use the same lures and bait but fish them deep. Rainbows will come up in the morning and evening during warm weather and can be taken with night crawlers, spinners, wet flies, and nymphs.

Directions: From South Fork, go west on U.S. Highway 160 for 11.5 miles, then turn right on Forest Road 410 and drive 1.5 miles.

Contact: Colorado Division of Wildlife, Colorado Springs; (719) 473–2945.

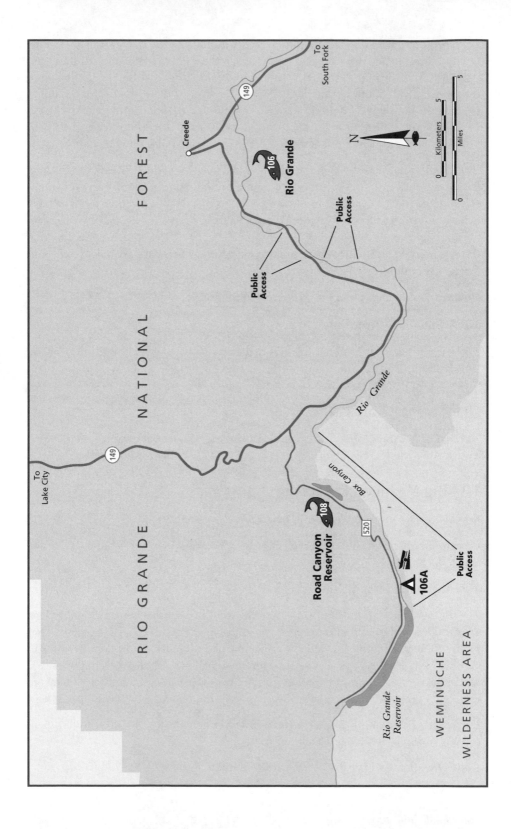

107A Camping: Big Meadows Reservoir Area

This popular campground is an RV favorite, with tables, fire grates, drinking water, and a boat ramp. From South Fork, go west on U.S. 160 for 11.5 miles, then turn right on FR 410 and drive 1.5 miles.

108 Road Canyon Reservoir

Key species: Rainbow trout.

Description: Road Canyon Reservoir is a 135-acre high-altitude reservoir in the headwaters of the Rio Grande on the northeast corner of the Weminuche Wilderness.

Tips: Catchable-size rainbows are still being stocked in this reservoir.

The fishing: This reservoir is a favorite with bait and spinner anglers, with plenty of medium-size fish and a few big ones. Fish with PowerBait, salmon eggs, or night crawlers from the shore. Use flashy spinners and spoons from a boat or float tube.

Directions: From South Fork, take Colorado Highway 149 northwest for 43 miles, then turn west on Forest Road 520 and drive 6.25 miles.

Additional information: Only wakeless boating is permitted on the reservoir.

Contact: Colorado Division of Wildlife, Colorado Springs; (719) 473–2945.

109 Poage Lake

Key species: Rio Grande cutthroat trout.

Description: Poage is a 29-acre natural lake at 11,000 feet in the San Juan Mountains.

Tips: This is one of the few lakes in the state stocked with Rio Grande cutthroat with no special restrictions.

The fishing: Night crawlers, PowerBait, and small spinners or attractor dry flies dragged behind a clear plastic bubble should all work well. The fish average 8 to 10 inches.

Directions: From South Fork, take U.S. Highway 160 west for 1 mile, then turn south on Forest Road 360 (Beaver Creek Road) and drive 17 miles to the lake.

Contact: Colorado Division of Wildlife, Colorado Springs; (719) 473–2945.

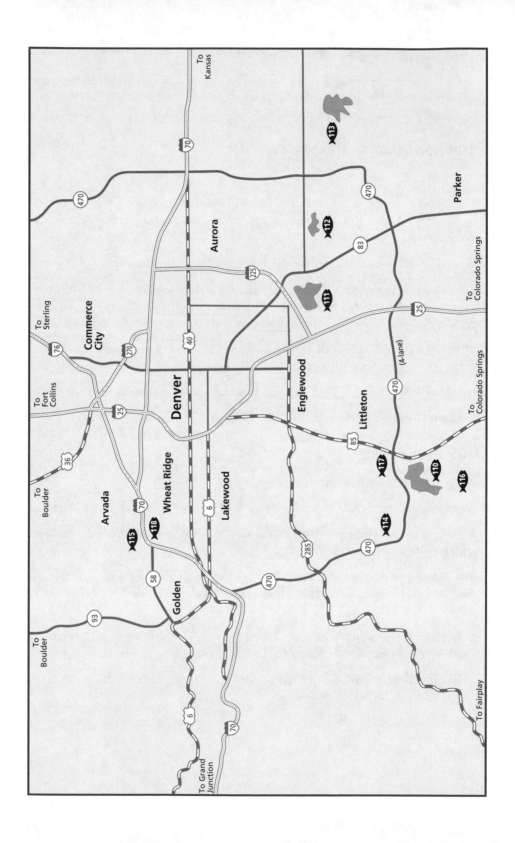

Denver Metro Area

110 Chatfield Reservoir

Key species: Rainbow trout, brown trout, smallmouth bass, largemouth bass, walleye, panfish, channel catfish.

Description: Chatfield Reservoir is a 1,400-acre impoundment nestled against the foothills in southwest Denver.

Tips: This is a good smallmouth bass fishery for fly anglers. Prime feeding times are morning and evening.

The fishing: With the stocking of 78,000 10-inch rainbows in 2000 and additional stockings annually, Chatfield Reservoir has become a prime Front Range trout fishery. Salmon eggs or PowerBait fished from shore in the northwest area is effective for these fish. The big ones, 18 to 20 inches, are caught that way, too, but most of the bigger trout fall to trolling with bait-tipped Rapala or Kastmaster lures behind cowbells. For largemouth bass throw a Hula popper or bass bug into weedy areas or cast a rubber worm or buzz bait around submerged structures. For smallmouth bass, some exceeding 15 inches, try throwing small streamers or crayfish patterns into rocky subsurface areas. For channel cats use stink bait at night in one of the inlet coves. Trout can also be caught in the South Platte River above and below the reservoir.

Directions: From I–70 in Denver, take Wadsworth Boulevard (Colorado Highway 121) south 15 miles to Colorado Highway 470, then go 0.5 mile on CO 121 until you reach the Deer Creek entrance.

Additional information: A Colorado State Parks season pass or daily use fee is required, as well as camping fees. The reservoir has wheelchair access to a fishing pier and an access trail. The bag limit for walleye is four fish 18 inches or larger. The minimum size for smallmouth and largemouth bass is 15 inches.

Contact: Chatfield State Park; (303) 791–7275.

110A Camping: Chatfield Reservoir Area

This cluster of four campgrounds is located on the south side of the reservoir and offers 153 sites, some with electrical hookups, and dump stations, a laundry, showers, a marina, and boat and jet ski rentals. From I–70 in Denver, take Wadsworth Boulevard (CO 121) south 15 miles to CO 470, then go 0.5 mile on CO 121 until you reach the Deer Creek entrance. Go south around the South Platte River inlet and follow the road 0.75 mile to the campgrounds.

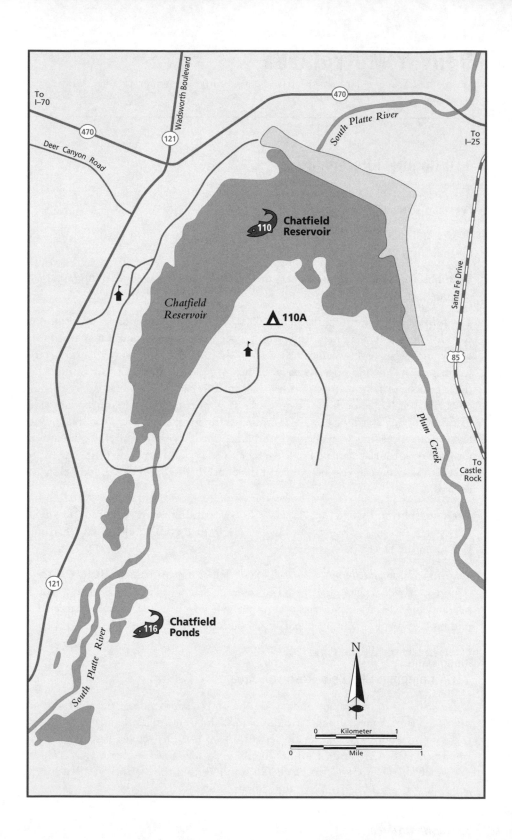

111 Cherry Creek Reservoir

Key species: Walleye, largemouth bass, smallmouth bass, wiper, rainbow trout, panfish.

Description: This 800-acre impoundment is in a state park surrounded by the suburbs of south Denver.

Tips: Fish the submerged stumps and logs at the south end of the reservoir for bass, wipers, and trout.

The fishing: Large walleye, some over 16 pounds, inhabit this reservoir and can be taken with worm harnesses and lures with lots of hardware slowly trolled near the bottom during the day. At night try lures or live minnows in shallower water. Largemouth bass up to 4 pounds inhabit the stump beds and can be caught on popping bugs, frog imitations, and rabbit-fur streamers. Wipers up to 8 pounds feeding on shad can be taken in the shallows in the spring. Anything that resembles a large minnow, including a large live minnow itself, can be cast into the feeding frenzy and will draw hard strikes. Smallmouth bass and crappies should be fished with crayfish imitations around the structure on the west side of the reservoir. Panfish and trout will take dry flies, worms fished with a bobber, or small spinners cast from the shore. About 50,000 10-inch rainbow trout were stocked in 2000, and additional stockings are done annually.

Directions: In Denver, get off I–225 at Parker Road and drive south 1 mile to the park entrance.

Additional information: A Colorado State Parks season pass or daily use fee is required, as are camping fees. A wheelchair-accessible fishing pier is available. The minimum size for walleye is 18 inches, and for largemouth and smallmouth bass it's 15 inches.

Contact: Cherry Creek State Park; (303) 699–3860.

111A Camping: Cherry Creek Reservoir Area

This 100-site campground is located on the east side of the reservoir and offers showers, a laundry, some electrical hookups, tables, fire grates, modern toilets, and a boat ramp. In Denver, get off I–225 at Parker Road and drive south 1 mile to the park entrance. From the entrance station, follow the road north 0.5 mile to the campground.

112 Quincy Reservoir

Key species: Tiger muskie, brown trout, rainbow trout, largemouth bass, smallmouth bass, yellow perch, black crappie.

Description: Quincy Reservoir is a 160-acre impoundment in the suburb of Aurora.

Tips: Secure yourself in the boat if you're going after tiger muskies.

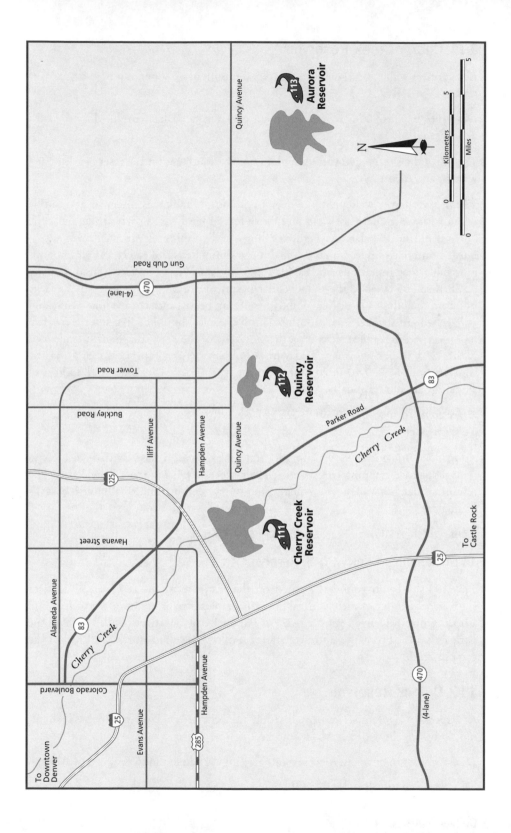

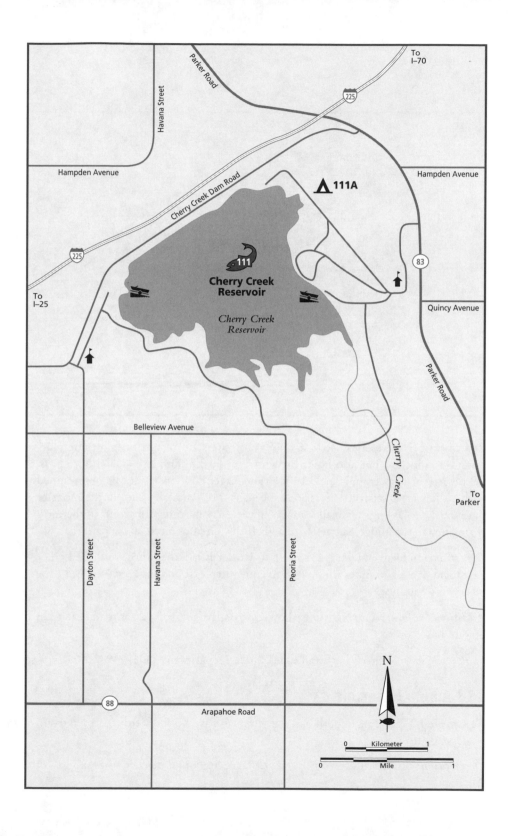

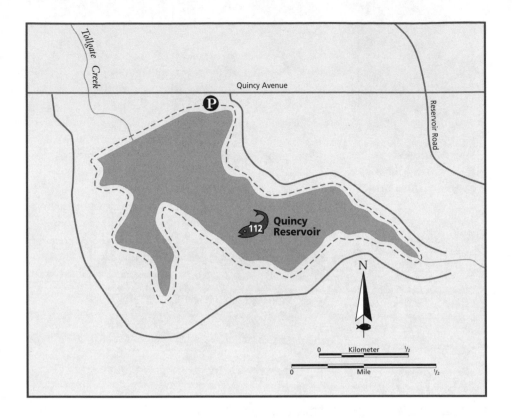

The fishing: This reservoir is best known for the state record tiger muskie (40.1 pounds, 53 inches) but also holds brown trout, largemouth and smallmouth bass, yellow perch, black crappies, and 10-inch and larger rainbow trout. Big plugs tipped with sucker meat retrieved at various speeds can occasionally haul in the monster tiger muskies. Use jigs or small spinners in the early morning for trout. In the early spring match the midge hatches with a Griffith's Gnat or a red larvae pattern.

Directions: In Denver, take I–225 south to Parker Road, then turn south on Parker Road and drive 1.75 miles to Quincy Avenue, turn east and proceed 3 miles to the reservoir's entrance.

Additional information: No bait is allowed. A daily or season pass is required; it can be purchased on site.

Contact: City of Aurora Park and Open Space Department; (303) 739–7160.

113 Aurora Reservoir

Key species: Wiper, smallmouth bass, largemouth bass, rainbow trout, brown trout, walleye, panfish.

Description: Aurora Reservoir is an 820-acre impoundment in the suburb of Aurora.

Tips: Bring heavy gear if you're fishing for wipers. An 8-pounder will fight like a 15-pound trout.

The fishing: An estimated 76,000 10-inch rainbow trout were stocked in this reservoir in 2000, and similar numbers will likely be planted here in future years. The ones that survive the first year will be smart but can still be caught by using lures and bait from the bank or by trolling deep. Wipers range from 8 to 12 pounds and in the spring are vulnerable near the shoreline as they forage for minnows. Cast streamers and top-water or shallow-running lures into boiling water to catch these fish. Walleye, rainbow trout, and brown trout can be taken in the summer by deep-trolling minnow imitations tipped with bait. Largemouth bass can be caught by casting buzz bait into weed beds or subsurface structures like trees and stumps. A highlight of this reservoir is its population of smallmouth bass, some exceeding 20 inches. Small streamers or lures, such as a rabbit-strip jig, cast into rocky areas and hopped along the bottom can be effective. Both smallmouth and largemouth bass are extremely aggressive during spawning, which generally occurs when the water temperature reaches between 60 and 70 degrees.

Directions: In Denver, take I–225 south to Parker Road, then turn south on Parker Road and drive 1.75 miles to Quincy Avenue, turn east and proceed for 6 miles to the reservoir's entrance.

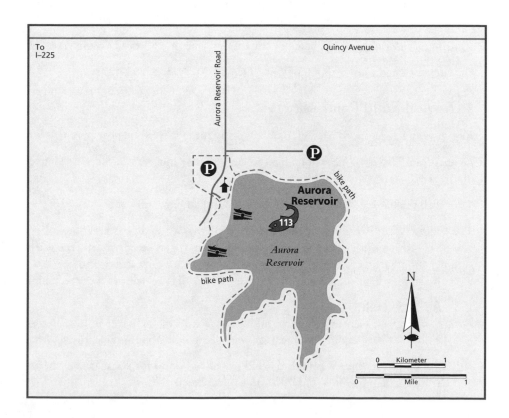

Additional information: No camping is allowed, and an entry fee is required. Gas-powered boats are not allowed on the reservoir. Handicapped-accessible facilities, including a fishing pier, are available.

Contact: City of Aurora Park and Open Space Department; (303) 739–7160.

114 Hine Lake

Key species: Largemouth bass, panfish.

Description: This 50-acre, 20-feet deep suburban lake is bordered by a hiking trail, condos, and a tennis court and just happens to have lunker largemouth bass and oodles of panfish.

Tips: Hine Lake is a closely kept secret of the bass-fishing community.

The fishing: This "secret spot" has big bass, which congregate around the artificial habitat created by the Colorado Division of Wildlife. Work the weed beds and structures in the evening with Hula poppers and popping bugs on top and weighted rubber worms down in the water. Worm-tipped spinners or weighted live minnows can also land a few of these bass, as well as the numerous varieties of panfish.

Directions: From Colorado Highway 470 in west Denver, take Bowles Avenue east for 0.3 mile, turn south on Coal Mine Road and drive 1 mile to West Meadow Park, then turn north on Van Gordon Way and proceed 0.25 mile to the lake.

Additional information: No boats or flotation devices are allowed on the lake.

Contact: Colorado Division of Wildlife, Denver Area; (303) 297–1192.

115 Ward Road Pond

Key species: Largemouth bass, crappie, bluegill, pumpkinseed, yellow perch.

Description: This is a 7-acre pond next to an interstate highway in the west Denver metro area.

Tips: Fish the habitat structures for 3- to 5-pound largemouth bass.

The fishing: Ward Road Pond (the pond east of here is a marsh) has great belly-boat fishing for largemouth bass, big crappie, and panfish. It gets weedy during the warm summer months, so try to be on the pond after the sun goes down and work the weed beds with bass plugs, mice or frog imitation flies or rubber worms behind spinners.

Directions: In west Denver, exit north off I–70 to Ward Road. Go 0.25 mile, then turn east onto West Forty-eighth Avenue, then immediately south into the parking area.

Additional information: Ward Road Pond is a brood pond for warm-water species and has flies-and-lures-only and catch-and-release restrictions.

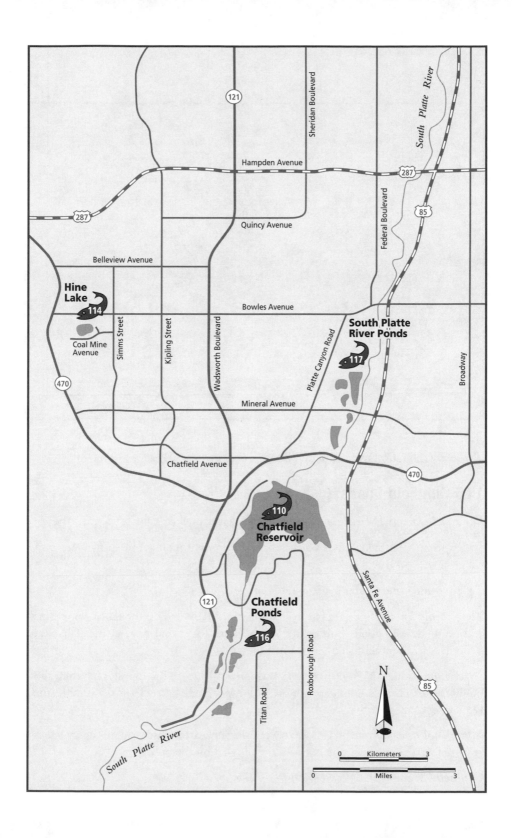

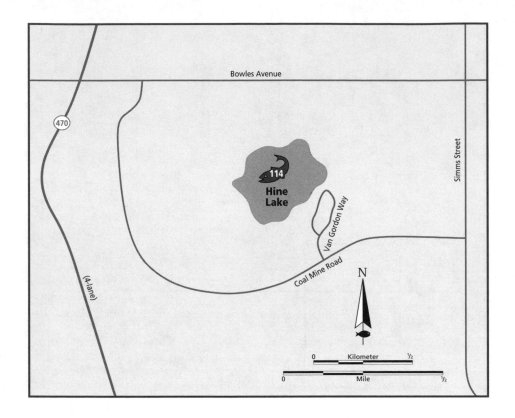

Contact: Colorado Division of Wildlife, Denver Area; (303) 297–1192.

116 Chatfield Ponds

Key species: Panfish, largemouth bass, bullhead, channel catfish.

Description: Chatfield Ponds consists of five ponds totaling 140 surface acres of water.

Tips: Nothing spectacular here, just lots of fish.

The fishing: These ponds are family-fishing fun. Many fish can be taken on worms and bobbers. The ponds border the South Platte River and have artificial habitat structures to maintain fish populations.

Directions: From I–70 in Denver, go south on Wadsworth for 15 miles to Colorado Highway 470, then continue south on Colorado Highway 121 for 0.5 mile to the Deer Creek entrance.

Additional information: A Colorado State Parks season pass or daily entry fee is required. No boats except belly boats are allowed on the ponds.

Contact: Chatfield State Park; (303) 791–7275.

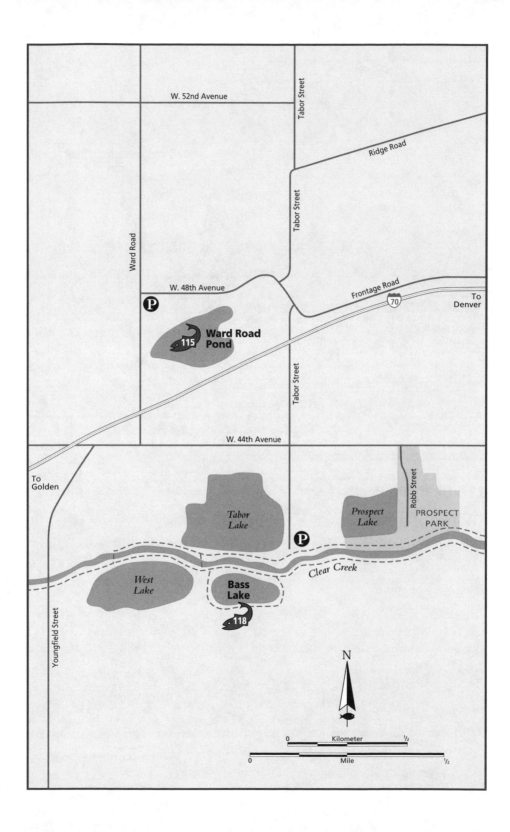

W. 52nd Avenue

Tabor Street

Ridge Road

Tabor Street

Ward Road

W. 48th Avenue

Frontage Road

70

To Denver

Ward Road Pond

115

Tabor Street

W. 44th Avenue

To Golden

Tabor Lake

Prospect Lake

Robb Street

PROSPECT PARK

Clear Creek

West Lake

Bass Lake

118

Youngfield Street

N

0   Kilometer   ½

0   Mile   ½

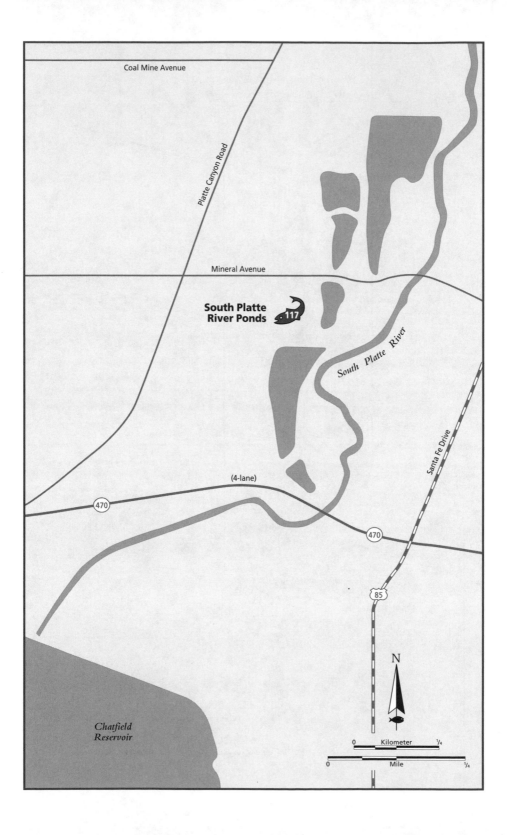

Coal Mine Avenue

Platte Canyon Road

Mineral Avenue

**South Platte
River Ponds** 117

South Platte River

Santa Fe Drive

(4-lane)

470

470

85

Chatfield
Reservoir

N

| 0 | Kilometer | ¼ |
| 0 | Mile | ¼ |

117 South Platte River Ponds

Key species: Panfish, rainbow trout, largemouth bass.

Description: The five South Platte River Ponds total 80 surface acres and are located along the South Platte River below Chatfield Reservoir.

Tips: The ponds' small size makes for good bank-fishing.

The fishing: These ponds have good fishing for largemouth bass around the artificial habitat structures, where they lie in ambush for panfish.

Directions: From I–70 (in west/central Denver), take Federal Boulevard south for 8 miles, then go west 0.5 mile on Bowles Avenue. Turn south onto Platte Canyon Road and proceed for 1.5 miles to the Platte River Park entrance.

Additional information: No boats, including belly boats, are allowed on the ponds. All largemouth bass must be 15 inches or larger to be kept.

Contact: Colorado Division of Wildlife, Denver Area; (303) 297–1192.

118 Bass Lake

Key species: Largemouth bass, crappie, panfish.

Description: Bass Lake is a 3-acre cattail-rimmed impoundment along Clear Creek in west Denver.

Tips: Work the weed beds that ring the lake just outside the cattails. Be ready to get mucky.

The fishing: This lake is a hidden jewel for largemouth bass, but don't expect any action until evening. Throw a Hula popper or a mouse imitation into the water between the cattails and the weed beds and retrieve it in short bursts.

Directions: In west Denver, exit I–70 onto Ward Road, then go south for 25 yards to Forty-fourth Street; turn east and go 0.4 mile to Tabor Street. Turn south onto Tabor Street for 150 yards to the parking lot.

Additional information: Only artificial flies and lures are allowed. All bass must be 15 inches or larger to be kept. No boats, including belly boats, are permitted on the lake.

Contact: Colorado Division of Wildlife, Denver Area; (303) 297–1192.

Appendix: Colorado Angling Resources

Colorado Division of Wildlife Offices

Denver Headquarters and Central Region Office—Denver Area
6060 Broadway
Denver, CO 80216
(303) 297–1192

Northeast Regional Office
317 West Prospect Road
Fort Collins, CO 80526
(970) 484–2836

Northwest Regional Office
711 Independent Avenue
Grand Junction, CO 81505
(970) 248–7175

Southeast Regional Office
2126 North Weber Street
Colorado Springs, CO 80907
(719) 473–2945

Southwest Regional Office
2300 South Townsend Avenue
Montrose, CO 81401
(970) 249–3431

Fishing Information Sites on the Internet

- www.coloradofishing.net (general fishing information for warm-water and cold-water sport fish)

- nwis.colo.cr.usgus.gov (current river and large stream flows)

- dwr.state.co.us/hydrology (detailed Colorado stream flow and reservoir water level information)

- wildlife.state.co.us/fishing (Colorado fishing news and very detailed fishing reports for the entire state)

- www.duranglers.com (thorough fly-fishing reports, including stream flow and lake levels, for Southwest Colorado)

About the Author

Ron Baird is a professional writer and an avid fly angler who lives in Boulder, Colorado. His fishing column for the *Boulder Planet* won first place from the Colorado Society for Professional Journalists in 1999. He worked for the Colorado Division of Wildlife for two years as a contract writer on issues related to fishing and currently works for a coalition of environmental groups as a cutthroat trout researcher. His first novel, *Dark Angel*, was published by iUniverse.com in 2001. Ron says it's a mystery about "murder, mayhem, and fly-fishing in the Rocky Mountains."

NANCY MORRELL